Practice-Led Theology

 **McMaster Divinity College Press**
McMaster Studies in Practical Theology, Volume 1

The learning paradigm at McMaster Divinity College is summarized and guided by three deceptively simple words: Knowing, Being, Doing. In many senses, Knowing and Doing are significantly easier to qualify and quantify, while Being is notoriously elusive. Nonetheless, in practical theology—a discipline that is difficult to narrowly define but inevitably has something to do with what can be learned theologically and theoretically from our practice(s)—it is the study (Knowing) of our practice (Doing) that ultimately has an impact on who we are (Being) and how we relate to God. Many could argue that it is our practices and our approaches to practices (of ministry, of service, of reflection, to name a few) that both reveal and shape who we are. In this series, the McMaster Studies in Practical Theology, we offer space for those who are investigating practices that offer something to theology, even if they are not overtly theological, to publish significant work on this exciting and diverse discipline, and to draw on investigations and observations of practice(s) to contribute to the larger conversation and related fields of research. Recent graduates who have invested their academic research in this broad area are welcome to submit manuscripts for possible inclusion in the series, but we also invite both new and well-seasoned academic writers from around the world to submit their work for possible publication.

Practice-Led Theology
A Model for Faith-Based Research

Neil K. Ferguson

☙PICKWICK *Publications* · Eugene, Oregon

PRACTICE-LED THEOLOGY
A Model for Faith-Based Research

McMaster Studies in Practical Theology, Volume 1
McMaster Divinity College Press

Copyright © 2024 Neil K. Ferguson. All rights reserved. Except for brief quotations in critical publications or reviews, no part of this book may be reproduced in any manner without prior written permission from the publisher. Write: Permissions, Wipf and Stock Publishers, 199 W. 8th Ave., Suite 3, Eugene, OR 97401.

Pickwick Publications
An Imprint of Wipf and Stock Publishers
199 W. 8th Ave., Suite 3
Eugene, OR 97401

McMaster Divinity College Press
1280 Main Street West
Hamilton, Ontario, L8S 4K1
Canada

www.wipfandstock.com

mcmasterdivinity.ca/mdc-press

PAPERBACK ISBN: 978-1-6667-6025-5
HARDCOVER ISBN: 978-1-6667-6026-2
EBOOK ISBN: 978-1-6667-6027-9

Cataloguing-in-Publication data:

Names: Ferguson, Neil K., author

Title: Practice-led theology : a model for faith-based research / Neil K. Ferguson.

Description: Eugene, OR: Pickwick Publications, 2024 | McMaster Studies in Practical Theology | Includes bibliographical references.

Identifiers: ISBN 978-1-6667-6025-5 (paperback) | ISBN 978-1-6667-6026-2 (hardcover) | ISBN 978-1-6667-6027-9 (ebook)

Subjects: LCSH: Theology, Practical--Methodology. | Theology, Practical--Research.

Classification: BV3 F47 2024 (paperback) | BV3 (ebook)

03/04/24

Contents

Lists of Illustrations or Tables | vii

Abbreviations | viii

Chapter 1
Introduction | 1

Chapter 2
Methodology | 14

Chapter 3
A History of Practice-Led Research | 47

Chapter 4
Defining Practice-Led Research: Foundations | 91

Chapter 5
Defining Practice-Led Research: The Definition | 119

Chapter 6
Application: Principles | 158

Chapter 7
Application: Preparation and Assessment | 202

Chapter 8
Application: A Project Proposal | 223

Chapter 9
Conclusions | 247

Appendix 1
Interview Guide Questions | 259

Appendix 2
Plain Language Statement | 262

Appendix 3
Consent Form | 263

Bibliography | 265
Index of Names | 281

Lists of Illustrations or Tables

Table 1. Levels of Interpretation | 43

Figure 1. Interpretative Interaction | 44

Figure 2. Hierarchy of Research | 102

Figure 3. Interrelationship between Research Styles | 103

Figure 4. Relationship between Knowledge Styles | 200

Figure 5. *The Holy Trinity* or *Hospitality of Abraham.*
Andrei Rublev (ca. 1410) | 235

Figure 6. *The Hospitality of Abraham.*
Theophanes the Greek (ca. 1378) | 236

Abbreviations

AB	*Art Bulletin*
AL	*Applied Linguistics*
ADCHE	*Art, Design & Communication in Higher Education*
AHRCRR	Arts and Humanities Research Council Research Review
AJC	*Australian Journal of Communication*
ANCTRTBS	Ashgate New Critical Thinking in Religion, Theology, and Biblical Studies
ASTIA	Ashgate Studies in Theology, Imagination, and the Arts
BCCS	Blackwell Companions in Cultural Studies
BCP	Blackwell Companions to Philosophy
BCR	Blackwell Companions to Religion
BGGW	Blackwell Guides to Great Works
BHC	Baker History of the Church
BPB	BridgePoint Book
BRL	Baker Reference Library
CGWEP	Chicago Guides to Writing, Editing, and Publishing
CIP	Cambridge Introductions to Philosophy
CSCD	Cambridge Studies in Christian Doctrine
CTRS	Contemporary Thinkers Reframed Series
DI	*Design Issues*
EAR	*Educational Action Research*
EIPR	Evaluations and Investigations Program Report

Abbreviations

EJAE	*European Journal of Arts Education*
EJP	*European Journal of Philosophy*
ELPT	*Everyman's Library: Philosophy and Theology*
ESP	*English for Specific Purposes*
FP	*Faith and Philosophy: Journal of the Society of Christian Philosophers*
FCI	Foundations of Contemporary Interpretation
HES	*Higher Education Studies*
HTCL	Harper Torchbooks: The Cloister Library
HUS	*Harvard Ukrainian Studies*
IETI	*Innovations in Education and Teaching International*
IJADE	*International Journal of Art & Design Education*
IJPR	*International Journal for the Psychology of Religion*
IVPBDS	The IVP Bible Dictionary Series
JCC	*Journal of Cognition and Culture*
JCS	*Journal of Consciousness Studies*
JP	*Journal of Pragmatics*
JR	*Journal of Religion*
JVAP	*Journal of Visual Art Practice*
JWCP	*Journal of Writing in Creative Practice*
LMC	Library of Medieval Civilization
LRC	Library of Religion and Culture
MIA	*Media International Australia*
MT	*Modern Theology*
NGC	*New German Critique*
NSCRS	New Studies in Critical Realism and Spirituality
NUSPEP	Northwestern University Studies in Phenomenology & Existential Philosophy
OAJ	*Oxford Art Journal*
OED	*Oxford English Dictionary*. 6th ed. Oxford: Oxford University Press, 2008.
OHA	Oxford History of Art

OLS	Open Linguistics Series
PC	Penguin Classics
PAPS	*Proceedings of the American Philosophical Society*
PHA	Pelican History of Art
PP	Princeton Paperbacks
PS	*Post-Script*
PSG	Palgrave Study Guides
QI	*Qualitative Inquiry*
RCARP	Royal College of Art Research Papers
RM	*Rethinking Marxism*
RMAH	Research Methods for the Arts and Humanities
RR	*Rhetoric Review*
RS	*Religious Studies*
SH	*Studia Humana*
SHE	*Studies in Higher Education*
SJCS	*Spiritus: A Journal of Christian Spirituality*
SJT	*Scottish Journal of Theology*
SPT	Studies in Practical Theology
SSJ	*Social Science Journal*
SDHAS	Sources and Documents in the History of Art Series
TC	*Tertium Comparationis*
TKJ	Taideteollisen Korkeakoulun Julkaisusarja
TST	Traditions in Social Theory
TVM	*Tijdschrift Voor Muziektheorie*
WBCP	Wiley-Blackwell Companions to Religion
WC	The World's Classics
YSH	Yale Studies in Hermeneutics
ZJRS	*Zygon: Journal of Religion & Science*

Chapter 1

Introduction

"Religion," according to Herman Bavinck, "is not limited to one single human faculty but embraces the human being as a whole."[1] Other disciplines such as art, science, and morality might be centred in one or more individual faculties; however, religion encompasses them all.[2] As religious faith affects all areas of the human life, every Christian believer wears multiple hats. First, every believer is a theologian as each individual "embraces a belief system . . . [and] in a deliberate manner or merely implicitly, reflects on the content of these beliefs and their significance for Christian life."[3] This is very much the historical task of theology, pondering what is right to believe based on the Scriptures, reflecting on them and on what has come down to us from those that have gone before. Yet the intellectual task is also a spiritual one; Evagrius observes that "a theologian is one who prays, and one who prays is a theologian."[4] Second, every believer lives the life of a Christian to one degree or another. These are what might be called the visible outworkings: the believer may attend church, pray, engage in worship, play a part in various community activities, meditate, or participate in some form of rituals. Faith also affects how the believer lives life: believers make decisions to do, or refrain from, actions based on these beliefs,

1. Bavinck, *Prolegomena*, 268. Bavinck here means the Christian religion.
2. Bavinck, *Prolegomena*, 269.
3. Grenz, *Theology for the Community of God*, 1.
4. Wilken, *The Spirit of Early Christian Thought*, 26.

sometimes consciously and sometimes unconsciously. However, these hats are not worn independently, but simultaneously—belief is an intellectual activity and, *at the same time*, a lived life.

PROJECT MOTIVATION

Sometimes the two hats of intellectual reflection on faith and the lived life of the Christian present a tension for the believer: a tension between thinking the faith and living the faith. It is summarized through a regularly appearing question on the *usefulness of theology*. Variously phrased by different writers, but well-illustrated by a paraphrased question one author received from his students, it is:

> Why do we need to bother with this? Isn't the gospel really more simple? After all, even a child can understand Jesus' message. All theology does is unnecessarily complicate matters and create an intellectual elite. It's a recipe for spiritual pride and deception. Can we skip it altogether and get back to the message of Christ?[5]

It certainly is the case that there is such a "thing as unfruitful, abstract theology that gets lost in a labyrinth of academic trivialities."[6] However, should the response be a return to some kind of simple devotion to Christ?

The tension could also be illustrated in various historical periods such as the Protestant scholasticism that began at the end of the sixteenth century. It was a time when "the dogmatic treatment of dogma acquired the aura of inviolable authority."[7] One theologian at this time was accused of "diverting the filthy lake of the scholastics into the [pure] fountain of Siloam."[8] In response to this, Justo González notes that "the seemingly endless debates on dogma, and the intolerance of Christians among themselves, led many to seek refuge in a purely spiritual religion."[9] One early proponent, Jakob Boehme, advocated

---

5. Hall, *Learning Theology*, 31.
6. Migliore, *Faith Seeking Understanding*, 7.
7. Bavinck, *Prolegomena*, 181.
8. Bavinck, *Prolegomena*, 181. Bavinck is quoting Maresius.
9. González, *Story of Christianity*, 2:196.

Introduction

for the freedom of the spirit, the inner life as well as direct individual revelation from God.[10]

Again, the pull between the views might also be illustrated by the tension Grenz and Olson identify in *20th-Century Theology* between a focus on transcendence and immanence.[11] They argue that the Bible "presents God as both beyond the world and present to the world."[12] The theological task—and good theology—seeks to maintain a balance between these two areas. The twentieth century, they argue, has been a "seesaw of transcendence and immanence" with the emphasis on one leading to a swing in the other direction, followed again by a reaction and a swing back again.[13]

This project is motivated by these tensions, seeking at least one way for theology to incorporate both these ways of seeing the task. Importantly, for many research projects, part of the motivation lies in the drive and interests of the individual researcher. Both the aims and the motivation of this project can be illustrated most effectively with some brief biographical sketches as aspects of my faith walk reveal a swinging of the pendulum between the *thinking* and the *doing* of faith.

I was saved in 1992, becoming a Christian in a small Baptist church in the southern suburbs of Perth, Western Australia. I had originally been on the trip simply to support family. A typical Sunday service at that church followed a standard model, the *hymn sandwich* or sometimes called the *hymn–prayer sandwich*. That is, one or two hymns, followed by the offering and prayer, another short hymn followed by the sermon, and finally ending with another hymn. The faith was presented in a reasonable, ordered, and sensible way (but could still be life-changing). Often despite the best efforts of the pastor, the God of this little Baptist church was generally well-behaved, polite, civilized, and a little unobtrusive: the faith had been largely intellectualized and externalized.

By the start of about 2001—after numerous changes in pastors—the little Baptist church had completed a *charismatic turn*. Over

---

10. González, *Story of Christianity*, 2:198.
11. Grenz and Olson, *20th-Century Theology*, 12.
12. Grenz and Olson, *20th-Century Theology*, 11.
13. Grenz and Olson, *20th-Century Theology*, 12.

a period of twelve to eighteen months the focus of the Sunday service moved from the sermon—Scriptural exegesis and application—to worship of God. The emphasis was on prayer combined with personal and community healing of a physical and spiritual nature. Charismatic practice included the various gifts of the Spirit, such as healing, words of knowledge, and words of wisdom, as well as *glossolalia* (speaking in tongues). This represented a shift from the earlier emphasis on the interpretation and application of the Scriptures centred in the sermon.

Sunday mornings saw a greater flexibility than had been the case in past years. Sometimes there would be a period of worship and then a message. Sometimes it would be the other way around—a message first and then an extended period of worship. Sometimes worship would start first and the pastor would decide not to bring a message but to continue in worship. These times of worship were rich and deep and seemed to me at least to be spontaneous and free-flowing. I continued attending this church for another four years.

One characteristic of the church that became apparent as the months went by was a tendency to separate *head knowledge* from *heart knowledge* or *faith knowledge*. It was thought that *too much* thinking interfered with the ability of the person to experience the Holy Spirit in the person's life. It has been argued in this section that there is truth to this—an over-intellectualized faith is one lost in its own reason and may be lacking in a relationship with the one at the centre of it—Jesus Christ. This swing toward a more experiential faith was a reaction to the intellectualized faith of the past, a faith that was thought about but not acted on.

This separation of the experiential dimension from the intellectual elements of faith—the heart from the head—is recognized as a potential weakness of the charismatic movement. Peter Hocken makes this observation in an extended article on the movement: "As an experiential movement, CM–CR has always been strong on faith-affirmation and short on critical reflection."[14]

This led to a *two knowledges* approach to Christian faith. On the one hand there was head knowledge, but this was often trumped by

---

14. Hocken, "Charismatic Movement," 517. CM and CR represents "charismatic movement" and "charismatic renewal."

Introduction

heart knowledge or the knowledge that was revealed by the Spirit. This separation tendency was amplified after a later move to a nearby Pentecostal church where people were told from time to time that the mind was an impediment to faith.

The *two knowledges* approach, however, is not peculiar to Pentecostals, charismatics and their theological relations. In the hermeneutical tradition, a representative is Wilhelm Dilthey (1833–1911). Dilthey wanted to find a firm basis for the humanities, one "that would make them truly *Geisteswissenschaften* (literally, "sciences of the spirit")", a way to give the humanities "objective validity."[15] At the same time, he reacted against the trend to "adopt the norms and ways of thinking of the natural sciences and apply them to the study of man."[16]

Ultimately, Dilthey's solution to this question lay in establishing a "fundamental distinction between all human studies and the natural sciences" and this difference lies not in a "*special way of knowing* but differs in content."[17] Dilthey argued that the key term for the natural sciences was *explanation*, but for the human sciences the key idea was *understanding*: "The sciences explain nature, the human studies understand the expressions of life."[18] Hans-Georg Gadamer sums up Dilthey's strategy in the following way:

> Dilthey was trying to explain "how one's inner life is woven into continuity" . . . in a way that is different from explaining the knowledge of nature by appeal to the categories. He used the concept of structure to distinguish the experiential character of psychological continuity from the causal continuity of natural processes. Logically "structure" is distinguished by its referring to a totality of relationships that do not depend on a temporal, causal succession but on intrinsic connections.[19]

Essentially, Dilthey drove a wedge between the natural sciences and human studies, claiming that while they may use the same

---

15. Gillespie, "Biblical Authority," 211.
16. Palmer, *Hermeneutics*, 98.
17. Palmer, *Hermeneutics*, 103, 105 (italics original).
18. Palmer, *Hermeneutics*, 105.
19. Gadamer, *Truth and Method*, 223.

methods, their final results are different. Dilthey's assessment is that the "fullness of human life in its social and historical manifestations, not nature, is the subject matter of hermeneutics."[20] Critics observe that a consequence of this is that theology cannot be objective and propositional.[21] Even an understanding of God, in this view, is a "projection of human inner experience as the interpreter seeks existential self-understanding."[22] This is, potentially at least, problematic according to some Pentecostal and charismatic approaches to reason. That is, a faith based on individual experience is one based in that individual and can only be internally objective to the individual—or possibly a group—and will certainly be prone to the idiosyncrasies of individual histories.

What is characteristic of these views is a privileging of one type of knowledge over the other, almost to the point that there is only one knowledge of any value—the knowledge favoured by the position one takes. On the one side lies a kind of *naïve rationalist* position which includes the possibility of a *God's eye view*—an individual can be detached from the world and see it how it is. In theological terms, it is not so much a God's eye view as the belief that we have full access to God's view. On the other is a kind of *naïve experientialist* position where it is the experience—the practice—that has sole precedence.

As a researcher and Christian believer, this project is motivated by my desire to find a way to bring these two perspectives into discussion and co-operation. Many of these ideas will be significantly expanded on in later chapters and these themes will reoccur in a variety of disguises.

OBJECTIVES

This tension between a strong intellectualism and an equally strong experientialism in the Christian church broadly provides the background to the objectives of this book as there are other areas where this division is present. This project is an attempt to avoid these two extremes. It is a project that aims to honour the conclusions of rational theological analysis as well as those of the lived faith experience. However, it does so within a narrow framework.

20. Gruenler, *Meaning and Understanding*, 59.
21. Gruenler, *Meaning and Understanding*, 59.
22. Gruenler, *Meaning and Understanding*, 59.

Introduction

The broad aim of this book is to present a relatively new research methodology—one that is certainly new to theology—that recognizes the value of both perspectives and understands them as complementary, connected, and required in combination. It makes an attempt in the particular domain of academic research to combine the intellectual and the experiential, recognizing both approaches and types of knowledge as providing a full understanding of an issue. It also presents the justification for its validity and the theoretical support for its use. It is not my aim to argue that it is better than other methods in theology, only that it offers an alternative that comes with additional advantages.

This is essentially a project on methodology. In this book I expand upon a methodology originally developed outside theology that in its application combines both the intellectual approach to research and knowledge as well as an embodied, experiential and practice-driven approach to research.[23]

There were originally two basic objectives of the project. The first was to take the definitions of practice-led research and modify them to suit a theological framework and the second was to conduct a practice-led research project as a part of this work. However, the early stages of the project encountered a significant issue. While some of the general concepts connected to practice-led research are independently understood, this is often only the case outside the disciplines that adopt practice-led research. The broad form and structure of a practice-led project in a practical sense has gained some standardization but what it specifically means to say "this is a practice-led research project" is not by any means clear if at times it means anything at all. It became necessary then to return to first principles and develop a definition from the ground up, and, in addition, modify existing available models to suit the definition that emerged and the situation to which it was to be applied.

The final result leads to a stronger and more rigorous version of the methodology, but it is important to note that this project is a theoretical development and expansion of practice-led research. It is not a practice-led research project itself although it does present (especially in chapter 6) theoretical examples of what a practice-led project

23. These concepts will be defined and expanded in later chapters.

in theology might look like. Chapter 8 is a fully worked example of a practice-led research project in theology.

BROAD PLAN OF THE BOOK

This book originated in a dissertation I completed in 2014 for a PhD at the University of Notre Dame, Australia. This chapter provides the broad underpinnings of the original project. Apart from some adjustments to this introduction and other minor corrections, the content remains otherwise unchanged. The following sections present the original research questions, the perceived limitations and significance along with a brief overview of the chapters.

RESEARCH QUESTIONS

This project aims to achieve practical goals associated with the following research questions:

1. Does practice-led research provide an additional methodology for theology?
2. Can a robust definition and model of practice-led research be developed while maintaining its flexibility as a methodology?
3. How might key concepts such as *research*, *knowledge*, and *practice* be defined and expanded to support the process of developing a robust definition?
4. Can practice-led research be theoretically demonstrated as a viable methodology in a theological context?

These questions are answered in the book as a whole. Chapter 8 also provides a direct answer to question 3.

LIMITATIONS

The limitations presented here at the outset of the project are potential ones related to the project as a whole. The first limitation of this project relates to the nature of practice-led research itself. The investigation in chapter 3 will show that it was originally developed as a way for creative practitioners to do research in a university environment without

Introduction

having to abandon their practice. This fundamental characteristic of the methodology is maintained throughout this project and its application is framed in a way that reflects this restricted field. This is a limitation in the sense that much of the background work as well as the development of a model and the definition of key terms is done within this narrower frame. This is somewhat less true of the core definition of chapter 5, but still can be seen.

A second limitation of the project is that practice-led research is framed in this book within a Christian faith context. This limitation may be relevant to the immediate application of the methodology and some of the assumptions of the project. It is not a limitation on practice-led research in a broader sense.

Finally, a third limitation relates to my approach and situation as a researcher: I am not a practice-led researcher myself, but rather, as the progress of this book will reveal, a strong sympathizer. This is a limitation in the sense that I am working at least partly from the outside and the application could be considered informed speculation. It may be also considered an advantage in that it gives me a different perspective.

These potential limitations will be revisited at the end of the project (in the conclusion) and the extent to which they have been addressed as the arguments developed are evaluated. There is one point to be addressed that, although not a specific limitation, may be seen as an unusual step.

This project is approached as an interdisciplinary study of a *traditional* nature. In this context an *interdisciplinary* project is one where "integration of the contributions of several disciplines to a problem or issue is required. Interdisciplinary integration brings interdependent parts of knowledge into harmonious relationships through strategies such as relating part and whole or the particular and the general."[24] There is an attempt to draw on various disciplines in order to fully develop the project and its outcomes.

The overview presented in the next section reveals no dedicated literature review chapter. However, due to the interdisciplinary nature of the project, a decision was made at the start to review the literature for each area of the project as it was developed rather than having a

24. Stember, "Advancing the Social Sciences," 6.

single chapter which could become large and disjointed. Chris Hart suggests that a literature review contains "information, ideas, data and evidence written from a particular standpoint to fulfil certain aims or express certain views on the nature of the topic and how it is to be investigated, and the effective evaluation of these documents in relation to the research being proposed."[25] With this purpose in mind, each particular section has a literature review embedded within it, presenting and analyzing as necessary.

OVERVIEW OF CHAPTERS

Chapter 2 expands the logic of the arguments. It outlines the methodological groundings and assumptions of the research and the adopted theoretical perspective. Given that the methodology focuses on the academic environment, the chapter presents an argument regarding the validity and legitimacy of theology as a discipline in the public sphere and in the university, a position argued to be not as sure as it once might have been. The chapter continues with the framework of analysis and the process related to a number of practitioner interviews conducted.

Chapter 3 outlines the changing relationship of the artist and the theologian to the society and culture in which they live, respectively. This chapter provides important foundational work for the following chapters and provides some justifications (taken up in later chapters) for decisions made in the definitional process and the development of the model for implementation.

The main goal of chapters 4 and 5 is to develop a robust definition, but they begin by analyzing in detail the key concepts related to practice-led research. Chapter 4 examines the meaning and nature of *research*, *practice* and *knowledge* in preparation for the broad-based definition of the methodology. The process considers three areas: the external regulatory frameworks (primarily governments and funding agencies); internal regulatory frameworks (within the universities themselves); and finally, the debates in the literature on practice-led research. Chapter 5 then expands on these ideas, returning in a sense

---

25. Cited in Silverman, *Doing Qualitative Research*, 323.

to first principles to build a rigorous definition. It concludes by distinguishing the methodology from others with which it has been, or maybe, compared.

Chapters 6 and 7 form two parts in the development of a model to implement the definition worked out in chapter 5. Chapter 6 presents the typical structure of a practice-led research project and considers some of its frequent issues. It then presents and critiques the *standard* models of practice-led research, examining in detail the purposes and aims of the components. It then elaborates on how the standard ideas might be reinterpreted and presents a reformulated model present in some institutions. To assist in understanding the nature of the model and how it operates, some theological applications are suggested. The chapter continues some of the arguments of chapter 5, discussing *meaning* and *understanding*. The aim is to expand on how knowledge might be best understood from a practice-led research perspective and as the outputs of research in their fullest understanding.

Although chapter 8 is based on all the previous chapters, it brings together the work of the previous four chapters in particular by presenting a hypothetical practice-led research project. It is presented as a research proposal prepared for a postgraduate degree at an unnamed university. The purpose is to attempt to put the model and definition developed in this book into practice and to see how it might look in the field. It aims to integrate the practical and theoretical elements of practice-led research into a single worked example.

SIGNIFICANCE

This study is significant in two areas. Firstly, and broadly, this project is significant in the contribution it makes to the theorizing and definition of the methodology. Secondly, and more specifically, the project is significant in the preliminary steps it takes in applying the methodology to the theological process. This second task depends upon the completion of the first.

As will be demonstrated especially in chapters 3 and 4, practice-led research was not the result of the work of an individual, nor did it result from the publication of a book or similar easily identifiable event. Rather, it developed incrementally over years, being expanded upon as researchers and students continued to explore. There were indeed external events that helped to begin this process, but practice-led research does not have a *birthday*. Although there are other reasons as well, partly as a result of this, the methodology has been inadequately defined or defined very generically. This has meant that the methodology has had a limited ability to make a contribution of research and knowledge beyond each project's narrow frame.[26]

The first significant contribution this project makes is in developing a single broad based detailed definition on the nature of practice-led research. Key terms such as *knowledge, research* and *practice* are defined and integrated into the definition. These terms, and others similar ones, are often left undefined and unanalyzed, the assumption being that all involved already know what they mean. However, given the diversity of meaning, and the often incomplete understandings of what practice-led research is, at least one fully developed definition is needed. The process is also significant in that it acknowledges but does not depend upon existing phrasings of practice-led research and the definition from the ground up. Related to this is the development of a model as well as general principles related to its application dealing with documentation, compilation and examination. It is hoped that this definition and model are sufficiently flexible yet rigorous enough to be applicable to the research of many who wish to employ practice-led research.

The second area of significance for this project is its application to the theological enterprise. One of the motivators of this project discussed earlier was the recognition that theology is not merely intellectual exploration of *God concepts* but is closely connected to the lived experience of the believing theologian.[27] For this reason, it seems apparent that in the same way researchers grounded in the creative disciplines developed the methodology to integrate their practice into their research, theologians need that opportunity as well.

---

26. Definitions and how the terms "research" and "knowledge" are understood in this work are explored in later chapters.

27. Even the non-believing theological researcher is affected by their experiences and beliefs. This is further developed in the next chapter.

Introduction

Numerous connections are made between theology and the creative disciplines—positively and negatively—throughout this monograph. This serves to show the general relevance of the methodology to theological thinking. Specific attempts are also made to apply the methodology. First, chapter 8 is an extended worked example of a practice-led research proposal. Second, a number of suggestions are made in other chapters, most notably, chapter 6.

This work presents a foundation, a starting point for later application. The fullest realization of the methodology in theology, and therefore its fullest significance, will have to wait for faith practitioners to implement, explore and expand on the model themselves.

CONCLUSION

This introduction has presented the basic goals and motivations of this book as an attempt to blend two methodological approaches into a useful whole. Practice-led research is developed and defined in this book within a university context. The project develops a robust definition and model for its use. This chapter also presents a broad plan of what is to follow and introduces the general story line the chapters will follow. The next chapter begins the process by laying out the methodology adopted for the investigation as well as a number of important foundational steps.

Chapter 2

Methodology

INTRODUCTION

THE FIRST CHAPTER OUTLINES the motivations driving this project, presents the research questions, and introduces issues to be investigated in coming chapters. A key point in chapter 1 is that practice-led research enables in the research process the combination of multiple ways of knowing and understanding the world. The different ways of knowing and experiencing the world are often seen as opposites and there is a swing between them over time. This is seen in historical periods, in the contemporary intellectual situation as well as in faith communities.

Although briefly covered in the introductory chapter, the question immediately arises: what is practice-led research? An examination of the contexts leading to its development in chapter 3 reveals it is a relatively recent innovation. It has been developed by artists and academics as they experimented with methods in a changing research environment. Although there is increasing literature on practice-led research, there is no clear definition or approach available, and no seminal texts exist. There is wide variation in the application of the method, including the very use of the term *practice-led research*.

Later chapters (especially chapters 4 and 5) go into that question in more detail by exploring the literature as well as the views of practitioner/researchers and supervisors. In order to develop a definition

Methodology

that does justice to this variety, it has been necessary to sift through the various arguments in articles and books as well as talk to people who have used the methodology or supervised researchers that have used the methodology.

This raises the further question of methodology. Essentially, the dilemma is this: in order to apply the methodology in theology, it is necessary to first understand its nature and use. To do so, a methodological framework is required within which to operate. To resolve this dilemma, an approach of halving the methodological task is adopted. This chapter will outline a strategy to investigate what practice-led research is as well as establish a broader framework within which this project situates itself. Chapter 3 investigates the history and development of the idea and explores the contexts that have influenced it. This chapter also explores the links between theology and the creative community within which practice-led research developed, and reasons why it did so. Chapters 4 and 5 develop the definition.

The second part of this division begins in chapter 6. This chapter will outline how the methodology functions in the field. The format and structures of a practice-led project will be outlined and two detailed examples will be presented. These will be given in the form of research proposals. Chapter 7 addresses additional questions arising out of the applications.

The main goal of the present chapter is to present the broad theoretical foundations on which this project is grounded. The first task of this chapter is to make clear my position as a Christian and outline the Christian framework within which this project operates. The second task is to present the theoretical position for this book, *critical realism*, and explain what it is and why it has been adopted. Thirdly, a clear case will be presented for the continued place of Christian theology in the *public sphere* as a contributor to debate. This section contains arguments for the right and responsibility to pursue questions of interest to Christian theology.[1] This step will also narrow the scope of investigation to theology in an academic environment. The fourth task will be to outline a preliminary hermeneutical method drawn primarily from N. T. Wright and his notion of *stories*. Fifthly, the process for conducting

---

1. I will also explain what I mean by *public sphere*.

a small set of interviews with practice-led researchers and supervisors will be outlined. Finally, I will adopt and develop a strategy, *reflexive interpretation*, as a way of keeping all the elements together, in play and interacting with each other.

A CHRISTIAN PERSPECTIVE

The fundamental grounding of this project is within a Christian worldview. It would be clear from the nature of the topic and the content of the first chapter, that I am "some type of Christian." There are three important reasons why a more specific statement is needed.

Firstly, it can no longer be assumed that Christianity is a cultural and theoretical baseline for discussion and public debate. A religious faith of any colour (or lack of one) will have an impact on the questions a person asks or does not, and the answers that are possible to consider. For this reason, it is important for researchers to state clearly their theoretical positions in which faith is one element. The third section below addresses this question and attempts to present a case why religion (and Christianity specifically) has a legitimate and important role to play in the community as a whole, in its social, political, and intellectual life.

Secondly, a more explicit statement on what *Christian* means is necessary because to say someone is Christian is only slightly more informative than saying a person is an Australian. There is a great diversity within the term *Christian* (as there is in the term *Australian*), and so it is important to be clear.

Thirdly, the importance of making my Christian position clear will become more apparent in later chapters when I examine the history, background and uses of practice-led research. Some of its underlying assumptions and the intellectual environments in which it is being developed can be somewhat antithetical to Christian understandings.

Statement of the Christian Perspective

I understand Christianity in a way similar to the following description presented by Alister McGrath. At the outset, he says his scientific theology project "is based on the affirmation of the intellectual resilience

Methodology

of traditional creedal Christian orthodoxy, whose fundamental ideas are stated in the classic creeds of Christianity and defended as living experienced realities by the great traditions of Christian theology—Catholicism, Orthodoxy, and evangelicalism."[2]

McGrath gives two reasons for this position. He suggests Christian orthodoxy is the "most authentic" form of Christianity as it represents "the consensus of the Christian communities over an extended period of time" something "governed both by Scripture and a long tradition of theological reflection, embodied and expressed in the creeds."[3] It is these classic creeds that define Christian orthodoxy. Although at this point, McGrath does not specify which creeds he means, he talks elsewhere of at least two creeds that received "increasing authority and respect throughout the church" in the patristic period.[4] They are namely the Apostles' Creed and the Nicene Creed.

McGrath's second reason is a note of caution. He argues that "alternatives to Christian orthodoxy tend to be transient developments, often linked with specific historical situations whose passing leads to an erosion of plausibility of the variant of Christian theology being proposed."[5] If Christian theology is formulated in a way too dependent on the conclusions of a current philosophical or cultural trend, then the theology will be discredited as intellectual climates change. Although McGrath is an evangelical, this position is broadly true for the Eastern Orthodox and the Roman Catholic. David Bentley Hart, an Orthodox theologian, presents a *dogmatica minora* in his book *The Beauty of the Infinite*. In the preamble he states that his project proceeds "in strict reliance upon the most elementary and binding canon of catholic confession, the Nicene-Constantinopolitan symbol (in its unadulterated Greek form); as the authoritative précis of the faith of catholic orthodoxy, East and West."[6] It is worth noting that Hart uses the terms catholic and orthodoxy with lower case letters. This indicates

---

2. McGrath, *Scientific Theology*, 35.
3. McGrath, *Scientific Theology*, 36.
4. McGrath, *Christian Theology*, 20.
5. McGrath, *Scientific Theology*, 36.
6. Hart, *Beauty of the Infinite*, 153.

he means these broadly rather than as references to Roman Catholicism and Eastern Orthodox.

To be more specific, I situate myself in a broadly *conservative* stream of Christianity. "Conservative" can be both a term of description and, frequently, one of abuse, ridicule and derision. Its use here is along the lines of the following quote from Donald Bloesch in describing evangelical Christianity:

> Evangelical theology has been impelled to uphold and defend certain tenets of the historic faith that palpably conflict with modern life . . . Among these are the absolute authority of and transcendence of God; the divine authority and inspiration of Scripture; the radical sinfulness of man; the deity of Jesus Christ; His vicarious, substitutionary atonement; the eschatological and superhistorical character of the kingdom of God; a final judgment at the end of history; the realities of heaven and hell; and evangelization as the primary dimension of the Christian mission.[7]

Theologians from this stream that are frequently cited throughout this book are mainly from an evangelical and reformed tradition. The main representatives include Alister E. McGrath,[8] Donald G. Bloesch,[9] Millard J. Erickson,[10] Herman Bavinck,[11] and J. Rodman Williams.[12]

THEORETICAL PERSPECTIVE: CRITICAL REALISM

This project is essentially *qualitative* in nature. Qualitative research is numerous and varied, but the following definition expresses its core principle:

> The term qualitative methods refers to a variety of research techniques and procedures associated with the goal of trying to understand the complexities of the social world in which

---

7. Bloesch, *Essentials of Evangelical Theology*, 1:14.
8. McGrath, *Christian Theology*.
9. Bloesch, *Essentials of Evangelical Theology*.
10. Erickson, *Christian Theology*.
11. Bavinck, *Prolegomena*.
12. Williams, *Renewal Theology*.

Methodology

we live and how we go about thinking, acting, and making meaning in our lives. [Its] research practices ... emphasize getting close to participants and trying to understand how they (and we) view the world ...[13]

Denzin and Lincoln make the following observation about qualitative methods: "Qualitative research is a situated activity that locates the observer in the world. It consists of a set of interpretive, material practices that make the world visible. These practices transform the world."[14]

At one level, this statement would suggest some accord with the practice of being a Christian. The apostle James, probably writing to Jewish Christians, understands the faith as something to be lived and not just acknowledged.[15] Bloesch, speaking as a "socially concerned evangelical," sees the gospel as a "stick of dynamite in the social structure."[16] According to James, a faith without action—one not attempting to transform the world—is "dead" and useless.[17] The Christian task is to proclaim the whole gospel to economic and political life—it is a means of change.[18] However, there are significant issues in making such a simple connection. All knowledge is influenced by the researcher and their context: "Every researcher speaks from within a distinct interpretive community, which configures, in its special way, the multicultural, gendered components of the research act."[19]

Typically, qualitative researchers "stress the socially constructed nature of reality, the intimate relationship between the researcher and what is studied, and the situational constraints that shape inquiry."[20] Denzin and Lincoln here dismiss tensions in qualitative research and posit an essential link between qualitative research and the notion of *social construction*. According to Michael Crotty, constructionism "is the

13. Ellis and Ellington, "Qualitative Methods," 2287.
14. Denzin and Lincoln, "Introduction: The Discipline," 4.
15. Keener, *IVP Bible Background Commentary*, 695.
16. Bloesch, *Essentials of Evangelical Theology*, 1:xi.
17. Keener, *IVP Bible Background Commentary*, 695 (cf. Jas 2:17).
18. Bloesch, *Essentials of Evangelical Theology*, 1:xi.
19. Denzin and Lincoln, "Introduction: Entering the Field," 11.
20. Denzin and Lincoln, "Introduction: The Discipline," 14.

view that all knowledge, and therefore all meaningful reality as such, is contingent upon human practices, being constructed in and out of interaction between human beings and their world, and developed and transmitted within an essentially social context."[21] Social constructionism is considered to be "central to the social sciences of today."[22]

This argument demonstrates that there is a clear link between how I might understand the world and the context within which that understanding is formed. There are obvious examples of this within theology. One example is the so-called first quest for the Historical Jesus. Albert Schweitzer dates the "quest" from 1778, and it ends with the publication of his own reconstruction in 1906.[23] The quest attempted to reconstruct a complete historical portrait of Jesus including his thoughts and motivations. The project was based on a set of naturalistic assumptions which restrained the conclusions that could be reached.[24] It produces a "desupernaturali[z]ed" Jesus.[25] Bringing this enterprise to an abrupt end, Albert Schweitzer noted that this reconstructed Jesus was a "figure designed by rationalism, endowed with life by liberalism, and clothed by modern theology in an historical garb."[26] In its essence, the "questioner's questions and outlook helped shape the answers that were given."[27] In the social constructionist terms of Berger and Luckman, theologians externalized and objectified contemporary social and religious categorizations and then read them back as a definite reality.[28]

As this project progresses, the importance of clarity in the close relationship between the researcher, what is studied, and what conclusions can be reached will become clear. This is in addition to affirming the presence of situational constraints influencing research. While this project fits broadly within the qualitative realm, any *emphasis* on social

---

21. Crotty, *Foundations of Social Research*, 42.

22. Alvesson and Sköldberg, *Reflexive Methodology*, 50; Sullivan, *Art Practice as Research*, 60.

23. Brown, "Historical Jesus," 326.

24. Ladd, *Theology of the New Testament*, 176.

25. Brown, "Historical Jesus," 328.

26. Erickson, *Christian Theology*, 1164.

27. Brown, "Historical Jesus," 341.

28. Alvesson and Sköldberg, *Reflexive Methodology*, 26.

Methodology

construction is problematic. There are theological and philosophical reasons for this and although expanded on in later chapters, it is necessary to begin to address them at this stage.

As outlined in an earlier section, this project is grounded in a broadly conservative Christian theistic position. One implication of this position is that it affirms the reality of an eternal God independent of, and separate from, human existence.[29] It also affirms a creation that is independent of God and of the human person. It further implies that some things, therefore, are sourced in God and are not social constructs.[30] It is *meaningful* to say, for example, that the human person is valuable, that there are ways of relating to each other and to God that are better than others. These attitudes are the product of the Triune God rather than human society. They are sourced in God rather than the characteristic of a society at a particular time and place, and so in their basic core, are independent of time and place. This perspective refuses anti-realist accounts of reality. These accounts—such as social constructionist conceptions—suggest that ethics and morality are produced by the society to which they apply.

However, the Christian perspective adopted here also affirms the fallibility of human reason and human attempts to fully come to grips with the world and with God. Since the Fall, the image of God in humans "has been darkened but not destroyed."[31] Humans still have "natural talents, intelligence, and also a moral sense, though because of sin it cannot be regarded as a safe or sure guide"—it has been impaired.[32] Essentially, humans are able to relate to God and with each other as well as reason about the world, however, there is an element of unreliability to these functions. In other words, sin has had an effect on the proper functioning of our cognitive faculties which in turn impacts our abilities to develop a noetic structure.[33] This conclusion refuses positivist and hard realist accounts of reality. These views can be understood as collectively taking the view that any proposition must be capable in

---

29. Erickson, *Christian Theology*, 403.
30. Moreland and Craig, *Philosophical Foundations*, 131.
31. Bloesch, *Essentials of Evangelical Theology*, 1:91.
32. Bloesch, *Essentials of Evangelical Theology*, 1:91.
33. Plantinga, "Justification and Theism," 165, 186.

principle at least of being empirically verified.[34] That is to say, all human knowledge must have some basis in the physical world. Further, data are something "that *exists, is (already) there*, and the task of the researcher thus becomes to gather and systematize them."[35] There is a reality *out there* that can be measured and known objectively.

The problems these two approaches raise for the Christian position of this book call for a different approach. Therefore, a version of *critical realism* will be adopted. Although this view might be thought of as merely a middle ground, it more fundamentally addresses the ontological and epistemological conclusions of the Christian position outlined earlier in the chapter. Andrew Wright argues that critical realism

> seeks to map a path beyond the extremes of modern certainty and postmodern skepticism via a triumvirate of core philosophical principles: ontological realism, epistemic relativism and judgmental rationality. Ontological realism asserts that reality exists for the most part independently of human perception, epistemic relativism asserts that our knowledge of reality is limited and contingent, and judgmental rationality asserts that it is nevertheless possible to judge between conflicting truth claims while recognizing that all such judgments necessarily remain open to further adjudication.[36]

Critical realists argue that the world is independent of us, that there is a reality to be known. However, our ability to access that world, what we can know of it for certain is *filtered*; it is understood through our cultural context, historical circumstances, but also limited by the tools and understandings available at a particular time. Given these constraints, it is possible to make contingent assessments of truth claims that might be considered to be more probable than alternatives. A return to the earlier example of the quest for the historical Jesus will help to illustrate the idea. It is true that the *real* Jesus is obscured by history and chronological distance. The critical realist position adopted in this book would argue that it can be accessed to a point, with the

---

34. Moreland and Craig, *Philosophical Foundations*, 154.
35. Alvesson and Sköldberg, *Reflexive Methodology*, 17 (italics original).
36. Wright, *Christianity and Critical Realism*, 9.

awareness that some conclusions reached should be viewed as provisional and open to modification or being discarded.

Benton and Craib suggest that the critical realist position is often lumped in with realist positions as claiming "an absolute certain, one-to-one correspondence between existing belief and the supposed reality of which it is the knowledge."[37] It is helpful to outline the four reasons they give as to why critical realism is different from the caricature. Firstly, they argue, that any cognitive practice makes sense only if they are about something that exists independently although the critical realist does not make any decision on the finality of the truth claims of a discipline.[38] The Christian perspective of this project would argue that it is the nature and understandings of God and the created world that is open to investigation. Secondly, critical realism holds to a "reflexivity" about the ability of thought and language to represent the world.[39] This point has been alluded to in an earlier section when it was suggested that our access to the world is restricted by the impairment or *darkening* of our cognitive faculties. Thirdly, critical realism suggests that the "surface appearance of things as potentially misleading as to their true character" that is, reality has "depth."[40] There is, at bottom, a God to whom we can relate, certainly, but about whom only limited knowledge is available—work has to be done in the words of Benton and Craib.[41] These three reasons lead to the fourth: any belief is open to revision after more cognitive work is done—critical realism is a "fallibilist" position.[42]

Summary of Implications of Critical Realism

By adopting this position, it is possible to affirm both the reality of God and creation as well as the noetic effects of sin on the human person. The Apostle Paul, writing to the Corinthian church, says that now "we see but a poor reflection . . . now I know in part, then I shall know fully"

37. Benton and Craib, *Philosophy of Social Science*, 120.
38. Benton and Craib, *Philosophy of Social Science*, 120.
39. Benton and Craib, *Philosophy of Social Science*, 120.
40. Benton and Craib, *Philosophy of Social Science*, 120.
41. Benton and Craib, *Philosophy of Social Science*, 120.
42. Benton and Craib, *Philosophy of Social Science*, 121.

(1 Cor 13:12). There is a reality accessible to the individual. But it is imperfectly formed and indistinct; there is a limit to the human ability to access it.

A further implication is that due to the dominance of social constructionism within the qualitative research field, it will be necessary to view the conclusions of some writers with discernment. Critical realism may also impact ways of understanding the relationship between an artist or theologian and the artefacts they produce. This question is clarified and examined later in this work.

THE ROLE OF FAITH IN ACADEMIC AND PUBLIC DISCOURSE

An underlying assumption of this monograph is that religious faith has a role to play in intellectual life. To this end, it is broadly speaking engaged in both a *private* project and a *public* project. The private project is one that is aimed at Christian believers by examining a methodology which permits intellectual work incorporating faith and aimed at the community of faith. The public project also targets the Christian believer but intends to allow them to do important and relevant works for a wider secular community. For the private element, I draw on the work of Alvin Plantinga, and for the public one, the work of Jürgen Habermas.

Superficially, it would seem that these two thinkers are somewhat opposed to each other. According to James Sennett, one "of Plantinga's most prominent qualities . . . is the steadfastness with which he holds to theistic, Christian and evangelistic convictions."[43] Habermas, however, has been described as an "atheistic and secular philosopher."[44] Adams also suggests Habermas is "unusual" in the sense that he "makes positive claims about religion in modern society."[45] Despite clear differences, it is this last comment on Habermas that reveals a thread they have in common: a view that recognizes the important role faith plays in decision making for the individual and the larger community. The

---

43. Sennett, ed., *Analytic Theist*, xiii.
44. Adams, *Habermas and Theology*, 1.
45. Adams, *Habermas and Theology*, 1.

Methodology

following outline will summarize two articles, one each from Plantinga and Habermas and then draw some conclusions.

Alvin Plantinga (b. 1932)

Plantinga is "widely recognized as one of the world's leading figures in metaphysics, epistemology, and the philosophy of religion."[46] He considers himself to be neither a Christian who happens to be a philosopher, nor is he a philosopher who happens to be a Christian—he is a Christian philosopher, and the terms are inseparable. This is made clear in an address he gave to the faculty at the University of Notre Dame, Indiana, after moving there in 1982. The address was later published as "Advice to Christian Philosophers."[47]

While his audience is Christian philosophers, he thinks that his advice may equally apply to other philosophers who believe in God, whether they are Muslim or Jewish.[48] I think it is also valid to suggest Plantinga's advice in the paper may also be applied to (at least) Christians in other disciplines, and, perhaps remarkably, also to those in theology and religion departments. Grenz, for example, notes that theologians function "within the context of the Christian community by articulating the conceptual framework and belief structure we share."[49] In his paper, Plantinga is making a call for a greater degree of attention to Christian issues and a greater Christian self-confidence.

Plantinga starts by noting that most of the "so-called human sciences, much of the non-human sciences, most of non-scientific intellectual endeavor and even a good bit of allegedly Christian theology is animated by a spirit wholly foreign to that of Christian theism."[50] He suggests when a person enters a university and begins to learn philosophy they will come into contact with all the burning questions of the day but will be hard-pressed for any guidance on how to be a Christian in philosophy.

---

46. Clark and Rea, eds., *Reason, Metaphysics, and Mind*, 3.
47. Plantinga, "Advice to Christian Philosophers."
48. Plantinga, "Advice to Christian Philosophers," 254.
49. Grenz, *Theology for the Community of God*, 7.
50. Plantinga, "Advice to Christian Philosophers," 253.

Practice-Led Theology

Christian philosophers, however, are "the philosophers of the Christian community" and it is a part of their task to serve the Christian community which "has its own questions, its own concerns, its own topics for investigation, its own agenda and its own research program."[51] So, while it may be important to attend to the questions that are important among the non-Christian philosophical community, a Christian philosopher who only does this will be neglecting a "crucial and central part of their task."[52] Further, Plantinga argues, a Christian philosopher has the "perfect right to the point of view and pre-philosophical assumptions" they bring to the task and if these are not shared by others, that would be "interesting but fundamentally irrelevant."[53] It is not the role of the Christian philosopher to engage in the "common effort to determine the probability of philosophical plausibility of belief in God." Rather, the Christian philosopher "*starts from* the existence of God, and presupposes it in philosophical work."[54] Plantinga thinks it is important for an individual to listen to and learn from the wider philosophical community—to be a part of it—but their work is not to be "circumscribed by what either the skeptic or the rest of the philosophical world thinks of theism."[55] I certainly would argue that it is important that Christians do engage in the work connected to the justification of theism, the existence of God and related questions (part of the task I am engaged in this book), that it is one dimension of the apologetics task, but that it is not to be the sole focus of the Christian in the disciplines.

Plantinga concludes his paper by saying that the Christian philosophical community has its own agenda, does not need to take its main focus from projects considered important in the philosophical centres of the day, and should be wary about assimilating currently popular philosophical ideas and procedures.[56] We are, he says, not "philosophers who happen, incidentally, to be Christians; we must strive to be

---

51. Plantinga, "Advice to Christian Philosophers," 255.
52. Plantinga, "Advice to Christian Philosophers," 255.
53. Plantinga, "Advice to Christian Philosophers," 256.
54. Plantinga, "Advice to Christian Philosophers," 261 (italics in original).
55. Plantinga, "Advice to Christian Philosophers," 264.
56. Plantinga, "Advice to Christian Philosophers," 271.

Methodology

Christian philosophers" and "pursue our projects with integrity, independence, and Christian boldness."[57] Apart from Plantinga's own work, contemporary philosophical representatives of this approach include Dallas Willard, James Porter Moreland, and William Lane Craig. There are also examples in other disciplines.

With Plantinga's advice in hand, it still remains for the Christian to negotiate a place for their work within the secular environment, be that in the public sphere or in the university. This will partly be established by the integrity and rigour of the intellectual tasks in which an individual engages. It is also helpful to illustrate the relevance of Christian perspectives to the wider intellectual project. One thinker to address this issue is Jürgen Habermas.

Jürgen Habermas (b. 1929)

As "arguably the most influential social theorist of the second half of the twentieth century," Jürgen Habermas's work has covered a wide range of problems and disciplines, including historical analyses, epistemology and philosophical anthropology, social theory, moral philosophy, legal theory, political analysis, and literary criticism.[58] William Outhwaite argues that Habermas's work is "central to many of the most pressing intellectual and practical concerns of the contemporary world."[59] Of his wide-ranging interests, I will draw on his development of *the public sphere*.

In Habermas's own words, the notion of the public sphere has been an interest of his for his whole life.[60] He has written on this question on numerous occasions starting with his first major work *The Structural Transformation of the Public Sphere* (1962)[61] to one of his more recent discussions on the topic, an article titled "Religion in the Public Sphere" (2006).[62] The primary focus of this section will be on this article.

57. Plantinga, "Advice to Christian Philosophers," 271.
58. Pensky, "Society, Morality, and Law," 49.
59. Outhwaite, *Habermas Reader*, 3.
60. Habermas, *Between Naturalism and Religion*, 12.
61. Originally published in German as *Strukturwandel der Öffentlichkeit*.
62. Habermas, "Religion in the Public Sphere." Although this article appears to be a reprint of a chapter in his book *Between Naturalism and Religion*, the version I

What does Habermas mean by the term "public sphere?" He does not intend this term to describe a large ball accessible to all citizens in the local mall but rather a translation of the German word Öffentlichkeit, which can mean either *publicness* or *publicity*.[63] It does not describe a physical location but rather "a realm of our social life in which something approaching public opinion can be formed. Access is guaranteed to all citizens. A portion of the public sphere comes into being in every conversation in which private individuals assemble to form a public body."[64]

The public sphere describes "the arena within which public debates take place."[65] He traces the idea back to the growth of a "literate bourgeois public" in the 1700s that started to take a "political role in the evaluation of contemporary affairs and, particular, state policy."[66] These discussions which took place in clubs, salons and coffee-houses were supported by a "growing and increasingly free press."[67]

His argument on the role of religion in this public sphere rests on a number of assumptions. The first assumption is what he sees as the self-understanding of the constitutional state, by which he means the modern liberal state. For all its decision making, the modern state relies on *natural* reason—that is to say, arguments made in public using language and concepts to which all persons supposedly "have *equal access*."[68] Habermas claims there to be a "common human reason" that underlies the state which no longer needs religions for its legitimation.[69] Within this context it is up to individual participants in public debate to find agreement between the "positive liberty" to practice one's religious beliefs and the "negative liberty" to be spared from the practices

---

am using is more easily accessible.

63. Outhwaite, *Habermas Reader*, 370.
64. Habermas et al., "Public Sphere," 49.
65. Adams, *Habermas and Theology*, 4, 5.
66. Outhwaite, *Habermas Reader*, 7.
67. Outhwaite, *Habermas Reader*, 8.
68. Habermas, "Religion in the Public Sphere," 4 (italics original).
69. Habermas, "Religion in the Public Sphere," 4.

Methodology

of others.[70] This relies on the equal participation of all citizens and a common epistemic understanding that grounds the decisions.

This first assumption is closely related to the second: the necessity for neutrality of the state in political decision making. He argues that to maintain an equal freedom of religion for all its members, the state must remain neutral regarding competing world views. He restricts this neutrality to the parliament, the courts, government ministries and administrations.[71] The ability for the representatives of the state to actually achieve this might be a different story. As writers from a range of perspectives have observed, it may indeed be impossible to make decisions in this way.[72] Habermas recognizes these objections but believes his project to be a practical one.[73]

The third assumption is the potential added value Habermas sees religions providing to the wider community although it must be recognized that Habermas may have a somewhat two-dimensional view of religion. Nicholas Adams notes that Habermas is not interested in whether religions are "bearers of substantial ethical positions" but rather in how to "feed on" the normative power of religions while "keeping one's distance" from their authority.[74] It is this normative power possessed by religions that leads Habermas to conclude that "religious commitments will persist as long as modern forms of life are unable to generate within themselves the same richness of motivation and identity."[75] A more fully developed understanding of faith would only strengthen this understanding although it is not a question explored in this book as much as whether it is actually *possible* for modern forms of life to generate the richness of motivation and identity that Habermas talks about.

Nevertheless, Habermas does think religions "have a special power to articulate moral intuitions, especially with regard to vulnerable

70. Habermas, "Religion in the Public Sphere," 4.

71. Habermas, "Religion in the Public Sphere," 9.

72. See, for example, Denzin and Lincoln, *Collecting and Interpreting Qualitative Materials*, 31.

73. Outhwaite, *Habermas Reader*, 134.

74. Adams, *Habermas and Theology*, 14.

75. Adams, *Habermas and Theology*, 11.

forms of communal life." He also articulates the "hidden" moral intuitions of the non-religious person.[76] As will be shown shortly, it is then the job of the religious believer to present these in a language that can be understood by those outside the tradition. With these three elements in place, it is possible to move on to the core of his argument.

In "Religion in the Public Sphere," Habermas is arguing for a middle ground between John Rawls and Robert Audi on one side and Nicholas Wolterstorff and Paul Weithman on the other. The former pair argue for the use of only secular reasoning in decisions relevant to the public sphere while the latter pair say it is legitimate to have decisions based only on religious reasons in the public realm. Habermas recognizes the centrality of faith for believers and wants to allow for their right to participate in public debate from their place of faith, and they need not and should not abandon the religious way of thinking. He takes a position somewhere in the middle ground presenting a way for this to occur. Before considering his position, it is necessary to summarize the views of the two sides of the discussion as Habermas sees them.

Habermas thinks the work of Rawls places a too restrictive burden on the religious members of the community. Rawls requires that reasons must be detachable from the doctrines to which they are initially connected for a decision to be regarded as legitimate in the public sphere. There are two problems with this restriction. Firstly, as Habermas sees it, religious communities contribute to the "stabilizing and advancing [of] a liberal political culture."[77] As an example, Habermas cites Martin Luther King and the US civil rights movement. He notes that "the religious roots to the motivations of most social and socialist movements in both the United States and European countries are highly impressive."[78] In a similar vein, Bloesch argues that the Gospel "entails not only taking up the cross in service to the unfortunate in society but also engaging in political programs for social change."[79]

---

76. Habermas, "Religion in the Public Sphere," 10.
77. Habermas, "Religion in the Public Sphere," 7.
78. Habermas, "Religion in the Public Sphere," 6.
79. Bloesch, *Essentials of Evangelical Theology*, 2:168.

Methodology

Secondly, and more importantly, the very nature of the liberal state, the idea Rawls wishes to defend, cannot "encumber its citizens, whom it guarantees freedom of religious expression, with duties that are incompatible with pursuing a devout life—it cannot expect something impossible of them."[80] I will return to this point a little later in the discussion.

Habermas rejects the idea that it is only wholly secular justifications which count in the liberal state and recognizes faith to be more than a set of doctrines but a "source of energy that the person who has a faith taps performativity and thus nurtures his or her entire life."[81] For these reasons, he argues it is not reasonable for the liberal state to expect all its citizens to justify political statements apart from their faith as this goes against the states' commitment to protecting religious expression. For the state to do this would be going from its secular neutrality into imposing a secular worldview on its citizens, a move that would be claiming too much ground.[82] However, Habermas argues that this separation is still expected of people in public office.[83]

For the religious believing citizen seeking to participate in the decision making process of the state, the first thing Habermas requires of them is to view their faith "reflexively from the outside and relate it to secular views."[84] Habermas calls this the "institutional translation proviso."[85] Whatever truth a religious statement may carry, it can only be included as part of the public debate if it is translated into language and concepts that are accessible by all citizens. Only when this occurs can the content of religious statements be "taken up in the agendas and negotiations within political bodies and in the broader political process."[86] To particularize this position for this project, Habermas is allowing Christians to be informed by their beliefs in decision-making

---

80. Habermas, "Religion in the Public Sphere," 7.
81. Habermas, "Religion in the Public Sphere," 8.
82. Junker-Kenny, *Habermas and Theology*, 136.
83. Habermas, "Religion in the Public Sphere," 9.
84. Habermas, "Religion in the Public Sphere," 9.
85. Habermas, "Religion in the Public Sphere," 10.
86. Habermas, "Religion in the Public Sphere," 11.

but expects them to present the results of their deliberations in language that is at least intelligible to all members of the state.

At the other end of the spectrum to Rawls and Audi are Paul Weithman and Nicholas Wolterstorff. Habermas thinks their views (particularly those of Wolterstorff) undermine the necessary neutrality of the state in decision making. Weithman believes citizens should be confident the state is justified in carrying out certain actions and they should be prepared to say why they think this is the case. Habermas sees this as a "milder" version of the translation proviso which is essentially a universalization test—decisions are grounded in concepts of justice that can come from their religious conceptions.[87] Wolterstorff thinks the political process should be free to use religious reasons in its deliberations. This concerns Habermas as it might make government the instrument of the religious majority; government enters the battle of religions.[88] Habermas sees Wolterstorff's argument as a violation of the neutrality principle "according to which all enforceable political decisions *must be formulated* in a language that is equally accessible to all citizens, and it *must be possible to justify them* in this language as well."[89] Although unstated by Habermas, this opposite should also be a problem—that is, if government became the instrument of a devout *anti*-religious minority. This concern is implicit in the position taken by Rawls and Audi since they argue that religious beliefs must be wholly secularized, other belief systems that are already wholly secularized are admitted unquestioned.

The religious citizen who is participating in the democratic process is contributing to the wider community a public version of conclusions reached in the private debate of a faith community. Habermas recognizes that there is an additional burden here for the believing citizen that the secular citizen is spared: having to think through an issue and then also having to translate it into a language and concepts for wider use. The obligation then on the secular citizen is that they recognize that they live in a "post-secular society that is epistemically adjusted to the continued existence of religious communities" and can expect

---

87. Habermas, "Religion in the Public Sphere," 11.
88. Habermas, "Religion in the Public Sphere," 11.
89. Habermas, "Religion in the Public Sphere," 12 (italics original).

Methodology

disagreements along these lines to be a part of the modern secularized environment.[90] They are not something that will, or should, disappear. The secular view would be to refrain from passing judgment on religious truths, insisting (non-polemically) on a line between faith and knowledge but rejecting "scientifically limited conception of reason and the exclusion of religious doctrines from the genealogy of reason."[91] A secular understanding accords religious convictions a status other than "irrational."[92]

Implications

There are a number of implications to be drawn from this discussion. Christians should be motivated, and legitimately so, by the faith to which they subscribe—it generates its own questions to which there may be uniquely Christian answers. Further, it generates answers to questions that are posed by those outside the faith but in ways that draw on the Christian tradition. This is part of my own motivation: there are questions presented to believers and I seek to contribute to the ways these questions might be answered.

Reasons based on faith are also legitimate. They are obviously valid for the faith community but as Habermas indicates (for whatever reason) the particular logic and answers that believers bring to the public debate are of value to the wider community and contribute in a positive way to the discussion. However, they are only of value if they are understood and so must be presented in the public sphere in a way comprehensible to that public. This translation needs to be done by the faith community for the sake of those of other faiths or no faith. Habermas envisions a situation where all follow a principle of neutrality in decision-making. It is important in this context to read *secular* as neutral to religious and non-religious views and not as being atheistic. To make the claim of atheism is to make a positive assertion on the non-existence of God; it is a claim to knowledge.[93] To conflate atheism with non-theist would lead to atheism ceasing to be a view,

---

90. Habermas, "Religion in the Public Sphere," 15.
91. Habermas, "Religion in the Public Sphere," 16.
92. Junker-Kenny, *Habermas and Theology*, 136.
93. Moreland and Craig, *Philosophical Foundations*, 156.

as then babies would be *atheists*,[94] as well as cats, birds and insects. It is therefore important not to confuse the terms and this is an obligation that rests on all the communities involved in public debate. This argument also means that the questions that arise out of the Christian community have answers that are relevant to both the faith community and the wider community and could be presented in ways that speak to both.

Habermas pointed out that for a believer, their faith is a central source of motivation and energy for all aspects of life.[95] Importantly for this project, this means that all aspects of the faith life are important in the decision process and a part of the knowledge base. This includes aspects such as the life of prayer and meditation, worship and ritual.

This book, then, is both a public and a private project—private in that it seeks a method to allow the Christian to work with faith questions and public in that it attempts to include in that method a process for the Christian to *translate* those question/answer sets into a form that is understandable and useful to those outside the faith community; for all in the secular public sphere. It will be a central contention of this work that practice-led research—as formulated here—provides a methodology to achieve this end: it allows researchers to answer the questions of the Christian community (what Plantinga sees as the main task for the Christian academic) and for negotiating a place in the public sphere (a place where Habermas argues they have a legitimate role).

There is one final task for this section: to provide the project with a specific understanding of the public sphere. Habermas understands the public sphere to be the *space* where debate takes place on all and every issue of concern to the modern liberal democratic state. He is attempting to establish a set of rules for civilized common discourse among people of differing contexts and worldviews. Of the many and varied participants the university is one of the places included in the public sphere. For the argument I make in this book, *public sphere* will be restricted to the university context. As will become clear after chapters 3 and 4 which consider the history and definition of practice-led research, it is in the university environment it was developed and, for

---

94. Moreland and Craig, *Philosophical Foundations*, 156.
95. Habermas, "Religion in the Public Sphere," 8.

Methodology

this project at least, it will be restricted to this situation and more particularly, applied to theology in the university.

AN ANALYTICAL TOOL: HERMENEUTICS

The previous section provided a set of arguments for the legitimacy of this project. Firstly, religious believers have a right and an obligation to pursue questions of relevance and interest to them, and secondly, that the conclusions of these deliberations have relevance to the wider community in which believers live. The purpose of this section is to provide a more specific theoretical framework within which to pursue the goal of developing the practice-led research model into one usable by theology.

At its most basic level, the word *hermeneutics* is understood as "to explain, interpret or to translate."[96] In a broader sense, it is the "science of interpretation, especially the principles of proper textual exegesis."[97] However, although in essence true, these brief statements hide the complexity of its use. For example, Richard Palmer talks of six modern definitions of hermeneutics: the theory of biblical exegesis; a general philological methodology; the science of linguistic understanding; the methodological foundation of *Geisteswissenschaften*; phenomenology of existence; the systems of interpretation used to reach the meaning of myths and symbols.[98]

However, fueling the interpretive process is an individual's *worldview*. According to James Sire, a worldview

> is a commitment, a fundamental orientation of the heart, that can be expressed as a story or in a set of presuppositions (assumptions which may be true, partially true or entirely false) that we hold (consciously or subconsciously, consistently or inconsistently) about the basic constitution of reality, and that provides the foundation on which we live and move and have our being.[99]

---

96. Klein et al., *Introduction to Biblical Interpretation*, 4.
97. Palmer, *Hermeneutics*, 33.
98. Palmer, *Hermeneutics*, 33.
99. Sire, *Universe Next Door*, 20.

Practice-Led Theology

A world view addresses the most basic issues, answering questions such as what is real, what can we know, what is right and wrong, and what is the nature of the person.[100] Anthony C. Thiselton observes that everything "is understood in a given context and from a given point of view."[101] Given the fundamental nature of what a world view addresses, this, it would seem, is inescapable. They are, according to N. T. Wright, the "grid through which humans perceive reality."[102]

A key element in the construction of a worldview is *stories*. They are a basic part of human life and stand alongside other essential elements of a worldview (symbol, praxis, and fundamental questions and answers).[103] Given the centrality of stories—of narratives—all of life involves hermeneutics. Social interactions are replete in narrative and will always involve some work in discerning the meaning of what people are saying to us. Wright's understanding of narratives will be developed in more detail in chapter 6 as a part of a model for understanding the outcomes of a practice-led research project.

In addition to narrative, Wright employs critical realism. In *The New Testament and the People of God*, Wright writes that critical realism

> is a way of describing the process of "knowing" that acknowledges the *reality of the thing known, as something other than the knower* (hence "realism"), while also fully acknowledging that the only access we have to this reality lies along the spiraling path of *appropriate dialogue or conversation between the knower and the thing known* (hence "critical") . . . Knowledge, in other words, although in principle concerning realities independent of the knower, is never itself independent of the knower.[104]

A critical realist approach, suggests Wright, seeks to "be true to itself, and to the public world, while always open to the possibility of challenge, modifications, and subversion."[105] Texts will be approached

---

100. Sire, *Universe Next Door*, 22.
101. Thiselton, *Two Horizons*, 105.
102. Wright, *New Testament and the People of God*, 38.
103. Wright, *New Testament and the People of God*, 38.
104. Wright, *New Testament and the People of God*, 35.
105. Wright, *New Testament and the People of God*, 67.

Methodology

from the relation of reader to text, of texts to their authors, and "beyond that to the realities they purport to describe."[106] This means considering the content of the text as well as the historical and situational context of, and influences on, the author. A critical realist perspective can act as a counterbalance to "oversocialization" of research where everything might be seen as construction.[107]

INTERVIEWS: HEARING FROM THE PRACTITIONERS

I began this project with a general understanding of the key features and potential benefits of practice-led research but without a detailed understanding of the method or any kind of definition. It will become clear in a later chapter that a significant reason for this is that definitions of practice-led research as well as its applications are still fluid. However, one thing was clear from the earliest stage: it is a tool developed by those from the creative arts in the university or college context as a means of doing research. It seemed likely that individuals and individual institutions will be able to provide more detailed descriptions of the methodology and how it operates.

Purpose

This, then, was the first purpose of the interviews. To speak to practitioners and see examples of the methodology in action; to see how it was structured, what it looked like in the field, and most importantly, to get an understanding of how the idea of practice-led research might be articulated. A second reason was to see different ways it might be implemented by individuals engaged in different types of research. The goal here was to get an overview of the flexibility of the methodology and how it had already been adapted. A third reason was that by listening to practitioners, it would be possible to gain an insight into the important literature which was often written from within. Speaking to individuals who wrote about practice-led research and/or were practice-led researchers might provide access to a different perspective

---

106. Wright, *New Testament and the People of God*, 64.
107. Alvesson and Sköldberg, *Reflexive Methodology*, 269.

and allow me to engage with the methodology in ways different to the one-way monologue of a journal article.

In line with the general argument of an earlier section of this chapter, time and place have an impact on research. My geographical location, Perth in Western Australia, is central to the genesis of this project. Local universities contain a number of theorists who have published in the area and/or have wide experience supervising postgraduate students using the methodology. Further, Australian institutions have been involved from the earliest stages in developing practice-led research as a legitimate approach.[108] By conducting interviews, it was *not* my purpose to reach general conclusions from them alone, but rather to gain a fuller understanding of the methodology from those speaking the "original language." The interview process began with these goals in mind.

Selection of Interviewees

The potential pool of interviewees was small—those in postgraduate study or having completed postgraduate study that use or that have used practice-led methodology. For this reason, I decided to use a *purposive sampling* method to select participants. Purposive sampling is "[a] form of non-probability sampling in which decisions concerning the individuals to be included in the sample are taken by the researcher, based upon a variety of criteria which may include specialist knowledge of the research issue, or capacity and willingness to participate in the research."[109] It is a strategy especially suited to a situation where only a small sample is selected from a restricted population,[110] enhancing the likelihood of finding "participants who would be most likely to contribute appropriate data, both in terms of relevance and depth."[111]

This was the primary approach adopted, although it was restricted further to include only those who had completed or were late in their research. Individuals early on in their research tended to be less clear

---

108. Questions of the origins of the method and the role of Australian universities in the debate will be explored in the next chapter.

109. Oliver, "Purposive Sampling," 245.

110. Battaglia, "Nonprobability Sampling," 524.

111. Oliver, "Purposive Sampling," 245.

Methodology

on what the methodology meant for their project. Participants were initially selected from existing contacts. Further contacts were made through recommendations from this initial set as well as individuals met at conferences and at seminars.

Structure of the Interviews

My initial strategy was to adopt an interview guide approach.[112] This would help keep the interview within a reasonable time frame as well as ensure coverage of what I thought would be important foundational issues. It is a method with some structure but would allow a good deal of flexibility to follow leads as well as permit interviewees to raise the points that seemed important to them.

However, even the flexibility offered by this approach proved insufficient. As the information sheet made clear,[113] interviewees were aware I was attempting to apply practice-led research in a new area. For this reason, as well as a lack of familiarity with my disciplinary background, many of the interviewees had almost as many questions for me as I had for them. They hoped to answer the questions in ways that might support my task. Two additional issues arose. Firstly, the range of creative approaches used by researchers was quite varied, requiring a variety of directional and clarification questions. Secondly, the guide questions were inappropriate for talking to supervisors of postgraduate students. Although I retained some broad and general questions, a more generalized style was needed to allow me to pursue the person's understanding of how the process worked in their case, or how they directed their students.

As a result of these issues, a more conversational style seemed to be better suited to the individuals I was speaking to. It is an approach that Ellis and Berger have called *reflexive dyadic interviews*. This method still follows the protocol of an interviewer asking questions and an interviewee answering them, but

> the interview is conducted more as a conversation between two equals than as a distinctly hierarchical, question-and-answer

---

112. See Appendix 1 for sample guides from the initial interviews.
113. See Appendix 2.

exchange, and the interviewer tries to tune in to the interactively produced meanings and emotional dynamics within the interview itself . . . When telling the story of the research, the interviewers might reflect deeply on the personal experience that brought them to the topic . . . and/or how they used knowledge of the self or the topic at hand to understand what the interviewee was saying.[114]

This approach allowed a certain dynamic aspect to enter the interviews, the role of interviewer sometimes changing hands as I was asked how I became interested in this area or was asked questions that might help the interviewee better frame an answer. Much of this refinement was carried out after completing the first interview with a visual artist who had completed a practice-led PhD and was beginning to assist students commencing the same study.

Interviews were situated in locations selected by the participant (in a coffee shop, for example, or their own office). Many of the necessary administrative tasks were completed prior to the interview, usually by email, and included the request to record the discussion, information on their right to review the transcript, and a plain language statement containing ethical details, privacy information and an overview of the project. A consent form was completed at the very beginning of the interview.[115]

Concurrent with these interviews were a number of informal discussions, workshops and seminars. Particularly helpful were weekly seminars at Edith Cowan University conducted by the Centre for Research in Entertainment, Arts, Technology, Education and Communications (CREATEC).[116] The CREATEC seminars host speakers from within the university as well as other institutions, businesses or independent researchers. Practice-led projects and similar research projects regularly make an appearance. A second useful forum was also at Edith Cowan University. Called *This is not a Seminar* (TINAS), it is a

---

114. Ellis and Berger, "Their Story," 162.
115. These documents are provided in Appendix 2 and 3.
116. See *Centre*.

Methodology

weekly gathering of postgraduate students many of whom are engaged in practice-led projects.[117]

Assessment of Interviews

The initial intention of the interviews was to find out more about the nature of practice-led research. I believed a useful starting point was to speak to those who had used, or were currently using, the methodology. I spoke to individuals currently engaged in or who had recently completed practice-led projects as well as supervisors of students completing practice-led research. While I was able to gain familiarity with the way individuals conducted individual projects, and how they were presented and some of the themes possible, I did not find any clear or consistent answers to the question as to what practice-led research is. It must be noted that one interviewee acknowledged that their project was not strictly practice-led research but was centred on practice and that they had developed a methodology of their own that related to the particular project. In a sense the forums, workshops and informal discussions were of greater benefit as theoretical issues were often raised and lively debate ensued; in this I was an active participant. This was not really the case in the interviews.

For these reasons, little direct content from the interviews appears in this book. Since they were conducted with formal ethical approval it is important to detail the mechanics. The interview process did feed into the motivations of the project to contribute to the formal and more detailed definition of what practice-led research is and how it can be consistently implemented while still retaining much of its inherent flexibility.

MANAGING THE PUZZLE PIECES

This section provides a strategy for managing the various components of the research project as there are a number of elements feeding into the research: an interpretive framework, theoretical perspectives, as well as the *raw* data of interviews, articles, books and other *texts*.

---

117. At the time of writing, TINAS does not have its own webpage, but some information is available as a part of the CREATEC mailouts, as well as its own mailing list.

In any project, there is a danger that its many components may get lost in the process, or potentially at least, ignored or forgotten or simply glossed over at certain points. In order to ensure the interplay of various components of a research project, Alvesson and Sköldberg suggest a researcher establish a level of consistency at the metatheoretical level. They define a metatheory as "a comprehensive frame of reference for inspiring and structuring reflection."[118] The metatheory they offer to handle this task—*reflexive interpretation*—is not a theory by their own understanding but rather a framework.

According to the definition proposed by Alvesson and Sköldberg, the Christian perspective outlined earlier in this chapter fills the role of metatheory providing the comprehensive frame of reference. So, if reflexive interpretation were used alone, it could be argued that reflexive interpretation could become a metatheory when you do not have a metatheory—that is to say, when you are directionless. It is therefore my intention in this project to use their method as a *mechanism of coordination* for the various elements involved in this study.[119]

Following a "double hermeneutic" and a "triple hermeneutic" developed by other writers, Alvesson and Sköldberg call their method a "quadruple hermeneutics" which they describe as a "rather heavy term" and so shorten it to an allegedly less heavy term, *quadri-hermeneutics*.[120] They describe it as *qualitative, interpretive* and *reflexive* representing "the open play of reflection across various levels of interpretation."[121] It is a "framework for drawing attention to and mediating between core dimensions in reflection, for initiating acts of reflection and maintaining movement between reflective themes."[122] The table below summarizes the levels of interaction.

---

118. Alvesson and Sköldberg, *Reflexive Methodology*, 271.

119. It is important to distinguish between the use of the term metatheory as Alvesson and Sköldberg use it and the sociological discipline of metatheory.

120. Alvesson and Sköldberg, *Reflexive Methodology*, 271.

121. Alvesson and Sköldberg, *Reflexive Methodology*, 271.

122. Alvesson and Sköldberg, *Reflexive Methodology*, 270.

Methodology

Aspect/level	Focus
Interaction with empirical material	Accounts in interviews, observations of situations and other empirical materials
Interpretation	Underlying meanings
Critical Interpretation	Ideology, power, social reproduction
Reflection on text production and language use	Own text, claims to authority, selectivity of the voices represented in the text

Table 1. Levels of Interpretation[123]

An important key to understanding what they mean is the difference in their use of the terms *reflexive* and *reflective*. By reflective, they mean "the focused reflections upon a specific method or level of interpretation."[124] For example, reflection on the interviews might involve considering different ways of interpreting comments by a particular interviewee or, say, consideration of comments by different interviewees on the same issues. Or another example, critical interpretation, might involve the consideration of conflicting ideologies and world views in a document and how these are restricting or progressing the debate: for example, in what ways is a document attempting to control what is and is not *knowledge*?

Reflexive is related to reflective (and they are often confused) but the former has a broader reach than the latter. Reflexive refers to considering the ways each level or aspect influences and is influenced by the others. It is about how each level or aspect plays off against the other, the influence of one calling for a reconsideration of another. This interrelationship may be expressed diagrammatically (see Figure 1):

---

123. Alvesson and Sköldberg, *Reflexive Methodology*, 273.
124. Alvesson and Sköldberg, *Reflexive Methodology*, 271.

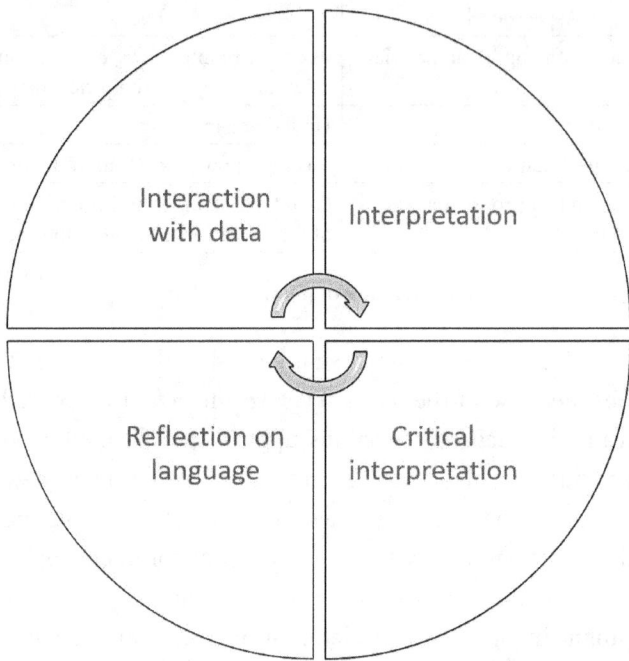

Figure 1. Interpretative Interaction

CONCLUSIONS

This chapter began by outlining a methodological dilemma. Practice-led research is a relatively new methodology. As such, definitions of what it means vary widely, are somewhat minimalist or, in some cases, are completely absent. In order to fully investigate the application of the methodology to theology, it is necessary to develop a strategy to undertake this task. The main aim of this chapter, then, is to outline a framework to solve this dilemma.

All academic discourse is undertaken within a worldview of some sort, whether that is acknowledged or not. It may be one sourced in a religious faith—Christianity, for example—or one sourced in a non-religious faith, such as Marxism. Whatever the case, it will have an impact on the questions asked and the answers which are acceptable. This first section made clear my position as a Christian and outlined the essential assumptions that accompany this position. It sets the tone for the type of questions asked and the tenor of answers sought.

Methodology

Next, the theoretical position for this book, *critical realism*, was outlined. In a nutshell, critical realism argues that "knowledge . . . although in principle concerning realities independent of the knower, is never itself independent of the knower."[125] This view allows the independence of God and a separate creation to be maintained—there is a world *out there* separate from human existence. The view also recognizes that any understanding of the world is impacted by culture and worldview as well as the impediment of sin on building a noetic structure.

Arguments were then presented for the legitimacy of academic projects flowing from a Christian framework. I argued that this project is engaged in both a *private* and a *public* project. The private project, grounded in work from Alvin Plantinga, suggested that Christians need to be approaching the academic task as believers by finding solutions to problems grounded in their faith as well as asking questions motivated by that faith. The public project, based in work of Jürgen Habermas, argued that Christian theology has a place in the *public sphere* as it has something to offer contemporary debates. Restricting the arena of the public sphere to an academic one, I suggested that the questions posed by Christians and the answers produced need to be translated so the wider academic community can have access to them.

A critical realist hermeneutic based on work from Wright was developed. Wright suggests that all individuals begin with presuppositions that make up their worldview. A key component is the stories we tell each other and are told by our culture. This is our raw material. Wright argues that texts came from a context and are not simply a window on the world. This is also true of the author who wrote with a purpose in mind and from within a particular cultural framework. However, to some degree, the text does have a life of its own that is not the author. The content of a text is, in principle, grounded in the events, time and situations of the world.

To assist in developing an understanding of practice-led research, a set of interviews with practitioners and supervisors were conducted. The aim was to see the method in the field, as it were, to see ways in which the methodology was being used. The interviewees were selected

---

125. Wright, *New Testament and the People of God*, 35.

using a purposive sampling method, seeking individuals with specialist knowledge of practice-led research. The style of interviews is described as *reflexive dyadic*, one where there is a greater interchange of information compared to a more hierarchical question and answer structure.

In the final task of this chapter, I outlined a strategy, *reflexive interpretation*, as a means of maintaining the interplay between the various components of the methodology. Two terms are key: *reflective* and *reflexive*. The first, reflective, describes the consideration of the issues of a particular element of the process, say, the interviews. The second term, reflexive, describes thinking about how the different elements relate to and influence each other. This model allows me to move between the content of the texts, relationships between them, and my role as interpreter and author. The next three chapters put the methods outlined in this chapter into practice by looking at the history of practice-led research and seeking a clear definition.

Chapter 3

A History of Practice-Led Research

INTRODUCTION

Practice-led research as a recognizable, discrete methodology is relatively recent in its development. Primarily for this reason, a comprehensive history has yet to be written, and indeed, that history is still in the making. However, it is possible to discern a number of key features of that history. This chapter will present these components and examine the many threads that run through and tie them together. Some of the drivers in the methodology's development have a long history but are still apparent in the form it has taken today. Some of these threads underlie the contemporary debates—if not always visible—and also underlie some of the directions in which writers wish to take practice-led research.

Broadly, the methodology's origins lie in the creative arts and are in response to practical and theoretical changes inside and outside that discipline. The central argument will be that the immediate causes for the development of practice-led research as a distinct methodology are a set of economic and political changes that began outside the creative community which impacted the structure and funding of universities and liberal arts colleges. These external influences motivated and crystallized intellectual, social, and economic ideas which had been developing in previous decades within the creative community itself. The interaction between these internal and external factors gave rise to the need for a new research methodology specific to the visual arts. This approach is a modification and significant expansion of one put forward by a number of scholars, most notably Fiona Candlin[1] and Rebekka Kill.[2] It will be argued beyond this, however, that the contemporary issues that fed into its formulation—the relationship of art and the artist to knowledge and research—are the most recent manifestation of a long-standing debate on these issues some of which go back millennia.

The argument will be expanded to illustrate the impact of similar external changes in the social, political, and economic environment in recent decades which has led to a re-evaluation of the role of the humanities (of which theology is a part) in the university. As the visual arts needed to adapt to their new role within the university, theology has needed to examine its own role in the academy, its purpose there and how it does its own work. It will be argued that the space created by the development of practice-led research is one into which theology can expand. With a specific focus on the Christian academic and student, it will be argued that practice-led research is a methodology readily adaptable to theology, and one that suits the very nature of theological reflection providing new opportunities for theological research in the academy. This idea will also be developed in later parts of this book.

Central to the debates surrounding the formulation of practice-led research, but often below the surface, is the question of the role and function of the *artist* in the public sphere. What is the social status of the artist? To whom, if anybody, and to what, if anything, is the artist responsible? The various ways these questions have been answered historically reveal much about the motivations directing the debates. This chapter will also provide important context to the sometimes fierce, sometimes polemical debates on what practice-led research is or what it should be. Practice-led research is very much a product of this historical context.

There are a number of reasons these issues are important for this monograph. Firstly, due to the economic and political debates occurring in universities over funding, there are connected debates on the legitimacy of disciplines and what role they have, or even should have, in

1. Candlin, "Dual Inheritance."
2. Kill, "Coming in from the Cold."

the academy. While practice-led research is to a large degree a product of these debates, they are equally relevant to theology and theologians. So, it is relevant to ask the same questions of theology as have been asked of creative disciplines: What is the social status of the *theologian*? To whom, if anybody, and to what, if anything, is the *theologian* responsible? Rather than these questions being asked as an ad hoc addition to the ones asked about artists, it will be further argued in this chapter that they are integral to each other and that there has long been a link between the two disciplines.

A second reason these historical points are important is expressed in the question: where is the role of the artist and the theologian in the public sphere, the arena of public debate? It was argued in the previous chapter that religion (and so theology) does have a role in the public sphere, but how might that function be expressed? Some of the answers to these questions revealed in the investigations of this chapter support my contention for the validity of practice-led research as a useful methodology for use in theology.

Finally, the historical context of the methodology provided in this chapter helps to lay the groundwork for later chapters where I define practice-led research, examine its relationship to theory/practice as well as how it can be employed in theology.

An important caveat: this chapter is not meant to be a history of art nor a history of theology. Its intention is to pick up threads in these histories that are important to the development of practice-led research within the last two decades or so. These threads will be used to put the methodology in an appropriate context as well as to highlight aspects of the methodology that are problematic for use in the disciplines it came from and for its application in a theological situation.

FOUNDATIONS

Plato

"The safest general characterization of the European philosophical tradition," according to Alfred North Whitehead, "is that it consists of a series of footnotes to Plato."[3] While there is certainly a degree of

---

3. Whitehead, *Process and Reality*, 63.

hyperbole in this observation, Whitehead is describing the vast array of topics Plato covers in his writing and that it is an "inexhaustible mine of suggestion."[4] The comment does capture an important truth relevant to the argument of this chapter. Even if Whitehead is correct in the additional observation that the systems scholars have extracted from his writings are doubtful,[5] it is nevertheless true that Plato's views on art have had a long-lasting influence and thinkers have had to engage with his ideas, positively or negatively. While he did not develop a clear artistic theory, Plato has had a "profound impact on artistic thought."[6]

Of particular interest to this chapter are the arguments Plato makes on the purpose of art and the role of the artist in society. The main point this section will explore is summarized in the following extract from his vision of a utopian state, *The Republic*. Socrates says to Glaucon:

> In that case, I would imagine, the art of imitation is a far cry from truth. The reason it can make everything, apparently, is that it grasps just a little of each thing—and only an image at that. We say the painter can paint us a shoemaker, for example, or a carpenter, or any of the other craftsmen. He may know nothing of any of these skills, and yet, if he is a good painter, from a distance his picture of a carpenter can fool children and people with no judgment, because it looks like a real carpenter.[7]

This idea that the arts are imitation—*mimesis*—and are, as a result, far removed from truth is underpinned by Plato's concept of the *forms* and so a brief overview is necessary. Plato wonders how we can recognize an object as a chair, for example, when there is so much variation within the type. What makes a chair a chair? Plato believed there "must be an essence—or Form—common to everything falling under one concept."[8] So, it is possible to describe an object as a chair because it

---

4. Whitehead, *Process and Reality*, 63.
5. Whitehead, *Process and Reality*, 63.
6. Barasch, *Theories of Art*, 1:4.
7. Plato, *Resp.* 598b–598c.
8. Crisp, "Form."

A History of Practice-Led Research

"participates in" the Form of *Chair*.[9] This also applies to more abstract concepts. A plate made by a potter is not perfectly round, but the Form *Roundness* is the ideal to which the plate aspires.[10]

To be able to say, "that is a couch" (to use one of Plato's own examples from book X), it is necessary to know what the Form of a couch is. In a more general sense, to know whether something is a particular object or not, it is necessary to know what the Form of that object is. The object's Form is only known by the reasoning of the mind or soul, whereas the representations of the object in the physical world are known by the senses—sight, touch and so on. Only when the Form is known is it possible to say that an object or concept is of that class of things.[11] In essence, Plato holds to a realistic ontology of universals;[12] the Forms exist independently of, and prior to, anything else.

The impact this has had on understanding art and artists arises out of the relationship of the Forms to the material world. This material world, the world of senses that humans occupy, is an imperfect representation of the perfect forms. It was shaped by the demiurge out of matter that pre-existed. The demiurge is only a crafter, shaping the world as an imitation of the Forms. There is no originality or creativity in the task they perform.[13]

The artist or other craftsperson then looks at the material world and, no matter how skilled they are, makes an imperfect representation through their craft based on their experience of the sense world. However, they are already looking at an inferior version, a copy, so anything they make is an imperfect representation of a world that is in itself an imperfect representation of the Forms.

Plato illustrates his argument in book X of *The Republic* by using an analogy of *three beds*. Penner sums up how Plato understands the relationship between the Forms, the physical object and the representation of that object:

---

9. Crisp, "Form."
10. Tiberius, "Blackburn, Simon."
11. Brown, "Plato and Aristotle," 602.
12. Crisp, "Form."
13. Allen and Springsted, *Philosophy for Understanding Theology*, 8.

As the painter stands to a painting of a bed, so the carpenter stands to the bed he manufactures, and so God stands to the Form of the Bed (God as the real maker of the really real bed: 597c–d). What God makes—"what the bed is," the thing itself which is "one in nature," whose Form both the carpenter's and the painter's bed possess—is made by God because he doesn't want just to make a bed, one of many physical beds. From this analogy, Plato tells us that we can see that the painter resides at "the third remove from reality" (*alêtheia*: truth) (And the carpenter, who presumably looks to what the bed is, comes in second, while only one with knowledge of the Forms comes in first).[14]

This aspect of the Platonic view—art was imitation; it served the community; and the artist as craftsperson held the corresponding status of a trade—dominated theory well into the Middle Ages.

It is important to realize that, according to Plato, artists were not creators but makers. The idea of an artist being *creative* does not arrive for some time (discussed later). Barasch observes there was no term in classical culture for what is now understood as art.[15] The terms nearest to a modern concept are the Greek *technē* and the Latin *ars*. "The word *technē* (traditionally translated "art") signifies the craft involved in the production of *mimemata* and pictures, not the modern Fine Arts as we know them. In general, any human activity founded on practice and experience and put into rules and habits was called *technē* (art), something that could be taught and learnt."[16] *Technē*, then, does not refer directly to the "fine arts" but rather "all kinds of human skills, crafts, or even knowledge."[17] It meant that all kinds of disciplines came under the umbrella of *technē* such as carpentry, agriculture and medicine.[18]

---

14. Penner, "Forms in the Republic," 244.
15. Barasch, *Theories of Art*, 1:2.
16. Sörbom, "Classical Concept," 24.
17. Barasch, *Theories of Art*, 1:2.
18. Barasch, *Theories of Art*, 1: 2.

Aristotle

Where Plato held that the product of a craftsperson was a copy of a copy and so somehow lacking, Aristotle ascribed full reality to the products of *technē*.[19] For Aristotle, "production" involves an agency, from something and shaped into something and involves following a set of general rules.[20] One consequence of this was that for Aristotle, the artist is completely separate from the thing they create.[21] This was to be significant in late antiquity (examined in a later section).

Aristotle discusses these issues at length in his *Nicomachean Ethics*. One goal of his text is to show the type of person an individual should aspire to be. What are the characteristics of this individual? It is "someone who has practical wisdom, and ideally someone whose practical wisdom is used in the service of philosophy—the activity that gives fullest expression to the virtues of theoretical inquiry. Aristotle discusses technical skill here only in order to emphasize the ways in which the other virtues of thought are superior to it."[22] So, while technical skill may be useful (and many of the examples Aristotle uses in describing practical wisdom revolve around *technē*),[23] the goal of the individual centres on practical wisdom, *phronēsis*, and theoretical wisdom, *sophia*. A significant goal of the Christian theologian is wisdom. There are numerous injunctions in the Scriptures to seek wisdom (most notably Proverbs). This question will be considered in a later section.

THE SITUATION OF THE ARTIST

However, for both Plato and Aristotle it was possible for artists to have a place in society. For Plato what was needed was for the artist to "encourage people to transcend their finite earthly condition and aspire to knowledge of the unchanging order of the cosmos."[24] For Aristotle "young men should be taught to look, not at the works of Pauson, but

---

19. Barasch, *Theories of Art*, 1:10.
20. Barasch, *Theories of Art*, 1:10, 11.
21. Barasch, *Theories of Art*, 1:12.
22. Kraut, "Introduction," 7.
23. Gottlieb, "Practical Syllogism," 218.
24. Harrington, *Art and Social Theory*. 10.

at those of Polygnotus, or any other painter or sculptor who expresses moral ideas."[25] For Plato and Aristotle, the artist had to, in some way, serve the community they were a part of. Jacques Barzun notes that

> in the beginning, art is the handmaid of religion. Temples, statues of the gods, rituals involving poetry, music, and dance form the cradle of the several arts. When the city is also the whole state, and the citizens all belong to one religion, which is a worship of the city's particular gods, the question of who shall pay for the arts does not arise. Religion, art, public office, and military service are duties which all citizens perform or pay for collectively.[26]

Artists and other related occupations were sometimes described by the term *banausos*; they were *banausoi* or mechanics.[27] The word also carried with it the idea of being vulgar people and "vulgar workers should not possess political rights although they are necessary for the city-state."[28] Aristotle argued, for example, that the "doing of manual labor and what [he], in general, describes as banausic work (roughly, anything physical or aimed at earning money) prevents the development of virtue, for which he thinks leisure is needed."[29] The task of the artist was largely a physical one and "there was an alienation of classical Greek society from any kind of manual work."[30] The reason this society was able to make this separation from work is not touched on by Barasch but it seems likely that it was only possible due to an economy reliant on slaves. This is supported by Jacques Barzun when he notes that "the craftsmen who made the art were not a separate group dependent on commissions for a living: they were slaves, already fully supported, already making pots and pans and other products of artistic skill."[31] This suggests that the situation of the artist has always been a social

---

25. Barasch, *Theories of Art*, 1:13.
26. Barzun, "Insoluble Problem," 121.
27. Barasch, *Theories of Art*, 1:23.
28. Miller, Jr., "Aristotle on the Ideal Constitution," 552.
29. Roberts, "Excellences of the Citizen," 559.
30. Barasch, *Theories of Art*, 1:23.
31. Barzun, "Insoluble Problem," 121.

A History of Practice-Led Research

and political issue. The artist was praised in antiquity for the product of their craft but they themselves, as a rule, were not.

In antiquity, there was an almost complete separation between the artist and the theorist. Aristotle argues that it is only the philosopher who "performs actions that are right and fine."[32] The work of philosophy is superior to that of politics,[33] and certainly that of the craftsperson, the one engaged in *technē*. Initially, philosophers determined the role and function of art in society and then later, as theology developed into a discipline with the work of Augustine,[34] it too guided the role and purpose of art and artists.

THE EASTERN EMPIRE AND THE ROLE OF ART

The Iconoclastic Controversy ran through the eighth and early ninth century and mainly in the east, the Byzantine empire.[35] While predominantly about the nature and role of images, it was also about attempting to reassert imperial power over the church.[36] Summing up the position of the Iconoclasts, Bredin states that they had two fundamental beliefs:

> Frst, that the widespread practice of venerating religious images was idolatrous (the mental habits of paganism were still prevalent at the time, and the charge of idolatry was sometimes justified); and second, that the very attempt to represent God or any aspect of the divine as a visual image was blasphemous, for it was an insult to God to think that one could represent His nature in material form.[37]

The iconodules—those in favour of the appropriateness of artistic images (literally, "worshipers of images")[38]—eventually won the day

---

32. Bobonich, "Aristotle's Ethical Treatises," 20.
33. Kraut, "Introduction," 10.
34. McGrath, *Christian Theology*, 13.
35. Barasch, *Theories of Art*, 1:48.
36. Beckwith, *Early Christian and Byzantine Art*, 78. Although purely a coincidence, it is worth noting the name of the series editor of this book. He plays a role in a later part of this account.
37. Bredin, "Medieval Art Theory," 31.
38. Barasch, *Theories of Art*, 1:53.

with the iconoclasts being condemned at the second Council of Nicaea in 787.[39] The general conclusions made at this time became the "standard justification for the visual arts throughout the Middle Ages."[40] Broadly, there were three:

> They had, firstly, an educational role, for visual representations of incidents in the Bible and of the lives of the Saints, were a method of instruction for an illiterate populace. Secondly, they were constant reminders of the life of the spirit and the ultimate purpose and destiny of humankind. Thirdly, they adorned the House of God by their beauty.[41]

One point particularly relevant here is that among "the many authors who participated in the Iconoclastic Controversy there was indeed not a single artist."[42] They were largely monks in monasteries under the direction of others. While Barasch observes that this may not be surprising given the status of the artist, what is surprising is that all the contributors on both sides of the argument seemed to lack any familiarity with the process of art, nor did they visit or consult with an artist. The nature of art was determined from outside the field. As was also the case with art's classical origins, the West was not directly involved in these debates. However, the impact of the controversy was felt, nonetheless. Generally, theologians in the West "relegated art to a rather limited didactic function."[43]

The general uncertain attitudes toward the artist, but specifically in the iconoclastic debates, is highlighted by the special status and power accorded *acheiropoietai*. These images are not created by an artist but are the "result of a direct contact between the wood, pigments etc. and the divine or holy person whose agency they host and embody."[44] That is to say, *acheiropoietai* are not created by an artist through their normal practice, but rather are the result of a spiritual and miraculous

---

39. Bredin, "Medieval Art Theory," 31.
40. Bredin, "Medieval Art Theory," 32.
41. Bredin, "Medieval Art Theory," 31.
42. Barasch, *Theories of Art*, 1:59.
43. Davis-Weyer, *Early Medieval Art*.
44. Tsakiridou, *Icons in Time*, 101.

process. These images are held in high regard not because they are exemplars of beauty (as they often are not) but rather for their "ontological peculiarity."[45] They have a special connection to the divine and are powerfully engaged with the community of faith, for example, weeping in anticipation of a disaster or in consolation for the faithful.[46]

As both Barasch[47] and Tsakiridou[48] observe, these types of images highlight the ambiguity with which art and the artist was viewed: the most revered icons are those where an artist is not involved and an artist is unable to produce an image of this stature and significance, it can only come from the divine directly. This ambiguity reinforces a key feature of the iconoclastic debate: it was conducted by the theologians and the philosophers with reference to the artefacts of art, with little if any engagement with artists or contribution from artists.[49] Yet, in an important way, the future of art was at stake.

THE TRAINING AND SUPPORT OF THE ARTIST

Art education continued much the same as it had been up until this time, and it would remain roughly the same up to the fifteenth century. Learning an art was a type of apprenticeship. According to Nikolaus Pevsner in his book first published in 1940, a boy would, at about the age of 12,

> enter a painter's shop as an apprentice and would in two to six years' time learn everything necessary from color-grinding and preparing grounds to drawing and painting [. . .] After the end of his apprenticeship he could go out as a journeyman and then, when some more years had passed, obtain his mastership certificate from the local company of painters or the company to which the painters happened to belong, and settle down as an independent painter.[50]

---

45. Tsakiridou, *Icons in Time*, 102.
46. Tsakiridou, *Icons in Time*, 101.
47. Barasch, *Theories of Art*, 1:59.
48. Tsakiridou, *Icons in Time*, 8.
49. Barasch, *Theories of Art*, 1:59.
50. This is cited in Borg, "Writing in Fine Arts," 86.

What had changed was the way the training was administered. Where once craftspeople had been characteristically slaves, they were now "usually organized in guilds and supported under uniform rules of pay."[51] Further, there was no artistic rivalry as prices were controlled and there was a guaranteed quality to be produced.[52] The artist was at the same social level as the other trades and, largely, anonymous.[53]

Theory was important, but was communicated verbally and focused on the skill and the techniques of the art process.[54] This is clear from the workshop manuals of the time which do not discuss subject matter only "such stages in the process of production that are still open as far as subject matter is concerned."[55] Possibly the most well-known of the workshop manuals is *The Various Arts* by Theophilus Presbyter.[56] The manual, published around the first quarter of the twelfth century, deals with technical issues although in a more detailed and expert way than others of the period.[57] The manual is intended to guide the artisan in the making:

> After doing this, take a flat thin piece of gold and fit it to the upper rim of the bowl. Measure this piece so that it extends from one handle around to the other; its width should equal the size of the stones you want to set on it. Now, as you arrange the stones in their place, distribute them in such a way that first there stands a stone with four pearls placed at its corners, then an enamel, nest to it another stone with its pearls, then another enamel; arrange it all so that stones will always stand next to the handles . . .[58]

The implication of accounts such as these is that the role of the craftsperson was the execution, to the best of their abilities, of a task for which they were commissioned and for which the subject matter and

51. Barzun, "Insoluble Problem," 122.
52. Barzun, "Insoluble Problem," 122.
53. Barzun, "Insoluble Problem," 123.
54. Borg, "Writing in Fine Arts," 86.
55. Barasch, *Theories of Art*, 1:79.
56. Barasch, *Theories of Art*, 1:74.
57. Davis-Weyer, *Early Medieval Art*, 172.
58. Davis-Weyer, *Early Medieval Art*, 173.

details were given in the commission. The commission in this period was, more often than not, received from the church.

Barasch suggests that there were certain traditions for the way figures were to be arranged or represented. For example, a face is to be painted in a certain manner and manuals assist by providing different ways that this can be achieved.[59] This appears, at least in part, to be a consequence of the iconoclastic period. The church designated the theology imaged in symbol and the artefact depicting these symbols was then produced by the craftsperson.[60] Here the theologians of the church were in the dominant position and the artists were the ones to carry out the task.

A second reason implied by Barasch's discussion of the workshop manual, but more specifically raised by others, leads into the question of patronage in this period. It is not necessary to wholeheartedly adopt a Marxist perspective to see the impact of economics on the status and possibilities available to artists on the one hand and theologians on the other.

Austin Harrington suggests a typology that summarizes three stages of how artists have been supported. The first stage is a "regime of private patronage by the church, the monarchy and the nobility, lasting from the Middle Ages until around the end of the eighteenth century."[61] Harrington does not go into any detail on the situation prior to the Middle Ages. However, as demonstrated earlier in this chapter, patronage was often from the wealthy, the church and the temple, and artists may have also been indentured servants.

In the medieval period "most painters, sculptors, architects and composers in Europe produced their works according to commission by private patrons."[62] Artists were "in close dependence on a small number of politically powerful individuals"[63] and the role of the artist

---

59. Barasch, *Theories of Art*, 1:77.

60. Tsakiridou, *Icons in Time*, 121.

61. Harrington, *Art and Social Theory*, 71. The other elements in his typology will appear at later points in this chapter.

62. Harrington, *Art and Social Theory*, 72.

63. Harrington, *Art and Social Theory*, 72.

was to produce work on demand.[64] The church and the state, which were often indistinguishable, were both "impresario and purchaser."[65] Discussion of subject matter was irrelevant as it was given to them by the commission and determined by tradition, for purposes "universally understood."[66] It was a case of art being produced by request for a particular situation and purpose.

The situation of the theologian at this time was quite different. For example, Thomas Aquinas was a Dominican monk and taught at the University of Paris and at the papal Curiae in Italy.[67] John Duns Scotus was a Franciscan monk and taught at the universities of Paris, Oxford and Cambridge.[68] This was the period of *scholasticism*, a movement that McGrath describes as "probably one of the most despised intellectual movements in human history."[69] It was regarded by the humanists at the beginning of the sixteenth century as "futile, arid intellectual speculation over trivia."[70] Whatever the caricature of scholasticism,[71] theology was at the centre of Western thinking and formation of opinion. This description is also quite revealing about the situation of the theologian in contrast to the artist of the day. That it was possible for these thinkers to delve deeply into the finer points of doctrine and have extensive written debates about them suggest that their livelihoods were not so fully linked to specific commissioned outputs as were those of the artist.

Summary

In the periods up to and including the Middle Ages, the status of the artist was low. The artist was a craftsperson, a *banausos*, a mechanic.[72] There was a separation between the product of art and the artist

---

64. Harrington, *Art and Social Theory*, 73.
65. Barzun, "Insoluble Problem," 122.
66. Harrington, *Art and Social Theory*, 123.
67. Geisler, "Thomas Aquinas," 1197.
68. Clouse, "Duns Scotus, John," 357.
69. McGrath, *Christian Theology*, 36.
70. McGrath, *Christian Theology*, 36.
71. Embarrassingly, I also once noted, somewhat rashly, in an undergraduate theology essay that reading the scholastics was like eating dry Weet-Bix.
72. Barasch, *Theories of Art*, 1:23.

themselves: it was possible to admire the art but not the artist. The medieval period saw this situation largely continue: the artist was at the service of the Christian community by adorning the house of God.

Theoretical input into discussions of art—its nature and purpose—is marked by the complete absence of the artist. Their intellectual contribution is, for all intents and purposes, non-existent. What art is and is not, what it should be like, subject matter, its purpose—all these aspects are determined, for the most part, by scholars *outside* the art community. What seems clear from these discussions is that the theologian was at the other end of the social spectrum to the artist.

THE BIRTH OF THE *ARTIST*

Up until the early Renaissance it is virtually impossible to separate the "artist" from the "craftsperson."[73] The task of the painter was "associated intimately with tasks which would today be judged menial."[74] However, in the transition period between the Middle Ages and the early Renaissance, the status and perceived function of the artist changed significantly and in a relatively short period of time. There were numerous social and economic factors at work in this process.

One of these factors arises out of the work of the artists themselves and is especially related to the nature of painting at the time. A key belief about art was that it imitates nature and, as is the pattern, the concept was originally formulated by non-artists dating back to at least Plato and Aristotle.[75] There arose a desire for "correctness" in painting with the artist attempting to depict nature as accurately as possible. This drive for accuracy in representing the world led to the need for the artist to study whatever skill or knowledge was necessary to achieve this end.[76] Sophisticated perspective systems developed a need for knowledge of geometry and optics as well as an understanding of anatomy for the correct representation of the human body.[77] Although

---

73. Martindale, *Rise of the Artist*, 15.
74. Martindale, *Rise of the Artist*, 15.
75. Barasch, *Theories of Art*, 1:114–15.
76. Barasch, *Theories of Art*, 1:127.
77. Barasch, *Theories of Art*, 1:155.

still within the guidelines of the church, early exponents such as Giotto (1267–1337) were praised for the achievement of "radical naturalism."[78]

This new level of learning that was now needed to be an effective artist included skills that generally fell under the umbrella of the *liberal arts*. The liberal arts gave "institutional form" to a hierarchical system of education grounded in Plato and in Aristotle.[79] The liberal arts consisted of the *trivium* of grammar, rhetoric and logic and the *quadrivium* of geometry, arithmetic, music and astronomy.[80] With the addition to this of anatomy in the training of artists, it was possible to develop an argument that artists were "superior to craft workers in society."[81] Essentially, artists "claimed a higher status, not because of any specifically artistic values . . . but because art is a science" and like the other liberal arts are a worthy pursuit.[82] Further, it has been suggested that the changing status of the artist at this time relates to a functional affinity with poetry, already recognized as valuable. The poet "bestowed fame and immortality upon the hero and ruler" in their poetry[83] (although the term *legitimizer* may be more accurate). The painter potentially did the same in their painting, recording for posterity the hero, the ruler and the famous. Even at the time a link was apparent: Bocchi in 1571 suggested that the higher placed the subject of an artist's work, the more elevated was the artist's own position in society.[84]

Harrington agrees suggesting that while artists in this period were acknowledged as more akin to the liberal arts such as philosophy and theology, they were still essentially little different from the crafting professions: "Their way of life was to produce work on demand. The idea of artistic labor as a personal quest for perfection in particular objects without immediate thought to buyers or clients did not arrive until the nineteenth century."[85]

78. Barasch, *Theories of Art*, 1:116.
79. Leff, "Trivium," 307.
80. "Liberal Arts."
81. Borg, "Writing in Fine Arts," 87.
82. Barasch, *Theories of Art*, 1:176.
83. Barasch, *Theories of Art*, 1:179.
84. Barasch, *Theories of Art*, 1:179.
85. Harrington, *Art and Social Theory*, 73.

The ambiguity, yet transitional nature of the status of the artist, is highlighted in Baldassarre Castiglione's *The Book of the Courtier* finished around 1516–1518 but not published until 1526.[86] Discussing the attributes of the good courtier, Count Lodovico Canossa says, "I should like us to discuss something else again which, since I consider it highly important, I think our courtier should certainly not neglect: and this is the question of drawing and of the art of painting itself. And do not be surprised that I demand this ability, even if nowadays it may appear mechanical and hardly suited to a gentleman."[87]

In the two centuries or so up to the time Castiglione is writing—the 1300s to the early 1500s—and in contrast to the social uncertainty faced by the artist, theology and theologians were in the ascendant position. It was a time when "the clergy was more numerous and influential in politics, economic, philosophy and other intellectual pursuits than it has ever been since."[88] The term "theology" meant something a little different from how the term is used today:

> The preponderant tendency of the Middle Ages was reflected in the use of the term "theologize" to describe the evangelization of the heathen, or in the decree of the Fourth Lateran Council in 1215, establishing the office of "theologian" as that of "one who is to teach priests and others about the Sacred Page and above all to inform them of those things that are known to pertain to the cure of souls."[89]

The intellectual activity encompassed by today's use of the word theology was described by phrases such as "sacred doctrine" or "divine science."[90] Peterson argues theologians were at the peak of their intellectual influence and power: "Theology, understood as the queen of the sciences, occupied the preeminent place in the university. Far from being peripheral to the educational process, it was understood that the

---

86. Castiglione and Bull, *Book of Courtier*, 11.
87. Castiglione and Bull, *Book of Courtier*, 96.
88. Lopez cited in Pelikan, *Growth of Medieval Theology*, 3.
89. Pelikan, *Growth of Medieval Theology*, 6.
90. Pelikan, *Growth of Medieval Theology*, 6.

educational process led to theological contemplation."[91] Theology was, then, the queen of the sciences, natural philosophy (what is now known as science) was viewed as the handmaiden to theology.[92]

Although church doctrine and the theologian influenced what was in art and the function of the artist, they had in common that both were in the service of the Christian faith and expected to support and enhance that faith. For example, speaking of icons specifically, Solrunn Nes notes that icons pass on the official teachings of the church and expresses the community's faith, a faith developed within that community.[93] It has a supportive and strengthening role for believers. In the same way, the theologian is in service to the faith and servants of the church (although not necessarily people of greater faith compared to the community they serve).[94]

Another development during the late Middle Ages and early Renaissance was the beginning of the construction of the *artist* as a distinct individual. The word *construction* is appropriate here as it was a deliberate attempt to improve the social position of the artist. This involved consideration of the personality of the *artist* and the application of ideas of *creativity* to the artist and the artistic process.

Important in this process was the notion that the visual arts were a part of the liberal arts. The artist should be as learned as possible in the liberal arts but also, according to Alberti writing at the time in *On Painting*, the artist "should be a good man."[95] Essentially, according to Barasch, the artist's behaviour should match the social group into which they want to be accepted.[96]

ART ACADEMIES

An important development for the position of the artist was what might be thought of as the *academization* of art education. Prior to the 1500s, artists were members of guilds as were the other trades. The guilds took

---

91. Peterson, "In Praise of Folly?" 564.
92. Peterson, "In Praise of Folly?" 564.
93. Nes, *Mystical Language*, 12.
94. Grenz, *Theology for the Community of God*, 9.
95. Barasch, *Theories of Art*, 1:181.
96. Barasch, *Theories of Art*, 1:181.

responsibility for all aspects of the lives of their constituents, "enforcing the religious observation of their members, controlling the education of apprentices and the teaching of masters, supervising contracts, and so on."[97] In addition the guilds aimed to protect the crafters from "unreasonable outside competition," from each other, and even "ensur[ed] that members' funerals should be well attended."[98]

The types of guilds artists were associated with and some of the ordinances of those guilds also highlight the differing status between them and the theologian/cleric. For example, in 1378, painters in Florence were granted the right to form an independent branch within the guild they were a part of, the Doctors' and Apothecaries Guild.[99] The painters' guild in London was considered an off shoot of the saddler's guild for a long period.[100] The ordinances of this guild from 1283 have nine clauses, four of which relate to the painting of saddles and are the only ones that relate to the craft.[101] The artist was expected to engage in tasks that today's mind might consider menial.[102]

However, with the growing idea that the visual arts is at least notionally equivalent to the liberal arts, a logical next step was the formalization of art education. The first academy of art, the *Accademia del Disegno,* was established in Florence in 1563. The immediate initiative for the *Accademia* came from Giorgio Vasari, an artist and writer famous especially for his book *The Lives of the Most Eminent Italian Architects, Painters, and Sculptors from Cimabue to Our Times* first published in 1550.[103] The *Accademia* was based on the then "moribund" Compagnia di S. Luca, a sodality of artists that was thought to have been founded in the time of Giotti.[104] The academy had as joint heads the "absent and aging" Michelangelo and Cosimo d'Medici.[105]

---

97. Barasch, *Theories of Art,* 1:175.
98. Martindale, *Rise of the Artist,* 12.
99. Barasch, *Theories of Art,* 1:177.
100. Martindale, *Rise of the Artist,* 15.
101. Martindale, *Rise of the Artist,* 14.
102. Martindale, *Rise of the Artist,* 15.
103. Preziosi, "Introduction," 23.
104. Dempsey, "Some Observations," 552.
105. Hughes, "Academy for Doing."

The first set of guidelines for the *Accademia* issued with its establishment in 1563 laid down the basic program: "Young artists were to have been visited in the workshops of their masters and encouraged by members of the Accademia. Regular lectures on mathematics were to have been instituted, and anatomical demonstrations periodically held at the hospital of S. Maria Nuova."[106] Hughes suggests that while this may not quite be replacing the workshop yet, it does seem to indicate the beginnings of a process to allow "academicians to intervene strategically in shop practice" as well as the introduction of theoretical knowledge normally associated with the liberal arts.[107] In terms of the argument being developed in the chapter, this represents a beginning for the independence of the creative community.

The style of art training developed in the *Academia del Disegno* continued to grow and was formalized by the establishment of the *Académie royale de peinture et de sculpture* of France in 1648. It had the support of the Regency Council who governed for Louis XIV, who was at the time only ten years old.[108] The petition describes painters and sculptors as "weary of the persecution that [they have] suffered these long year through the hostility of certain master craftsmen, who take the name of painters or sculptors only to oppress those who have spent their youth toiling at the study of beautiful things in order to merit this title . . ."[109] However, at the time, France was in deep in a series of civil wars and within a year of presenting the petition, the Royal Household was forced to leave Paris. It was not until 1652 when control was regained that the proper registration of the academy was possible, but it would take another 20 years of struggle for the Academy to take over from the guilds.[110]

It seems to have been a hybrid model: the students continued under a master, but their training was supplemented with lectures on perspective, geometry, and anatomy. This pattern continued through

---

106. Hughes, "Academy for Doing," 3.
107. Hughes, "Academy for Doing," 3.
108. Harrison et al., eds., *Art in Theory*, 11, 80.
109. de Charmois, "Petition," 81.
110. Harrison et al., eds., *Art in Theory*, 11.

the eighteenth century and well into the nineteenth.[111] In agreement with Borg on comments originally made by Nikolaus Pevsner, it is appropriate to add "and beyond"—as this pattern continued well into the twentieth century.[112]

There are positives and negatives from the establishment of the academies. It did eventually free artists and their education from the guilds, a system whose methods and ideas were firmly tied to the medieval period. The formalization of artists' education in academies also meant that they were closer to the model used in the other liberal arts—theory of one form or another was an integral part of the curriculum. However, it might be argued that it is at this point an enduring separation between the education of visual artists and other professions was formalized. It will be argued later in this chapter that this would not change until the late twentieth century.

Yet the break from one form of oppression led to a different sort. One goal of those establishing academies was "in the name of artistic freedom" and to be free of the oppressive guilds yet, because the French Academy was under the patronage of the king, and part of their role was the "glorification of the monarch and the visible projection of his achievements,"[113] this provision would, in time, allow for the greater state control of the arts.[114] In an important way, the situation of the visual arts did not change as the goals and aims of art shifted only in who was responsible for dictating the commissions. Although this period is still in the first phase of Harrington's typology of patronage, there is a beginning shift from the church to the wealthy nobility. Blaxandall describes artists as producing work on "a bespoke basis, tailor-made to the demands of a client" whose requirements were laid out in a legal contract.[115]

As artists were coming to understand the relationship between the art forms, unifying their education, and gaining greater status as a community, Christian theology was passing through a time of division

---

111. Borg, "Writing in Fine Arts," 88.
112. Borg, "Writing in Fine Arts," 88.
113. Harrison et al., eds., *Art in Theory*, 11.
114. Harrison et al., eds., *Art in Theory*, 15.
115. This is cited in Harrington, *Art and Social Theory*, 73.

and fracturing through the further rise of the nation state and some consequences of the Reformation. It is worth noting here the mixed impact the Reformation had on the arts.

During the reign of Edward VI, injunctions were issued ordering the destruction of all "pictures, painting, and all other monuments of feigned miracles, pilgrimages, idolatry and superstition so that there remain no memory of the same in walls, glasses, windows or elsewhere within their churches or houses."[116] In ways similar to the Iconoclasts in earlier history, Calvin and Zwingli believed that any images of divine things were idolatrous.[117] Of the churches, Calvin says that

> it appears to me more unbecoming their sacredness than I well can tell, to admit any other images than those living symbols which the Lord has consecrated by his own word: I mean Baptism and the Lord's Supper, with the other ceremonies. By these our eyes ought to be more steadily fixed, and more vividly impressed, than to require the aid of any images which the wit of man may devise.[118]

However, one consequence of this was that while in Catholic countries the energies of artists were still directed to the churches, artists in Protestant regions directed their attention to the development of new genres of secular art: "portraiture, the new art of landscapes, the pictures of everyday life known as genre paintings and still life" all flourished where Catholicism had restricted the use of art for sacred purposes.[119]

The same year as the establishment of the *Académie royale de peinture et de sculpture* was the signing of the Peace of Westphalia bringing to an end one of the bloodiest of the so-called religious wars of the period, the Thirty Years War, which ran from 1618 to 1648. The following sections will suggest that the War and its aftermath had important consequences for a future understanding of Christianity and theology in particular.

---

116. This is cited in Heinze, *Reform and Conflict*, 388.
117. Heinze, *Reform and Conflict*, 388.
118. Calvin, *Institutes*, 58.
119. Andrew Pettegree is cited in Heinze, *Reform and Conflict*, 389.

Pearse notes, firstly, that the war was not an accidental by-product but an "inevitable consequence" of a "politici[z]ed Christendom whereby churches have, and claim, a legal monopoly on entire populations."[120] The treaty signed in 1648 emphasizes state sovereignty and territorial independence and integrity.[121] In other words, "the throne was now mightier than the altar."[122] As such, it is seen as the beginning of the development of the secular state: the starting point for understanding modern international politics and the modern state.[123]

Secondly, the final peace reaffirmed the situation that existed after a previous conflict in 1555. At one level, therefore, the war had been fought to no good purpose.[124] Therefore, on "what grounds," González asks, "did theologians dare to affirm that they were correct, and that others were mistaken?"[125] The result was that Christianity stood "discredited in the rising generation of thinkers in the ensuing Enlightenment."[126]

ARTIST AS PERSONALITY

However, this move to understanding the artist as fitting into the liberal arts was, to a degree, slowly eclipsed from around 1500 with the emergence of a view of the artist as a "somewhat eccentric figure" which is more characteristic of a modern view of the artist—and as someone who is *creative*.[127] This development, parallel with the growth of the art academy and the social status of the artist, came with an increasing understanding of what it was an artist seemed to do:

> The painter is lord of all types of people and of all things. If the painter wishes to see beauties that charm him it lies in his power to create then, and if he wishes to see monstrosities that are frightful, buffoonish or ridiculous, or pitiable he can be

---

120. Pearse, *Age of Reason*, 160.
121. Pearse, *Age of Reason*, 162.
122. Pearse, *Age of Reason*, 163.
123. Pearse, *Age of Reason*, 162.
124. Pearse, *Age of Reason*, 161.
125. González, *Story of Christianity*, 2:140.
126. Pearse, *Age of Reason*, 164.
127. Barasch, *Theories of Art*, 1:181.

lord and god thereof... In fact whatever exists in the universe, in essence, in appearance, in the imagination, the painter has first in his mind and then in his hand...[128]

Deborah Haynes, in her book *The Vocation of the Artist*, identifies a number of "myths" in the vision of the artist.[129] Some she suggests include *artist as hero, semi-divine creator, mystic visionary* and a *prophet*.[130] Of especial interest in this section are the concepts that lead to Haynes concluding that "[b]y the end of the nineteenth century, the transition from the pre-modern theocentric craftsperson was complete: The artist had become an anthropocentric inventor, imitating God and creating the new world." A number of conceptual developments accompany these ideas, specifically understandings of creativity, imagination and *genius* as well as a shift in the nature of patronage to a market-based system.

Prior to the Renaissance, the idea of creation was something only the divine could do. Plato's demiurge *crafted* the world out of existing materials by *copying* the forms—there is no creativity here, only technical skill.[131] This was especially strong in the Medieval period: "creation" and "creativity" are terms reserved for God.[132] Unlike Plato's demiurge who created from pre-existing matter, Augustine saw this view as unacceptable, insisting that God had made the world from nothing which "became the standard Christian position for Western scholars."[133] In a strict Christian sense, this is true today. The paradigm creation event is the Genesis story of the beginning of the universe. When God creates it is "absolute origination," there was no pre-existing material, *creatio ex nihilo*—out of nothing.[134] J. Rodman Williams notes that this is "without analogy in human experience, because human creative activity always involves some shaping of material that is already in existence."[135]

128. da Vinci, *Notebooks*, 194.
129. Haynes, *Vocation of the Artist*, 112.
130. Haynes, *Vocation of the Artist*, 93.
131. Allen and Springsted, *Philosophy for Understanding Theology*, 8.
132. Barasch, *Theories of Art*, 1:186.
133. Evans, *Philosophy and Theology*, 71.
134. Williams, *Renewal Theology*, 1:98.
135. Williams, *Renewal Theology*, 1:99.

However, this view was changing, and theology was no longer able to maintain this distinction outside its own borders. Artists could be seen as "creators, on a level with poets and scholars in the revival of classical knowledge"[136] and increasingly described as divine and the things they create as virtually of divine origin.[137]

Some of the distance travelled to reach this idea and what it represents can be highlighted by briefly returning to the Iconoclasm dispute. Earlier in this chapter, the role of *acheropoietoi* was discussed. These were icons of high value because they were divinely created, untouched by human hands, and for this reason, were held up as confirmation of the validity of icons in worship.[138] The artist themselves had now begun to be thought of as at least semi-divine if not divine, and their creations were described in terms of the divine.

A second indication of the difference between the *old* and the *new* view of the artist is expressed in another quote from Leonardo da Vinci: "He who despises painting loves neither philosophy nor nature. If you despise painting, which is the sole imitator of all the visible works of nature, you certainly will be despising a subtle invention which brings philosophy and subtle speculation to bear on the nature of all forms."[139] This view of the painter—a view rejoicing in its power—is a considerable distance from Plato's condemning of the imitation of imitations.

The changing notion of the artist as a personality and the independence of the art and the artist were accompanied by changes in the patronage of artists. Haynes suggests that content would come to matter less than the signature of a particular artist, marking the beginning of art as a commodity for profit.[140] Austin Harrington's second patronage category is beginning to appear. It was a "regime of free sale of works of art on an open market, beginning in different European countries in the seventeenth, eighteenth and nineteenth centuries."[141] What the artist may have gained in a degree of artistic/intellectual freedom, they

---

136. Borg, "Writing in Fine Arts," 87.
137. Barasch, *Theories of Art*, 1:188, 190.
138. Barasch, *Theories of Art*, 59.
139. da Vinci, *Notebooks*, 195.
140. Haynes, *Vocation of the Artist*, 108.
141. Harrington, *Art and Social Theory*, 71.

also *gained* in economic freedom, if it was indeed a benefit. Harrington notes that artists had to rely on the open markets "without secure guarantees of buyers and sponsors."[142]

This situation expanded throughout the nineteenth century with the advent of the Industrial Revolution. Prior to this, it had been mainly nobles who had the money, but now there was the newly rich industrialist who was "unsure of their taste" and artists were responsive to the times.[143] What is important for this chapter is the broader situation the artist was finding themselves in as these two themes played out; one, the growing artistic independence of the artist and two, the growing economic insecurity of the artist. The situation is summarized well, if a little negatively, by Barzun when he says the stage is set "for the solitary *artist*, a new social species, who becomes an egotistical wanderer in search of a patron."[144]

The idea grew that the artist was a "self-shaping genius"[145] who is "completely on 'his' own."[146] Haynes emphasizes *his* in this quote as it was essentially a discipline largely dominated by men. She quotes Arnold Hauser saying, "From the romantic period on, art is the language of the lonely man, alienated from the world, seeking and never finding sympathy. He expresses himself in the form of art because—tragically or blessedly—he is not to be confused with his fellow human beings."[147] This is, however, a faulty paradigm left over from Romanticism, which Haynes argues is beginning to be broken down by more collaborative approaches.[148] Further, it was argued earlier in this chapter that theology is conducted as a part of a community and is in various ways referenced by the community of believers and the wider community as a whole.

It is necessary to highlight an important conclusion from the changing view of the artist, from anonymous tradesperson to

---

142. Harrington, *Art and Social Theory*, 74.
143. Borg, "Writing in Fine Arts," 89.
144. Barzun, "Insoluble Problem," 123.
145. Borg, "Writing in Fine Arts," 89.
146. Haynes, *Vocation of the Artist*, 109.
147. Haynes, *Vocation of the Artist*, 109.
148. Haynes, *Vocation of the Artist*, 109.

self-shaping genius. It is that these views are a product of the times. Any ideas of the artist as independent, one who should simply be supported and remains somehow unaccountable to anyone, are artificial.

Further, holding on to faulty views from the past may ultimately be unhelpful to art and artists. This needs to be borne in mind especially as some hand-waving becomes apparent in the rapid development of the next stages this argument follows. This is not necessarily to question to what degree art should be independent or what role it should play in culture. These are separate questions. One of the functions of practice-led research is to allow artists to investigate these questions—theoretically and practically—themselves.

CHANGES IN EDUCATION AND SUPPORT

The chapter has so far described a shift in the process for the education of the visual artist beginning with a master/apprentice relationship which was formalized into a system of guilds in the Medieval period. The guilds were gradually replaced by the development of the art and design academies in the Renaissance. Along with these structural changes have come attempts to improve the social position of the artist.

Yet, up to the end of the 1950s, and despite earlier changes, art was still fundamentally taught as a *craft*. Art was still seen as a skill with individuals needing to be taught the various techniques and processes required to produce a painting or sculpture or whatever was planned. Essentially, "design, sculpture and painting [were] based on good drawing skills and a firm knowledge of anatomy, composition and perspective."[149] More negatively, Graeme Sullivan describes the situation as "formalized instruction in canonical art content meaning that art knowledge was codified, and although it was based on nature, it was sifted through the theories of master teachers."[150] In a similar vein, David Thistlewood argues that art education involved "conformity to a misconceived sense of belonging to a classical tradition, [and] to a belief that art was essentially a technical skill" which later shifted to an education style focused on "devotion to individual creative

---

149. Candlin, "Dual Inheritance," 303.
150. Sullivan, *Art Practice as Research*, 6.

development."¹⁵¹ Although these two quotes reflect a tacit acceptance of the contemporary construction of *artist* and *individual* they do capture the significant shift in the attitude and function of art and the artist.

The situation for the artist in history is well summed up by following words from David Smith: "The artist has been told by almost everybody what art is, what the artist's function is, most often by people who do not perceive, love or make art, but who nonetheless presume the right, because they are laymen, historians or critics, or figure somewhere in the art fringe, to make definition."¹⁵²

ECONOMIC AND SOCIAL CHANGE

The aim of this section is to consider the most immediate circumstances impacting the creative community leading to the development of practice-led research. The contention is that rather than simply being a reaction to economic and political changes in the education sector (as is frequently claimed), practice-led research is part of a progression in the intellectual development and processes of that community. It will be argued that practice-led research may be viewed as the recognition by creative departments as an opportunity for practitioners to further integrate theory and practice to contribute to the ideas that impact on them.

The early stages of this history focus mainly on the UK as this is where the early development occurred. The first significant turning point can be traced to 1959. In that year, in the UK, the National Advisory Council on Art Education was formed to advise the government on art education issues. Appointed to chair the committee was Sir William Coldstream (1908–1987). Coldstream was a recognized artist in his own right¹⁵³ and had an active interest in the situation of artists.¹⁵⁴ At the time of his appointment to the chair of the committee, he was professor at the Slade School of Fine Arts (1949–1975). The Slade was one of the few art schools associated with a higher education institution, University College London, and may have provided

151. Kill, "Coming in from the Cold," 312.
152. Smith, "Economic Support of Art," 664.
153. Borg, "Writing in Fine Arts," 93.
154. Stephens, "Sir William Coldstream."

a unique perspective on education influencing some of the decisions the committee made. Further, Coldstream's appointment to chair the group is significant in that he is being asked to make recommendations to the government and is a practicing artist familiar with the workshop and with the education and training of artists.

In 1960, the committee published its first report recommending significant changes to the way art was to be taught. This report is generally known as the "Coldstream Report," or sometimes the "first Coldstream Report" because there was a second report, a revision and expansion of the first, published in 1970.[155]

Two changes implemented as a result of the report are important here. The first relates to the status of art education qualifications. In attempting to align art education with undergraduate degrees in all other areas, the report recommended introducing a new Diploma in Art and Design (DipAD) which later became roughly equivalent to an Honours degree.[156] The recommendation was that the qualification be "approximate in quality and standard and achievement to a university course of the same length" and makes recommendations for the curricula to establish its equivalence to a degree.[157] To support this goal, the report recommended that art schools have an "unprecedented level of control for institutions over their curricula."[158]

The second important change, and especially critical, was that the Coldstream Report wanted the degree to contain a "compulsory academic element"[159] with "about 15 per cent of the course to be 'devoted to the history of art and complementary studies.'"[160] The report itself had little detail on what this was to actually consist of, something that later became both a problem and an opportunity.

An important question needs to be asked: Why did Coldstream and his committee see the need to introduce a formal theoretical component into the art curriculum? A good part of the answer to this

155. Kill, "Coming in from the Cold," 312.
156. Borg, "Writing in Fine Arts," 96.
157. Kill, "Coming in from the Cold," 312.
158. Kill, "Coming in from the Cold," 312.
159. Candlin, "Dual Inheritance," 304.
160. Kill, "Coming in from the Cold," 312.

question lies in the situation of art education at the time. In Britain at least, "an education as an engineer and in other practical or applied knowledge had a lower status than an education in the theoretical, historical and philosophical subjects of the university."[161]

Evans and Le Grice go on to note that this "powerful and class-based division" was a reflection of the "lower status of these professions in Britain" one not so apparent in the rest of Europe.[162] It is also important to recognize that this was not a division aimed at artists but at the *practical* as opposed to the "theoretical" professions. In this respect, little had changed since antiquity. As discussed earlier, the painter or sculptor—representing the practical disciplines—was referred to as a *banausos*—a mechanic—and this carried with it a lower social status, a sense of lowliness and vulgarity.[163] The theoretical disciplines—represented in terms of this chapter by the philosophers and theologians—were to be above the practical disciplines. There was "alienation" in classical Greek society "from any kind of manual work."[164]

Architectural historian Nikolaus Pevsner (1902–1983) was on the committee with Coldstream and had published a "pioneering survey of art education" in 1940 called *Academies of Art, Past and Present*.[165] One of the conclusions Erik Borg believes Pevsner saw was that for artists to "achieve parity of qualification with undergraduate students of other, more traditional, subjects with the concomitant change of social status, there would have to be a theoretical component in their education, which would be text-based."[166] That is to say, equal status would come when the education of artists was intellectual as well as practical and skill-based.

This is reminiscent of the debate of the early Renaissance as to whether the visual arts should be considered one of the liberal arts, bringing with it an elevated social and intellectual status. Evans and Le Grice argue that the Coldstream Report "presented a view that art

161. Evans and Le Grice, "State of the Art," 105.
162. Evans and Le Grice, "State of the Art," 105.
163. Barasch, *Theories of Art*, 1:23.
164. Barasch, *Theories of Art*, 1:23.
165. Borg, "Writing in Fine Arts," 91.
166. Borg, "Writing in Fine Arts," 93.

education should have the credentials of a liberal and intellectual education as well as being a practical training in art and design."[167] The argument of the early Renaissance seems to be one of "equivalence"—the artist needs to learn geometry, for example, so they should have the equivalent status as one who has had a formal liberal education and learn theoretical aspects as appropriate to their discipline. In the mind of the writers of the Coldstream Report, the theoretical component is incorporated into the qualification and assessed in similar ways as any other university qualification and so is effectively the same as any other university qualification.

In the period following the Coldstream Report, theory was introduced alongside practice which brought an "increasing demand for some written dissertation to be produced for examination alongside the practical studio work."[168] This "increasing demand" for a written component in the assessment process will be important in the later development of practice-led research as a methodology. At this stage, however, it seems apparent that a written component was important to be recognized in the system to which art was seeking recognition from. Fiona Candlin suggests that this change "legitimized art education by introducing an element of academic work."[169] It is also worth flagging for later discussions that the written component sat *alongside* a creative component.

Candlin seems to draw two conflicting conclusions from her discussion of the changes introduced by Coldstream. The first is that the report "programmed a gulf between art theory and art practice into higher education."[170] The overview presented so far suggests that there had *always* been a gulf between art practice and theory—most of the theory and ideas on art and its function had already been coming from outside the discipline long before Coldstream. It certainly seems to be the case that failures in *implementation* may have meant the arts community did not or was not able to take advantage of an opportunity to narrow the divide as the theoretical content was often vague or poorly

---

167. Evans and Le Grice, "State of the Art," 105.
168. Evans and Le Grice, "State of the Art," 105.
169. Candlin, "Dual Inheritance," 304.
170. Candlin, "Dual Inheritance," 304.

implemented. However, this is not the same as *programming a gulf* between theory and practice. Although I just flag it here, arguments will be presented later in this book that the integration of a written component with the practical component in fact brings the two closer together due to the more intimate relationship between the two dimensions of research.

An alternative view draws on ideas from Donald Schön. An unstated underlying premise of the debate may be the presence of what Schön calls the *Technological Program* and its associated paradigm of *Technical Rationality*.[171] This view holds a hierarchical understanding of knowledge and sets a separation between the researcher and the practitioner as well as between real knowledge (which lay in theory) and skill (which was the application of the theory). It is this view that programs a gulf between theory and practice. Under this view,

> it was to be the business of university-based scientists and scholars to create the fundamental theory which professionals and technicians would apply to practice . . . this division of labor reflected a hierarchy of kinds of knowledge which was also a ladder of status. Those who create new theory were thought to be higher in status than those who apply it and the schools of "higher learning" were thought to be superior to the "lower."[172]

Under this view, rather than affirming a division between theory and practice, the objectives of Coldstream's reforms were preliminary steps in bringing the two closer by combining theory and practice in one course.

The second conclusion Candlin draws is that the Coldstream report enabled "the introduction of theoretical material into art education and . . . gave room to more marginal groups and critical stances."[173] It is this second element that is more important for a history of practice-led research as it is a move away from art as solely teaching the craft to the introduction of theory, viewing it also as an intellectual activity. The

---

171. Schön, *Reflective Practitioner*, 30.

172. Schön, *Reflective Practitioner*, 36–37.

173. Candlin, "Dual Inheritance," 304.

Coldstream Report opened a door allowing more wide-ranging critical elements into the art making process. An important consequence of this, according to Candlin, who is tracing the influence of feminist theory, is that feminism "formed one of the main intersections between theory and practice in art schools."[174] This led to the breaking of a barrier between theory and practice through conceptual art in the 70s.[175]

Very similar events were occurring in Australia. The Murray Committee of 1957 produced a report saying that universities—then almost the sole responsibility of the states—were "short-staffed, poorly housed and equipped, with high student failure rates, and weak honours and postgraduate schools."[176] The Murray Report was accepted by the government of the day and led to increased funding and increased level of federal government involvement in the funding process.[177] There was a strong link seen between the role of the university and the economy: "Economic theory was extrapolated into a conviction that improving the educational standards of the entire population would automatically improve the productivity of the nation. Following this line of reasoning the purpose of university education was to serve the meritocracy and the economic interests of the nation."[178]

This report was followed by a report chaired by Sir Leslie Martin in 1965. Martin's wish was to significantly expand the university sector, but the government of his day was not inclined to invest the money needed.[179] The report "upheld the view that tertiary education should be available to all who have the capacity to undertake it" but proposed a binary system—adding colleges of advanced education—instead of a straight expansion of the university sector.[180]

Similar changes were occurring in the UK, where a binary education policy was announced in 1965,[181] the same year as it was in

---

174. Candlin, "Dual Inheritance," 305.
175. Candlin, "Dual Inheritance," 305.
176. Laming, "Seven Key Turning Points," 244.
177. Laming, "Seven Key Turning Points," 245.
178. Laming, "Seven Key Turning Points," 245.
179. Laming, "Seven Key Turning Points," 247.
180. Laming, "Seven Key Turning Points," 247.
181. Pratt, "Higher Education," 20.

Australia. The system proposed 28 (later 30) polytechnics to "head the 'public sector' of higher education."[182] The "polytechnics would provide vocationally oriented degree courses."[183]

According to Susan Davies, this binary system, in Australia at least, was "based on a supposed division of pure from applied study and research."[184] The Colleges of Advanced Education (CAEs) came to accept their responsibility to engage in applied research as demonstrated by a 1982 joint statement by the directors of the Central Institutes of Technology and the Australian Conference of Principals of Colleges of Advanced Education. In a section titled "Applied Research and Development" the document notes that "the advanced education sector has established a substantial reputation in meeting the applied research needs of industry and its standing in applied research and development is reflected in the increasing funding support it is receiving from industrial and commercial sources . . . In expanding their functions to meet the increasing demand from industry, the colleges are assisting greatly in bridging the gap between scientific research and industrial innovation."[185]

Most art and design schools were in the Technical and Further Education institutions (TAFEs) where "their programs were often insular, conservative and provided a relatively narrow range of skill training."[186] Later they were moved to the CAEs which aimed to "place Australian arts in an international context, to increase intellectual and practical rigor, and to broaden the availability of specific subjects and course types."[187]

This system meant that art education—located in the colleges—was practically oriented and any research conducted was of an applied nature aimed at the technical aspects of the discipline. While it may appear that this was not really progress over the situation of art education of the past, future sections will reveal that this laid important

---

182. Pratt, "Higher Education," 20.
183. Pratt, "Higher Education," 21.
184. Laming, "Seven Key Turning Points," 248.
185. "General Informatioin."
186. Strand, *Research in the Creative Arts*, 14.
187. Strand, *Research in the Creative Arts*, 14.

A History of Practice-Led Research

groundwork. A link was clearly established between art practice, research and theory. Theology, on the other hand, can be seen as a theoretical discipline—located in the universities—the research being *pure*, that is, without thought to its immediate usefulness. Its weakness may be the idea that it is theoretical research and need not have immediate value to the faith community.

Concurrent with these developments in art education was a growing interest from economic and political forces relating to the role and funding of higher education which included universities and the Colleges of Advanced Education. The next section explores these in more detail.

These two factors, one internal (changes to education of artists) and one external (economic and political pressures), are so closely related that it is difficult—if not impossible—to say one was causing the other. In addition to these changes, are shifts in the support of artists. Austin Harrington's third division in his typology of patronage is one that consists of "a regime of state subsidies for the arts, in combination with charitable philanthropy and commercial sponsorship, beginning in the twentieth century."[188] He supports Moulin's argument that public art galleries and funding agencies have performed a *gatekeeping* role conferring on certain art and artists a "stamp of public cultural legitimacy" to art and artists that have already gained commercial recognition.[189] Art movements were driven by systematic targeted collecting by dealers and buyers.[190] Rather than representing a situation where the artist was free to pursue their own creative drive, they were to work on an *implied* commission, one given by the market, the state, and the buyer. In one sense, the change for the artist was the expansion of their commissioning base: from only the church and aristocracy to a situation that now included these patrons but also the addition of commercial entities commissioning art for their own purposes as well as any collector able to pay for the work. However, there was at least the potential for the artist to create work that became collectible and receive the imprimatur of legitimacy.

188. Harrington, *Art and Social Theory*, 72.
189. Harrington, *Art and Social Theory*, 80.
190. Harrington, *Art and Social Theory*, 82.

PRACTICE-LED RESEARCH: HISTORICAL TRIGGERS

Fiona Candlin suggests that practice-led research as a model can be thought of as the "logical consequence of the theoretically informed art practices that have emerged over the past three decades."[191] As the historical sketches up to this point have suggested, there has been an ongoing debate on the place and function of the *artist* in the community and in theory. It is therefore an incomplete understanding to say that practice-led research was only a product of changes that were occurring *within* art practice itself. However, since artists have generally been excluded from the academic and theoretical debate about their own discipline, it can be argued that practice-led research—as the means for including artists within the academic debate—would not have been fully possible if an appropriate externally determined environment was not available.

A number of political and economic changes affecting higher education began in the late 1970s extending through the 1980s–1990s. They provide the direct impetus for the development of practice-led research. These changes are often cast as a gross infringement on art and the artist. For example, Graeme Sullivan complains of "the cult of accountability moving relentlessly through most Western systems of higher education."[192] These changes are often also given the status of what made practice-led research necessary as a methodology. Although they did play their part, the changes can also be seen as the most recent development impacting the situation of the art practitioner. The focus will be on changes that occurred in the UK, Australia, and a number of European countries, particularly those of Scandinavia.

In December 1987, the Australian government issued a discussion paper on higher education which was followed in July 1988 with a white paper *Higher education: a policy statement*. The white paper announced the introduction of the Unified National System (UNS). This system was to consist of "fewer and larger institutions" than was the case at the time. It notes that size "is not an end in itself; rather, in most cases, it is a necessary condition for educational effectiveness and

---

191. Candlin, "Dual Inheritance," 306.
192. Sullivan, *Art Practice as Research*, 77.

financial efficiency."[193] Importantly for the development of practice-led research, the policy statement links funding with research performance.[194] The UNS marked the end of the binary education system that prevailed in Australia up to that time and through the late 1980s and early 1990s brought about the merger of many creative art schools with universities.[195]

There were positives to this for both the art school and the university. For example, universities were able to broaden their education base; they saw the introduction of new ideas and talent, as well as a higher community profile.[196] However, a negative result of this change, an important one for the development of practice-led research, was the view from the universities that the incorporation of the art schools meant "a case of the 'poor cousins coming to stay' and 'another hungry mouth to feed' as they brought little in the way of resources dedicated to research with them."[197]

The experience in Australia reflects several changes in several other countries. Reforms to higher education in the UK were similar to those in Australia. The Diploma of Art and Design introduced by Coldstream's reforms was converted to an undergraduate degree in 1974, and in 1991, the government proposed that "the 'binary line' between polytechnic and university education be abolished" and many polytechnics changed their name to include the word "university."[198] This was formalized with the 1992 *Further and Higher Education Act*.[199] The situation in the UK at this time is well summarized in the following from a report commissioned by the Arts and Humanities Research Council:

> Although many art schools became part of the Polytechnic system in the 1970s and developed CNAA degrees, most other disciplines in the Polytechnics already had one foot in the

193. Education and Training Department of Employment, "Higher Education."
194. Strand, *Research in the Creative Arts*, 6.
195. Strand, *Research in the Creative Arts*, 14.
196. Strand, *Research in the Creative Arts*, 14.
197. Strand, *Research in the Creative Arts*, 15.
198. Candlin, "Dual Inheritance," 307.
199. Pratt, "Higher Education," 20.

university sector and for them, arguably, the shift to university status in 1992 was not a fundamental challenge to the way that academics worked or perceived their roles. For Art and Design the period following 1992 has brought some dramatic changes and in many ways Art and Design can still be seen as emergent academic disciplines despite their long history.[200]

In Sweden, 1977, many art schools were incorporated into universities as a part of reforms to the higher education sector.[201] Those that were not had imposed upon them regulations that were designed for universities or research institutions.[202]

The result of these economic and structural changes was that universities were required to do the same things with less money overall. This put pressure on the newcomers, the art departments, to justify their actions in terms of the funding models imposed by governments and by the universities themselves. The predominant mode was *research*. There was research in the institutions they came from, but this was generally of an applied nature. Further, this chapter has argued that the historical pattern was that the justification for art and artists has been debated *outside* the creative community. What is significant about this development is that performers and artists were being asked *directly* to justify themselves. Although some argue how appropriate it is to ask the visual and performing arts to justify what they do, it remains clear that the question is one of long standing (dating back to antiquity) and that theoreticians from within the creative community were now in a position to address it themselves. Henk Borgdorff agrees, asking whether the introduction of research "is a dictate and threat coming from outside arts and arts education, or whether it is a chance and a challenge for art and arts education. My assessment is that introducing artistic research enables a free space to be created within arts education for what might be called 'material thinking.'"[203] Sullivan quotes Paul Carter as reaching a similar conclusion. Arguing that although it is "easy to simply say that the work speaks for itself" it

---

200. Rust et al., *Practice-Led Research in Art*, 14.
201. Kälvermark, "University Politics," 4.
202. Kälvermark, "University Politics," 4.
203. Kälvermark, "University Politics," 8.

A History of Practice-Led Research

actually "perpetuates a Romantic myth about the creative process—that it cannot stand up to rational enquiry—and ... cedes the terms of the debate to outsiders."[204] Further, Evans and Le Grice note that, although not thought of as research at the time, "the new concepts and directions being forged in the British art schools in the sixties and seventies were the direct equivalent to research in other fields. They fulfilled the same role in their field as research did in other subject areas."[205]

Early debates on PhDs and creative arts, such as those of the MATRIX conferences in 1988 at Central Saint Martins College of Art and Design,[206] seem to have initially focused on whether the arts should engage with research and then later shifted to how it should do so.[207]

Carole Gray argues that even in the early 1980s, it is possible to identify postgraduate research that could be termed practice-led. She cites fourteen completed PhDs and MPhils up to 1988 in the UK, and even argues for one completion from 1978.[208] Linda Candy states the first practice-led PhD in Australia begun in 1984 when creative writing was offered at the University of Wollongong and the University of Technology, Sydney, Graeme Harper being the first to graduate.[209]

While these examples may or not be examples of practice-led research as it is recognized in the current environment (and outlined in the following chapters), they do represent, to use Gray's term, "first generation" pioneers and a number of the key elements are present.[210] They are early attempts at integrating research and practice. To what extent this type of research would have continued, or to what extent it would have been accepted in the mainstream academic community without the concomitant economic and educational reforms, cannot be known, only speculated. In Australia, it is likely that practice-led research approaches would have remained minor players and external to the academic community until they were recognized by the major

204. Sullivan, *Art Practice as Research*, 85.
205. Evans and Le Grice, "State of the Art," 2.
206. Evans and Le Grice, "State of the Art," 3.
207. Combrink and Marley, "Practice-Based Research," 181.
208. Gray, "Inquiry through Practice," 4, 6.
209. Candy, *Practice Based Research*, 4.
210. Gray, "Inquiry through Practice," 3.

government funding and assessment agencies. Prior to November 1993, the Australian Research Council specifically excluded creative outputs, but modified their definition of research to allow for it.[211] These organizations and developments are discussed in more detail in the next chapter.

Practice-led research, then, occupies the *border lands* between on one side, what might be termed traditional understandings of what constitutes research and on the other side, what might be thought of as regular art practice, one that does not require any engagement with theory or that it be reviewed as *research*.

While these theoretical debates were going on inside the art research community and economic and reform movements were impacting from the outside, other disciplines were experiencing related pressures. Some are of a similar nature; some relate to issues arising at the end of the Renaissance.

Desiderius Erasmus's writing in 1509 observes of the theologians of his day: "And these most subtle subtleties are rendered yet more subtle by the several methods of so many Schoolmen, that one might sooner wind himself out of a labyrinth than [their] entanglements..."[212] That this view can ring true today is partly due to a general view of the futility of what might be seen as theological hair-splitting, and partly due to the portrayal of religion since the Thirty Years War as "obscurantist—the great impediment to the progress of knowledge and the advancement of human flourishing."[213] This is clear in Friedrich Schleiermacher's 1799 book *On Religion: Speeches to its Cultured Despisers*. In the opening "First Speech" subtitled "Defence" he says,

> Now especially the life of cultivated people is far from anything that might have even a resemblance to religion. Just as little, I know, do you worship the Deity in sacred retirement, as you visit the forsaken temples. In your ornamented dwellings, the only sacred things to be met with are the sage maxims of our wise men, and the splendid compositions of our poets. Suavity and sociability, art and science have so fully taken possession

---

211. Strand, *Research in the Creative Arts*, 7.
212. Peterson, "In Praise of Folly?" 563.
213. Pearse, *Age of Reason*, 367.

of your minds, that no room remains for the eternal and holy Being that lies beyond the world.[214]

The arts, in a broad sense, have taken precedence over religion and artists over clerics. This quote also well captures two themes of this book. The first is the attempts of art and artists to gain social acceptance, and Schleiermacher suggests, they were in a period of growing cultural recognition. The second is how the once dominant intellectual position theology and theologians once held was now at a point where justification of their community worth could not be taken for granted. The contemporary notion that religion is a private matter and should be kept out of the public sphere is one important manifestation.

It is not appropriate here to mount a full counter to this position, since there are many writers engaged in this task.[215] David Bentley Hart argues that, at the end of the day, "the most splendid and engrossing of modernity's self-aggrandizing fables is that of Western humanity's struggle for liberation, of the great emancipation of Western culture from political tyranny, and of Europe's deliverance from the violence of religious intolerance."[216] Further, chapter 2 presented a case for the inclusion of religious faith in the public sphere, and in terms of this book, the academic environment.

Rather, my purpose here is to reclaim some balance between the two approaches to understanding the world. The goal, then, of the remaining chapters of this book, is to present the case that practice-led research as a methodology has the ability to combine the insights of an embodied practicing faith with the intellectual reflection on faith in a way that is academically rigorous to give a fuller, or at least a different, account of the question under investigation.

IMPLICATIONS

The position of this book is that the notion of theology being an intellectual discipline separate from faith is alien. "According to Augustine," Migliore notes, "knowledge of God not only presupposes faith, but

---

214. Schleiermacher, *On Religion*, 1.
215. Pearse, for example, cites Stark, *For the Glory of God*.
216. Hart, *Atheist Delusions*, 75.

faith also restlessly seeks deeper understanding."[217] This idea is further expressed in Anselm's definition of theology as faith seeking understanding.[218] I make a distinction in this book between theology and religious studies. Theology is preceded by faith, and as is the investigation into that faith, the *who and what* of the belief as expressed by Augustine and Anselm. Religious studies attempts to account for religious faith in human terms:

> Religious beliefs and practices are concocted by humans, not revealed from on high. But humans purportedly concoct them in order to make contact with God. That is the irreducibly religious origin and function of religion. Humans do not happen to seek contact with God. They *need* to do so. Just as they come into the world with a need for food and for love, so they come into the world with a need for God. That need, like the need for food or love, is innate. Religion arises and serves to fulfill it.[219]

At various points in this chapter comparisons have been made between the situation of theology and theologians and that of art and artists. There is a level where a comparison between the practice of art and that of theology is natural as the chapter has suggested the presence of numerous historical links. Like the artist, there are many theologians that choose to work outside the government education system either as independent scholars or in one of the private theology schools.[220] It is also apparent that there has always been some relationship between *practice* and *theory*. While this has not always been positive, it has been present.

As argued in the previous chapter, all disciplines and the knowledge they produce are grounded in their historical, cultural context as well as that of the individual and communities' beliefs. Since theology, as understood here, is grounded in faith, it can never be detached from the faith community in which it is developed, nor can the attempt be

---

217. Migliore, *Faith Seeking Understanding*, 2.
218. Migliore, *Faith Seeking Understanding*, 2.
219. Segal, "Introduction," xiv (italics original).
220. Barnes, "Religious Studies and Theology," 232.

made to do so. Therefore, a significant aim in developing a practice-led research as a theological method is to establish a working relationship between the triumvirate of faith, intellect, and practice.

SOME CONCLUSIONS

The claim that the development of practice-led research is largely a product of political circumstances[221] is true only so far as the relationship between art and artists on the one hand and the wider community on the other has always been about power, status, and financial support. It is more accurate to say that the current situation is a progression in a series of changes—some beneficial and some not so beneficial—in the situation of art and the artist in the community.

The notion that the artist is a *self-shaping genius* or somehow independent of the social milieu that surrounds them is, at best, faulty. There has always been a close connection—again, sometimes for better and sometimes for the worse—between the artist, the art they produce, and the community that supports them. While it is beyond the scope of this book to explore the question of the mix between the extent art and the artist is a driver of public opinion or a responder to that public, it is safe to note the close link between the two. This is also true of the theologian, partly also due to the communal nature of Christianity. They are a part of the wider faith community to which they belong and to a degree at least, responsible to them.

Based on ideas from Alvin Plantinga, it was suggested in the previous chapter that an individual's faith and the faith of the religious community of which they are a part offers a legitimate source and motivator for research questions.[222] The individual and the community have a right to answer questions that are important to them, using the tools and the frameworks that arise out of it.

Further, based on writing from Jürgen Habermas, a religious community is entitled to its own views on social, cultural, and political issues and are not required to think in ways determined by others in the community.[223] These views and reasons are valuable to the wider

---

221. Kälvermark, "University Politics."

222. See chapter 1.

223. See chapter 1.

community. However, what is expected of faith communities is to translate these thoughts into language and concepts understood by the wider (secular) community. He calls this the "institutional translation proviso."[224]

With the possible exception of the Iconoclasts, it has not been argued by any of the writers in the historical sketch so far that art has *no* place in society. Rather, the arguments have tended to centre on two aspects: firstly, the nature and philosophical status of art and its artefacts, and secondly, the role and function of the artist and the art they produce.

It is the contention of this chapter that both the performing and visual arts as well as faith communities are entitled to pursue questions and draw conclusions using the methods and assumptions that are particular to them. It is also the case that the same obligation is on each of them to ensure that the thoughts and conclusions they reach are made available in language understandable to the community at large.

---

224. Habermas, "Religion in the Public Sphere," 10.

Chapter 4

Defining Practice-Led Research
Foundations

INTRODUCTION

UP TO THIS POINT, the term *practice-led research* has been used as if it was self-evident and uncontroversial. However, despite its wide usage, this is not the case. The previous chapter outlined a history of practice-led research and gave clues as to why a definition has not been readily available. It suggested that at least in part, practice-led research is a product of the new situation in which artists found themselves and there are, broadly, two reasons. Firstly, it was argued in the previous chapter that as a methodology, practice-led research developed largely in response to recent economic and political changes relating to the structure of higher education in a number of countries. Secondly, however, its relatively recent status as a recognizable methodology has been driven by long-standing debates relating to the role and status of art, the social standing of the artists themselves, the nature of art education leading to the contemporary environment of art schools and their relationship to universities.

No claim is made in the literature (nor in the previous chapter) that there is any individual who is responsible for its "birth" but, rather, that it is part of a largely communal response to longstanding discussions of a political, economic, social and cultural nature. Although there are common threads across the participants, there remain significant differences in perspective. There will be, therefore, variations arising from the stance a writer takes on the differing social, economic, and political position of artists and the other elements of the arguments (and, of course, my own views are no exception). These questions go to the heart of the nature of research and will be addressed in this and later chapters.

The historical thread running through the previous chapter argued that there has been an improvement in the understanding of the role and status of the artist over time. There have been differing and generally richer understandings of answers to questions such as what artists do, what their role in community is and what the intellectual status of art products and artist themselves are.

The previous chapter also attempted to show a parallel history of the changing status of theology and theologians. It also is in a state of change and the relationship it has with the academy and the wider intellectual and social community is shifting. Although already addressed to a degree in chapter 2, observations of a more historical nature were made in chapter 3 on the changing role of religion in the public sphere, and the place of Christianity as a particular focus of intellectual activity. One by-product of the fluid and diverse nature of the theoretical discussions on practice-led research is that agreed-on or even clear definitions of what it means to do research in this way are surprisingly scarce.

This chapter begins a two-step process in developing a robust definition of practice-led research. The aim of chapters 4–5 is to develop a clear understanding of practice-led research while still allowing for the flexibility that is inherent within the methodology. This flexibility, it will be argued, is more than a result of practice-led research being a recent addition to the scene and is not the result of its definitions being actively argued by scholars and therefore still in a state of flux.

The first step in the process will be to examine more closely the reasons a particular term, *practice-led research*, has been chosen. This will lay the groundwork for the next step, namely the foundations for developing a definition. The second step, and what amounts to the bulk of this chapter, will be taken up with an exploration of the various

Defining Practice-Led Research: Foundations

components of the methodology. The key ideas contained within the term practice and research will be explored as they are generally understood in writing about practice-led research. This includes a number of concepts that underpin the methodology—for example, questions of *knowledge*.

Although the history discussion demonstrated that the method is used and discussed in many countries and languages, the focus here will be on English speaking participants, primarily Australia and the United Kingdom, but also Canada and New Zealand. In addition to contemporary published journal articles, important documents will include those from national governments (especially Australia and the UK), documents from the OECD, as well as regulations and guidelines from universities where practice-led research is conducted. Where information is helpful from other countries (and available in English) these will also be included.

In the published literature on practice-led research, the US is notably absent. In the US, the idea of *research equivalence* is preferred over practice-led research approaches to incorporating creative research into the academy. Strand describes the idea of research equivalence as meaning that the "work of academic artists is the equivalent of scientific and scholarly research and of equal value to it in the advancement of knowledge and in terms of its legitimacy to access research funds."[1] It is, as he puts it, a "pragmatic solution" and a way of recognizing that what artists do in an academic environment allowing access to funding, promotion and tenure.[2]

There are two issues with this idea. The first is recognized by Strand in his analysis, although not really addressed. He notes "that the term 'research equivalence' might be misconstrued to denote activities that are 'not quite research' or are 'second grade research.'"[3] Although he says that this is not what the term means, it seems difficult to avoid the conclusion that this style of research is not of the same standard when the idea that it is not up to the standard of conventional research embedded in the description. Projects may be described as research

---

1. Strand, *Research in the Creative Arts*, 45.
2. Strand, *Research in the Creative Arts*, 44–45.
3. Strand, *Research in the Creative Arts*, 44.

for administrative reasons only: to gain access to facilities, support and grants. The second reason is that it sidesteps the real issue, one that practice-led research scholars address head on: what really is research and how can it be understood in an expanded way. This chapter contributes to the discussion on the way that a practice-led methodology is actually research in a traditional sense, but it also expands on the nature or what research is and does.

This chapter spends some time analyzing individual components of the concept and it could be asked: why is such detail necessary? At the commencement of this project, it became apparent that clear definitions of the methodology were elusive and those that were available were often vague, not generally agreed upon and mostly resting on numerous unstated assumptions. Frequently in research papers and articles, a statement of any sort on how a researcher understood the idea is entirely absent. While some may argue that contributing to this state of affairs is the comparative newness of the methodology and the fact that it is still in a state of formation and actively debated. However, while this is certainly the case, it is not a reason for the failure to define how the methodology is to be understood in individual cases. Practice-led research is being used in universities and art academies; degrees are being awarded on the basis of a practice-led methodology, and journal articles and books are being published. So, the newness of the method might account for *differences in the understandings of how the methodology is used and applied* but it does not account for the *absence of definitions*. Essentially, the methodology is being used without clear definitions of what it is about and what essential features differentiate its methodology from that of other forms of research.

The literature contains many examples of individuals recounting their research experience that fit broadly into a qualitative framework and use a variety of methods.[4] Mottram and Rust note in a review paper that a "worrying tendency emerging in the field is the propensity of a claim for an activity to be 'practice-led' research to assume that this is all that needs to be said on the matter."[5] When I offered this

---

4. Examples of this will be provided later in this chapter as the literature is examined.

5. Mottram and Rust, "Pedestal and the Pendulum," 149.

observation to one of the interviewees, they opined that one reason was that the method was not yet fully theorized. But there was evidently more to it:

> Do you think—is there an early conclusion to draw here that ... actually the reason they don't talk about it is that it hasn't been ttheorized and they're using it as a kind of shield to cover ... up a lack of an understanding of what they are actually doing, that it is an intuitive thing. My personal feeling is that ... practice-led research is another way of saying practice as research which lets everybody off the hook for explaining what it is they are actually doing.[6]

Therefore, to avoid this problem, as well as to present a useful methodology that can be utilized in theology, it is necessary to return to first principles. To this end, an understanding of practice-led research will be developed from the ground up, examining in the process how it meshes with the ideas of research in a university in general and with theology in particular.

TERMINOLOGY

The phrase *practice-led research* is not the only term used to describe the general methodological approach developed in this chapter. Some other examples prominent in the literature include: "artistic research; practice as research; practice-based research; arts based research; arts informed research; creative practice as research; art practice as research; performance as research; a/r/tography; arts-informed research; research through practice; arts practice research; studio-based enquiry and practice-led research."[7] Although extensive (and this list may still be incomplete), there are three recurring elements. The first is *research*,

---

6. Jeremy, interview by Neil K. Ferguson. Note that all names for interviewees are pseudonyms. The represented names were selected through the use of a random name generator (http://random-name-generator.info). The "practice as research" used by the interviewee is an equivalent one to practice-led research.

7. The terms in this list have been gathered from journal papers, books and book chapters, interviews, presentations, conference papers, and other sources in the course of research for this book. The list progressively expanded and was added over the duration of the project.

the second is *practice*, and the third is *art* or *arts*. The aim of this section is to consider each of these more primitive elements in turn but not to be all-encompassing or be of a purely abstract nature, but to address the issues only as they apply to the context of this book. The section will examine the key elements as they relate to the university and academic situation as well as the organizations that support, fund, and monitor them, or have some vested interest in their role and function.

Among the many terms available, the one adopted throughout this project is *practice-led research*. Why has this particular term been selected over the many others? Firstly, it is in common use in Australia and has a recognized currency overseas. Frequently contributors to the Australian debate generally prefer the term. Haseman,[8] Harper,[9] and Green,[10] for instance, all seem to prefer the term practice-led research. Haseman argued in 2007 that practice-led research has "become a prominent term for effectively describing the research approach that enables practitioners to initiate and then pursue their research through practice."[11] In a recent review of higher degrees by research awarded across Australian institutions, Hamilton and Jaaniste used the term in preference to other options[12]. This suggests that the term is preferred in Australian institutions.

Secondly, it contains the research concept. This is the case in common with nearly all the other terms in use and so links to them. As was seen in the last chapter, one key contributor to the origins of the methodology was the question asked by universities of the newly arrived art departments: how can what you do be justified as research? The concept and meaning of research is central to the debate.

Thirdly, the use of *practice* frees the concept from being tied too closely to art practice and—potentially at least—allows the inclusion of other disciplinary practices. This is important both for the flexibility of the idea as well as the uses to which it will be applied in this project. Terms that include the word *art* will tend to restrict it to the creative

8. Haseman, "Manifesto"; Haseman and Mafe, "Acquiring Know-How."
9. Harper, "Creative Writing."
10. Green, "Creative Writing"; Green, "Recognising Practice-Led Research."
11. Haseman, "Rupture and Recognition."
12. Hamilton and Jaaniste, "Connective Model."

arts. The term "art" also relates to skill as in "skill in doing something" of "a skill in doing a specified thing, typically acquired through study and practice."[13] However, this is not what the word means in the descriptive terms in the list on page—or in the practice-led research literature. Art in practice-led research discussions means the creative disciplines—for example, painting, sculpture and music. Although it will be understood more broadly later in this chapter, at this point, to use it in any other way in this discussion would be unnecessarily ambiguous.

Finally, it seems to be saying that it is research that is practice-*led*, as opposed to practice-*based*, affirming that it is the practice that is the driver and motivator of the research rather than simply being situated within it. These distinctions will be further clarified in the following sections of this chapter as I flesh out and develop a definition of practice-led research.

A PRELIMINARY DEFINITION

This section will present definitions from two different writers. The definitions will not be analyzed directly but provide a broad understanding of practice-led research and a general operating environment for the discussions to follow.

The first definition, often quoted by others, was formulated by Carole Gray in 1996.[14] She defines the methodology in the following way:

> By "practice-led" I mean, firstly, research which is initiated in practice, where questions, problems, challenges are identified and formed by the needs of practice and practitioners; and secondly, that the research strategy is carried out through practice, using predominantly methodologies and specific methods familiar to us as practitioners in the visual arts.[15] . . .
> With regard to epistemological issues the practitioner is the

---

13. See "Art," *OED*.

14. Some examples include Haseman, "Manifesto," and McWilliam et al., "Transdisciplinarity for Creative Futures." Although these two papers include Haseman as a common author, the difference in the nature of the journals indicates the broad use of the term and the interest in different disciplines.

15. Gray, "Inquiry through Practice," 3.

researcher; from this informed perspective, they identify researchable problems raised in practice, and respond through practice.[16]

For the second, I have selected one by Henk Borgdorff. He builds this definition over a number of stages in an article from 2007:

> Art practice qualifies as research if its purpose is to expand our knowledge and understanding by conducting an original investigation in and through art objects and creative processes. Art research begins by addressing questions that are pertinent in the research context and in the art world. Researchers employ experimental and hermeneutic methods that reveal and articulate the tacit knowledge that is situated and embodied in specific artworks and artistic processes. Research processes and outcomes are documented and disseminated in an appropriate manner to the research community and the wider public.[17]

There are two distinctive characteristics revealed in these definitions that need to be noted about the methodology at the outset. Firstly, the research is investigating a problem that has arisen from within practice or as a part of an individual's practice. In other words, the issue appears as a *result of their practice and would not be seen outside of that practice*. It would not have been seen by someone wholly outside the discipline nor by the practitioner when they were not engaged in the practice. While it will be argued later in this chapter that these are not the only questions suitable for investigation through practice-led research, this is certainly a unique feature of the methodology. Secondly, the problem is researched within the practice and using the methods and tools of the practice. So a visual artist would investigate the issue through painting, drawing, sculpture, installations and so on, whereas a dancer would do so through dance and performance, and a creative writer through a novel, short stories or poetry. It may be the case that, depending on the nature of the issue, a topic could be researched in ways separate from the practice which brought it to light. The results

---

16. Gray, "Inquiry through Practice," 13.
17. Borgdorff, "Debate on Research in the Arts," 18.

Defining Practice-Led Research: Foundations

from such an investigation may still add knowledge and understanding to the discipline. However, it would not be practice-led research unless the investigation was conducted in and through the very practice that manifested the issue. This idea is clearly framed in a question asked by Estelle Barrett in *Practice as Research: Approaches to Creative Arts Enquiry*.[18] The question potential researchers need to ask themselves is "What did the studio process reveal that could not have been revealed by any other mode of enquiry?"[19] The arguments presented in this and the following chapters will provide the means by which researchers can answer this question.

The next stage of this chapter investigates the core elements of these definitions and considers them in the university context, the site where the method is generally applied and it developed.[20] It will expand on the important elements in these definitions, considering the key components of *research*, *practice* and *art/arts* as well as a number of implied terms. The aim is to form a definition that allows entry of other disciplinary practices while maintaining the advantages of the methodology.

A significant number of government and university guidelines and policy documents will be examined. There are two reasons for this. Firstly, it highlights that the methodology has already been recognized and accepted in other disciplines, attracting funding and included in various metrics. Secondly, analysis of these documents provides important clues to how practice-led research might be firmly defined (this chapter and chapter 5) as well as the forms it might best take in its application (chapters 6–7).

RESEARCH

At its most general, research is an activity done "whenever we gather information to answer a question that solves a problem."[21] This definition covers any activity from an in-depth longitudinal study on a particular phenomenon to finding out what time the movie starts at

---

18. Barrett and Bolt, *Practice as Research*.
19. Barrett and Bolt, *Practice as Research*, 186.
20. See chapter 3.
21. Booth et al., *Craft of Research*, 10.

the local cinema. A more helpful introductory definition is offered by Clough and Nutbrown. They suggest that "all research, necessarily, is about asking questions, exploring problems and reflecting on what emerges in order to make meaning from the data and tell the research story."[22] An even more focused and succinct definition was offered by one of the interviewees when they described research as the "systematic process of asking and answering questions."

As demonstrated in chapter 3, the immediate stimuli for practice-led research were in a particular environment—the university—where the idea of research was generally well understood (if not always clearly defined). It is also the case that research is a part of the core business of the institution. It is the purpose here to concentrate only on an understanding of research in the academic and university context. Other ways of understanding research might be suggested—for example, in an industrial or other professional setting—however these are outside the scope of this study. Later discussions will consider other research styles and comparisons will be made at that point.

This section will look at various ways research is understood by key players in this discussion: government agencies (Australian and international), non-government advisory bodies (national and international), university administrations and academics. The underlying assumption of what counts as knowledge *in this context* will also be discussed.

An influential definition of what research (and development) means comes from the OECD. First published in 1963, the *Frascati Manual*, named after the town where the original committee met, is now in its sixth edition.[23] It was "originally written by and for the experts in OECD member countries who collect and issue national data on research and development (R&D)."[24] The Frascati Manual defines R&D in the following way: "Research and experimental development (R&D) comprise creative work undertaken on a systematic basis in order to increase the stock of knowledge, including knowledge of man,

---

22. Clough and Nutbrown, *Student's Guide to Methodology*, 4.
23. OECD, *Frascati Manual 2002*.
24. OECD, *Frascati Manual 2012*.

culture and society, and the use of this stock of knowledge to devise new applications."[25]

It is important to note at the outset that while the original understanding of the Frascati manual was for R&D, it will be shown in the following sections that this definition has been extended well beyond the original context. There are a number of key ideas in the Frascati definition. The first is that research is thought of as *creative work*. The manual does not say what it means by *creative*, but the intention is made clearer by the fact that what the writers think is not included in research and further by the distinction made from *innovation*. The authors of the manual do recognize that the exclusions they make are not hard and fast. Some of these are the education and training of personnel; others are various scientific and technological activities (for example, data collection, testing and standardization); and administration and other support activities.[26] Creative work is also different from *innovation*. The writers of the Frascati Manual refer to another OECD publication, the *Oslo Manual: Guidelines for Collecting and Interpreting Innovation Data*. This publication provides a definition of innovation: "An innovation is the implementation of a new or significantly improved product (good or service), or process, a new marketing method, or a new organizational method in business practices, workplace organization or external relations."[27] An important distinction from research is made clear when the manual states that the "minimum requirement for an innovation is that the product, process, marketing method or organizational method must be *new (or significantly improved) to the firm*."[28] That is, while it may include processes and products that the firm develops itself, it may also include those that have been adopted from elsewhere.[29]

The Frascati Manual distinguishes three categories: basic research, applied research and experimental development. *Basic research* is "experimental or theoretical work undertaken primarily to acquire new

25. OECD, *Frascati Manual 2012*, 30.
26. OECD, *Frascati Manual 2012*, 31–33.
27. OECD, *Oslo Manual*, 46.
28. OECD, *Oslo Manual*, 46.
29. OECD, *Oslo Manual*, 46.

knowledge of the underlying foundation of phenomena and observable facts" however, no practical application may be envisioned.[30] Applied research is defined as any "original investigation undertaken in order to acquire new knowledge" but in this case, it is "directed primarily towards a specific practical aim or objective."[31] Finally, experimental development is "systematic work, drawing on existing knowledge gained from research and/or practical experience."[32] Its goal is for the development of new or improved materials, systems procedures, processes and the like. There is a requirement, then, for research to add to the stock of knowledge in some way rather than to be only improving or refining existing knowledge, innovation, as described in the Oslo Manual.

It might be thought that these types of research fall into a hierarchy, and this relationship is illustrated in Figure 2.

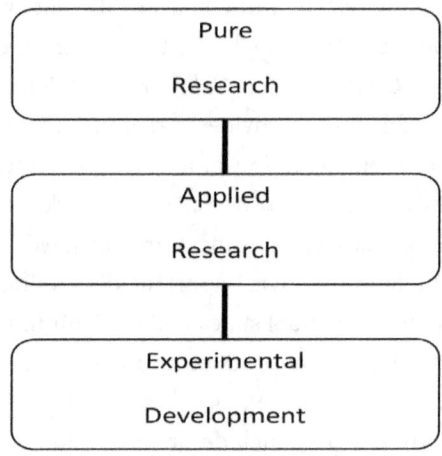

Figure 2. Hierarchy of Research

However, this hierarchical diagram obscures the relationships between research outputs and suggests that one research approach is better than another. A more accurate representation might be better expressed in Figure 3.

30. OECD, *Frascati Manual 2012*, 30.
31. OECD, *Frascati Manual 2012*, 30.
32. OECD, *Frascati Manual 2012*, 30.

Defining Practice-Led Research: Foundations

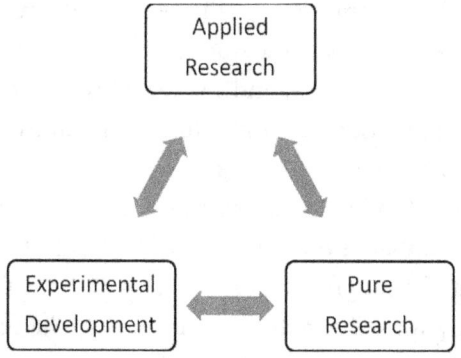

Figure 3. Interrelationship between Research Styles

This diagram illustrates how the different types of research interact with each other. A simple illustration is that pure research might discover particular understandings of the way a process works. This is then taken up and developed into a technology that enables pure researchers to discover something that was not possible before, and that tool is then developed and fine-tuned into an improved and more efficient machine. A later section in this chapter will explore this relationship in more detail. The Frascati understanding provides the basis for definitions of research developed by a number of government agencies who formulate or administer policies impacting on the creative industries.

Australia

The Australian Research Council (ARC) was established by an act of parliament in 2001 with a mission to "deliver policy and programs that advance Australian research and innovation globally and benefit the community."[33] The ARC is a significant funder for research projects providing almost AUD $709 million through its programs in some 4,900 research projects and more than 10,700 researchers.[34]

The ARC provides a glossary of terms on their website where they define numerous key terms important for researchers and grant applicants. According to this glossary, "research and (experimental)

---

33. Australian Research Council, "Factsheet," 1.
34. Australian Research Council, "Factsheet," 1.

development (R&D) comprises creative work undertaken on a systematic basis in order to increase the stock of knowledge, including knowledge of man, culture, society, and the use of this stock of knowledge to devise new applications."[35] This definition is almost identical to the current Frascati Manual.

As well as its funding tasks, the ARC administers the *Excellence in Research* (ERA) initiative on behalf of the Australian Government. The aim is to "identify and promote excellence across the full spectrum of research activity, including both discovery and applied research, within Australian higher education institutions."[36]

The 2012 ERA submission guidelines define research as "the creation of new knowledge and/or the use of existing knowledge in a new and creative way so as to generate new concepts, methodologies and understandings. This could include synthesis and analysis of previous research to the extent that it is new and creative."[37] The guidelines go on to say that this is consistent with a definition of research as "comprising creative work undertaken on a systematic basis in order to increase the stock of knowledge, including knowledge of humanity, culture and society, and the use of this stock of knowledge to devise applications."[38] The second quote is almost identical to that from the Frascati manual and is referenced in the guidelines as such.

The ERA document also identifies "four kinds of traditional research outputs" and for some disciplines "the following 'non-traditional' types of research output."[39] The traditional research outputs are books (authored research or book chapters), refereed journal articles, and refereed conference publications.[40] The non-traditional outputs include original creative works, live performance of creative works, recorded/rendered creative works, and curated or produced substantial public exhibitions and events.[41] The ARC provides a "discipline matrix" out-

---

35. Australian Research Council, "Glossary."
36. Australian Research Council, "Era 2012 Submission Guidelines."
37. Australian Research Council, "Era 2012 Submission Guidelines," 13.
38. Australian Research Council, "Era 2012 Submission Guidelines," 13.
39. Australian Research Council, "Era 2012 Submission Guidelines," 31.
40. Australian Research Council, "Era 2012 Submission Guidelines," 31.
41. Australian Research Council, "Era 2012 Submission Guidelines," 31.

Defining Practice-Led Research: Foundations

lining various codes and assessment categories. This document also includes a column of disciplines where non-traditional outputs may be submitted. For the ERA, both "HCA 2204 Religion and Religious Studies" and "HCA 2299 Other Philosophy and Religious Studies" are included for non-traditional research outputs.[42]

The ERA process of identifying excellence also implies the identification of poor research and the process adopts a number of strategies to achieve this assessment. The term "non-traditional" in the document is initially surrounded by quotation marks. Given that these are removed later in the document, it seems that the highlighting of the phrase in this way is only to identify the relative newness of the term and of the recent inclusion in the ERA system rather than to suggest any inadequacy of the research the term "non-traditional" represents. The inclusion of non-traditional research outputs by Australia's primary research assessment process is recognition of the validity of this mode of investigation.

The Higher Education Research Data Collection (HERDC) process is conducted by the Australian Government's Department of Industry, Innovation, Science, Research and Tertiary Education each year "to assess the relative research and research training performance" of higher education providers (HEPs).[43] The process has a direct impact on universities in Australia as the results drive the allocation of research block grant funding. This funding supports research and research capability of institutions, the training of research students, the indirect costs of research, as well as collaboration between higher education providers and the business and non-government sectors.[44]

In the Department's document that outlines what may and may not be included for assessment, research is defined as "the creation of new knowledge and/or the use of existing knowledge in a new and creative way so as to generate new concepts, methodologies and understandings. This could include synthesis and analysis of previous research to the extent that it leads to new and creative outcomes."[45]

42. Australian Research Council, "Era 2012 Discipline Matrix."
43. Australian Government, "Higher Education Research Data Collection," 4.
44. Australian Government, "Higher Education Research Data Collection," 4.
45. Australian Government, "Higher Education Research Data Collection," 7.

The document also gives a summary of the Frascati statement and concludes that their definition is consistent with this "broad notion" of research. The HERDC process, then, aligns itself to this recognized benchmark.[46] The following subsections will briefly examine the situation in a number of other countries.

The United Kingdom

As was noted in the previous chapter on the history of the methodology, the UK has played a central role in its development. Therefore, how research is understood in this context deserves scrutiny. The Quality Assurance Agency for Higher Education in the UK publishes a set of codes of practice for institutions to follow. The guideline for postgraduate programs states:

> Research for the purpose of the RAE [Research Assessment Exercise] is to be understood as original investigation undertaken in order to gain knowledge and understanding. It includes work of direct relevance to the needs of commerce and industry, as well as to the public and voluntary sectors; scholarship; the invention and generation of ideas, images, performances and artefacts including design, where these lead to new or substantially improved insights; and the use of existing knowledge in experimental development to produce new or substantially improved materials, devices, products and processes, including design and construction.[47]

The definition goes on to exclude testing and analysis as well as developing teaching material that does not involve "original research."[48] This definition, as well as the exclusions, is in line with the one from the Frascati Manual. It is important to note that it has been expanded to explicitly include the products of research characteristic of creative disciplines.[49] The two countries have a similar understanding of what research constitutes.

46. Australian Government, "Higher Education Research Data Collection," 7.
47. "Code of Practice," 4.
48. "Code of Practice," 4.
49. In Australia, the equivalent organization to the QAA in the UK is the Tertiary Education Quality and Standards Agency (TEQSA; http://www.teqsa.gov.au).

Defining Practice-Led Research: Foundations

New Zealand

The Tertiary Education Commission (TEC) has two broad functions: to administer the tertiary funding system in New Zealand and to monitor the performance of tertiary education organizations.[50] One of their key functions is the administration of the Performance-Based Research Fund (PBRF). This is a broad-based funding source aimed, among other things, at "increasing the average quality of research" and to "underpin the existing research strength in the tertiary education sector."[51] The definition of research that the guidelines provide is comprehensive and is intended to be "a broad characteri[z]ation that includes original investigation of a professional and applied nature."[52] The key points are that, for the purposes of the PBRF,

> research is original investigation undertaken in order to contribute to knowledge and understanding and, in the case of some disciplines, cultural innovation or aesthetic refinement ... It typically involves enquiry of an experimental or critical nature driven by hypotheses or intellectual positions capable of rigorous assessment by experts in a given discipline.[53]

This definition carries the common theme of original investigation to increase the stock of knowledge but adds innovation and aesthetic refinement. It continues by noting that research must be open to scrutiny and evaluation by experts in the appropriate fields. It includes the observation that "[i]n some disciplines, the investigation and its results may be embodied in the form of artistic works, designs or performances."[54] This statement, part of the definition of what research is, appears to be a direct reference to the type of investigation

---

50. "Tertiary Education Strategy."

51. Tertiary Education Commission, "Performance-Based Research Fund: Quality Evaluation Guidelines," 16.

52. Tertiary Education Commission, "Performance-Based Research Fund: Quality Evaluation Guidelines," 26.

53. Tertiary Education Commission, "Performance-Based Research Fund: Quality Evaluation Guidelines," 25.

54. Tertiary Education Commission, "Performance-Based Research Fund: Quality Evaluation Guidelines," 25.

characteristic of practice-led projects. This will be discussed further later in this chapter.

Research is evaluated when individual researchers submit through their institution an evidence portfolio (EP). These are then assessed by discipline specific review panels who allocate rankings. There is a *Creative and Performing Arts* panel as well as a *Humanities and Law* panel which covers theology and religious studies.[55] The Creative and Performing Arts panel expands on the definition of research in the primary PBRF guidelines by noting that "original creative work is in and of itself considered to be research and fulfils the criteria of the PBRF Definition of Research where it results in the generation of new knowledge, an enriched sense of the possibilities of the art form, or communicates in a meaningful and profound way through an artistic medium."[56] It also adds that "work in the creative and performing arts is regarded as research (rather than as exemplary practice) where it has an aesthetic or exploratory rationale and value (rather than relating to routine professional demands)."[57] This understanding has broad scope and allows many creative practices to be included under the research banner. The Humanities and Law panel also includes the expectation of receiving practice-led projects but wants to be confident that the projects have been through a quality assurance process:

> If a non-standard quality-assurance process has been used, e.g., in relation to practice-based research outputs (such as a commissioned report) or creative research outputs (such as a film, video or exhibition), staff members are expected to explain in the Description field precisely how quality has been assured for the NRO [Nominated Research Output].[58]

---

55. Tertiary Education Commission, "Performance-Based Research Fund: Quality Evaluation Guidelines," 83, 84.

56. Tertiary Education Commission, "Performance-Based Research Fund: Creative and Performing Arts Panel-specific Guidelines," 5.

57. Tertiary Education Commission, "Performance-Based Research Fund: Creative and Performing Arts Panel-specific Guidelines," 5.

58. Tertiary Education Commission, "Performance-Based Research Fund: Humanities and Law Panel-Specific Guidelines," 3.

Defining Practice-Led Research: Foundations

Summary

The emphasis of this section on the widespread use of the definition of research as presented in the Frascati Manual, and versions of it serves to illustrate that there is a common idea of what it means to do research and broadly what research outputs look like. The addition to the statement from the OECD of the policies of three countries further demonstrates that there is a common idea of research. Importantly, this section has also suggested that the common understanding of research is one that is open to the inclusion of a practice-led methodology. Also of importance is that it lays out some expectations that any research must fulfil. It further demonstrates that the outputs of practice-led research are a legitimate inclusion in the assessment and funding models of universities.

KNOWLEDGE

A second key term needing clarification is *knowledge*. The term seems to be used as if it was universally agreed on and, if asked, a standard framing could be pointed out, outlining what it meant and what it encompassed and did not include. However, neither the Frascati manual nor any of the agencies discussed define what they mean by knowledge. This ambiguity creates both arbitrary restrictions and potential opportunities. Before considering these, I will examine how the word knowledge is used in this context and what may be the underlying assumptions.

In both the Frascati Manual and in the various uses of its research definition, knowledge seems to be understood in a broad general sense; in what might be called a 'common sense' way. It seems to be the case for these writers that no deep ontological or epistemological discussion is needed as they assume their idea of what knowledge is can be easily grasped by anyone. At one level this may certainly be the case. For example, I have knowledge of something when I have some familiarity with it, or I have knowledge about the history of an event or person. However, the following discussion reveals there are a number of problems with this lack of any clear definition. The problems are revealed by clarifications added to definitions as well as by statements on what is excluded from definitions of research.

The first Frascati Manual was in response to an increase in the amount of statistical data being collected by member countries on R&D and the perceived need for standardization.[59] The Foreword notes that since its original release in 1963, the manual has become "a cornerstone of OECD efforts to increase the understanding of the role played by science and technology by analyzing national systems of innovation."[60] Further the primary measurement tool of the manual is through surveys. While the manual recognizes that there are weaknesses of the method as well as other ways to gather information on research and development—for example from annual reports—it argues that "statistics on R&D require regular, systematic and harmonized special surveys."[61] By survey, the writers do not mean a popular understanding of surveys—large numbers of investigators roaming streets and corridors ticking off questions asked from clipboards—but the systematic collection of data from government, industry and higher education institutions. The main output of the collection process is statistics on research and development inputs and outputs—it is in the form of information, of data, and data that is largely numerical.

The *Frascati Manual* operates, broadly speaking, from within a *quantitative* paradigm. It inherited this from the fields to which it was originally targeted: "manufacturing industry and research in the natural sciences and engineering."[62] The third edition incorporated the social sciences and the humanities into the manual,[63] however, the essential core assumptions remain unchanged, and the authors insert a discussion on the problems associated with the use of Frascati in these included areas.[64] Although Frascati operates within a quantitative paradigm, practice-led research fits broadly within a *qualitative*

---

59. OECD, *Frascati Manual 2012*, 151.
60. OECD, *Frascati Manual 2012*, 3.
61. OECD, *Frascati Manual 2012*, 126.
62. OECD, *Frascati Manual 2012*, 19.
63. OECD, *Frascati Manual 2012*, 153.
64. OECD, *Frascati Manual 2012*, 153.

Defining Practice-Led Research: Foundations

research paradigm.⁶⁵ A general definition of the qualitative approach is provided by Denzin and Lincoln:

> Qualitative research is a situated activity that locates the observer in the world. It consists of a set of interpretive, material practices that make the world visible. These practices transform the world ... Qualitative research is inherently multimethod in focus ... However, the use of multiple methods, or triangulation, reflects an attempt to secure an in-depth understanding of the phenomenon in question.⁶⁶

Thomas characterizes the differences between this framework and a quantitative one in the following way:

> The simplest way to distinguish between qualitative and quantitative may be to say that qualitative methods involve a researcher describing *kinds* of characteristics of people and events without comparing events in terms of measurements or *amounts*. Quantitative methods, on the other hand, focus attention on measurements and amounts (more or less, larger and smaller, often and seldom, similar and different) of the characteristics displayed by people and events that the researcher studies.⁶⁷

Although Thomas points out that there is no agreement from authors on how best to describe these methods, another key feature of the quantitative paradigm is raised when he cites Glesne and Peshkin: "Quantitative researchers seek explanation and predictions that will generalize to other persons and places. Careful sampling strategies and experimental design are aspects of quantitative methods aimed at producing generalizable results."⁶⁸

It is this general quantitative paradigm, largely dominant in the university and government understanding of research, that the

---

65. This view is not universally accepted and will be addressed in a later section (see chapter 5).
66. Denzin and Lincoln, *Collecting and Interpreting Qualitative Materials*, 4, 7.
67. Thomas, *Blending Qualitative and Quantitative Research Methods*, 1 (italics original).
68. Thomas, *Blending Qualitative and Quantitative Research Methods*, 2.

practice-led researcher, and a suitable definition, must negotiate. In reality, the two paradigms are complementary and the question a researcher needs to ask is "not whether one method is overall superior to another but, rather, whether the method a researcher employs can yield convincing answers to the question that the investigation is intended to settle."[69] It is a core claim of this book that practice-led research is particularly adept at answering certain types of questions.

This process of considering how research and knowledge is understood serves several related purposes. Firstly, it sets the limits—the borders—within which research in a university or academic setting must operate. This applies to all research, not just research in the creative arts. Secondly, however, it also provides room for change and shift, and demonstrates the flexibility inherent in the way research is understood. It permits a variety of ways of doing research. The implications of these two points will be considered after other components of practice-led research have been examined.

An important third purpose is that it also imposes a certain responsibility for some kind of validity and rigour within this flexibility. It helps to avoid nebulous definitions like this one: "Research is, yes, a process of *re*searching–that is, of coming back again and again to perceived phenomena, scrutinizing the world, and thereby re-experiencing it."[70] Later sections will return to the question of validity and rigour.

Fourthly, there seems to be a requirement for dissemination of research results. This is still a source of resistance in some quarters of the practice-led research debate. There is a strand in the literature that attempts to put the case that artist-researchers should not be required to make any written contribution as a part of their research—their creative output should stand on its own (e.g., Haseman, 2006).[71] However, for research to be assessed and validated, examined and critiqued, the results, conclusions, findings, whatever is *new* about the research needs to be reported to a community of scholars as well as those funding the research.

---

69. Thomas, *Blending Qualitative and Quantitative Research Methods*, 7.
70. Barone and Eisner, *Art Based Research*, 47 (italics original).
71. Haseman, "Manifesto."

ART/ARTS

In a similar way to the term knowledge, the phrase "the arts" is frequently used as if the term was self-evident. It is not the purpose of this section to investigate whether any particular condition is necessary and sufficient for something to be called 'art' nor is it the purpose to provide a clear definition on how art should be understood in the literature and a definition of practice-led research. Rather, since the aim of this book is to expand the use of the methodology to areas outside the art community, what I show here reinforces the existing ambiguity in the use of the term practice-led research highlighting the need for a richer definition. Further, since art is frequently used in literature as if everyone knows what it was describing, it is helpful to understand more clearly what authors are describing when using the term.

Generally speaking, writers in the field use the term in two ways. Firstly, it refers to one particular art form in which a writer is involved. It includes both traditional and non-traditional art forms. Traditional exemplars include painting, sculpture, textiles, dance, and music. Non-traditional forms include photography, digital imaging, soundscapes, installations, and animation. The second use of the term is a more general use and refers to the visual arts, performance arts, or even more generally creative arts. This use of the term encompasses all of the forms described in the more specific use of the word. To illustrate, one list of what constitutes the creative industries includes "advertising, architecture, art and antiques markets, computer and video games, crafts, design, designer fashion, film and video, music, performing arts, publishing, software, television and radio."[72]

In line with the form of discussion so far, one useful guide to what art means in a restricted sense comes from university departments. Some of the general terms used within schools include the following: the arts; creative industries; creative arts; culture, art and design; creative media; and visual arts. If it is a creative arts faculty, there may be individual schools within it that cover various arts—for example, a school of fine art.

---

72. Stock, "Approaches," 1.

Another pointer as to what is considered under the banner of art, in Australia at least, comes from the *Arts Funding Guide 2012*, a government funding initiative coordinated by the Australia Council for the Arts. There are nine boards that assess grant applications on behalf of the Council's, and these include ones for dance, literature, music, theatre, major performing arts, and visual arts.[73]

These understandings of art in literature are different to art in an expanded sense, or what may be phrased as "an art." That is to say, an art is any skill or ability that has been refined to a high level. While this is certainly true, understanding "art" in this way is too broad for the specific purpose of this chapter. Further, what is not covered by the term's use here are the liberal arts which would generally fall within the Humanities grouping.

PRACTICE

Practice is another term freely used in literature yet lacking a clear meaning. There are at least two obvious reasons for this absence. Firstly, as with the term "art," many contributors are writing from within a particular discipline and are either addressing the same discipline or to a wider audience but still within the art community. As was the case with earlier concepts, the assumption seems to be that everyone knows what is meant by the term practice.

Secondly, searching through documents from funding agencies and universities provides no description of how practice could or should be understood. Part of the reason for this is that the focus of these documents is the end result of the research. The funding agency is expecting publications, conference presentations, patents, commercialization results, or in some cases, art exhibitions or performances. The focus is on *outputs* and not on the specific way the researcher reaches the output.

The term practice seems to be a cover-all term, a place holder for the vastly varying activities of artists. There are in use a number of terms for the methodology which appear to avoid this issue; *arts-based research*, for example. Alternative phrasings have their own issues of

---

73. Australia Council for the Arts, "Arts Funding Guide 2012."

what is understood by the terms they use but this only reinforces the need for some degree of clarity.

However, while there is a significant reason to avoid fixing a definition of practice too tightly—it may prove to be restrictive and therefore defeat the arts themselves—some understanding is essential as an individual's practice is central to the methodology and still implicit in these other terms. A degree of rigour and the ability to disseminate the research necessitate some boundaries to what practice might mean.

There are some descriptions in the literature of how practice is understood. For example, McNiff defines artistic process as "the actual making of artistic expressions in all of the different forms of the arts."[74] Another clue to what is distinctive of practice is a reference made by Raein that studio practice is taught to students through *doing* and that "through the act of 'doing' students absorb knowledge."[75] It is an activity that involves the mind and the body. A definition of practice might be understood as the ways and means of what artists do when they engage in their creative enterprises.

There are obvious differences in the practices of various fields. For example, the materials used by a creative writer centre on words and the means of recording those words while a sculptor's materials would consist of wood, bronze, fiberglass, steel, and any number of others to complete their task. The skills and tools used in these two activities are very unlike each other. A second obvious difference is the means of presentation. A painter might hold an exhibition in a gallery, a writer could publish a book or an eBook sold in a physical or an online bookstore, while a digital artist may use an internet portal as the method of dissemination. While these differences are obviously important, "practice" in practice-led research must be understood in a more fundamental way. If this were not the case, the methodology could mean different things to different people and discussions would be at cross purposes, each understanding practice in different ways. Each individual understanding the area as only "my practice" with all the possible diversity this might entail. The methodology would be so diverse as to be meaningless. It would be a term so specific that it

---

74. McNiff, "Art-Based Research," 29.
75. Raein, "Where Is the 'I'?"

had meaning only within one discipline or sub discipline. This would undermine the methodology as well as the usefulness and meaning of research.

However, it is not just the term practice that is important, but the relationship between the researcher's practice and the knowledge that is generated as a result of that practice. Donald Schön argues that beginning with the work of Francis Bacon and Thomas Hobbes, the idea grew that "human progress would be achieved by harnessing science to create technology for the achievement of human ends."[76] Schön calls this the *Technological Program* and its associated paradigm, *Technical Rationality,* and which Schön further argues is the heritage of logical positivism.[77] Positivists held to a verification principle which stated that "an informative sentence, in order to be meaningful, must be capable in principle of being empirically verified."[78] Positivism had a negative impact on all disciplines that were not based on what the positivists considered meaningful.

Technical Rationality has a hierarchical understanding of professional knowledge and has led to two issues that are of interest to the argument of this chapter. The first issue lies in a separation between researcher and practitioner, and second, a separation between real knowledge and skills. Real knowledge "lies in the theories and techniques of basic and applies science" while skills, coming in later, are there to solve concrete problems:[79]

> Researchers are supposed to provide the basic applied science from which to derive techniques for diagnosing and solving the problems of practice. Practitioners are supposed to furnish researchers with problems for study and with tests of the utility of research results. The researcher's role is distinct from, and usually considered superior to, the role of the practitioner.[80]

---

76. Schön, *Reflective Practitioner*, 31.
77. Schön, *Reflective Practitioner*, 31.
78. Moreland and Craig, *Philosophical Foundations*, 154.
79. Schön, *Reflective Practitioner*, 26, 27.
80. Schön, *Reflective Practitioner*, 26.

Defining Practice-Led Research: Foundations

Using examples from the writing of others, Schön notes that the paradigm maintains that the so-called "minor" professions are "hopelessly non-rigorous" and "suffer from shifting, ambiguous ends and from unstable institutional contexts of practice."[81] These disciplines, then, are unable to develop a base of "systematic, scientific professional knowledge."[82] The sort of disciplines that fit this *minor* category include social work, librarianship, education, divinity, and town planning.[83] If they would be considered professions at all, the various creative disciplines would also fit here since ends are not fixed and agreed as technical rationality demands.[84] In this view, theory forms a kind of Procrustean bed into which practice is forced to fit.

Two final points are needed. In discussions on practice and praxis, the ideas of Antonio Gamschi and his "philosophy of praxis" are sometimes considered. However, if his philosophy of praxis does indeed refocus Marxism on its original "nucleus of Historical Materialism,"[85] then its inclusion in the argument of this book would be deeply problematic. A basic understanding of Marxism holds that religion is the result of economic and social conditions and that with the elimination of material needs, religions will also disappear.[86] Since this is in direct conflict with the assumptions of this book as outlined in chapter 2,[87] Gramschi's ideas will not be considered. Similar reasons can be given for the concept of praxis in liberation theology. Critics of liberation theology have noted its use of Marxist categories, some going so far as describing it as an "unholy alliance between Christianity and Marxism."[88] While it is certainly possible to draw on Marxian-like analyses and not be a Marxist (as some of the discussion in chapter 3 of this book demonstrates) including it here would require preliminary work to separate the liberation theology concept of praxis from

---

81. Schön, *Reflective Practitioner*, 23.
82. Schön, *Reflective Practitioner*, 23.
83. Schön, *Reflective Practitioner*, 23.
84. Schön, *Reflective Practitioner*, 41.
85. Haug, "From Marx to Gramsci," 71.
86. McGrath, *Christian Theology*, 100.
87. See the discussion that begins in chapter 1.
88. McGrath, *Christian Theology*, 116.

any Marxist roots. While this would be possible, the task is outside the purpose of this book and so will not be attempted in this project. More importantly, it will be the intention of a later section to return to a first principles approach for developing an understanding of the nature of practice.

CONCLUSION

The analysis of this chapter has provided a deeper understanding of the framework within which practice-led research must operate and is intended to address: a research environment in the university context. The discussion has further aimed to outline the basic principles with which any definition needs to contend. An overview of what research means in a university context and by the major government funding bodies was outlined. The basic understanding of what is meant by the term knowledge in a research context has also been examined. What is understood by art in this context was also considered in order to better understand the underlying thinking process. Finally I considered the rudimentary understanding of practice in the field.

The next stage, developed in the following chapter, is to consider how these concepts—research, knowledge and practice—have been expanded by scholars writing about the methodology as well as in other contexts. The work conducted in this chapter will allow the methodology to be defined more clearly and effectively. Importantly for the ultimate goal of this project, it will also allow the method to be used in other areas, specifically, theology.

Chapter 5

Defining Practice-Led Research
The Definition

INTRODUCTION

THERE ARE A NUMBER of key concepts that lie at the heart of practice-led research: *research*, *knowledge*, and *practice*. Each of these concepts needs to be understood clearly and proves it challenging to do so in ways that are meaningful and useful for research generally but also for practice-led research specifically. This chapter develops and expands these concepts and then draws them together in a robust definition of practice-led research. Each of the three concepts—research, knowledge, and practice—was examined in detail in the previous chapter and so a brief summary of those here will be useful.

Firstly, research was understood based on a widely used and adapted understanding originating from the Frascati Manual produced by the OECD.[1] The definition describes research as systematic creative work that is aimed at increasing the stock of knowledge relating to humanity, our culture, and society. This knowledge is then used for further research and for new purposes and innovations. Implicit in this view is the need to make the outcomes of research known to others.

Secondly, the concept of knowledge was explored. Ideas on what knowledge is or might be are already embedded in the understanding

---

1. OECD, *Frascati Manual 2012*.

of research. It was shown that the nature of knowledge was not clearly defined, but appeared to be most often understood in a general way or in what might be thought of as a *commonsense* way. However, influenced by the Frascati Manual, this understanding is underpinned by a *quantitative paradigm*. Thomas described a quantitative paradigm as being a focus on measurements and amounts and the relationship between them (for example, more or less, greater or smaller).[2]

The third component considered was practice. This term was shown to be the most ambiguous of the three in terms of what it actually means. There appears to be a common assumption within creative disciplines as to what practice is for them, but this assumption is never examined. Further, problems will emerge when there are discussions across disciplines as these assumed understandings may clash.

The aim of this chapter is to examine these concepts in greater detail and develop conceptual understandings of the terms. Firstly, each of the terms will be expanded in order to produce a richer understanding of the ideas and to allow them to be more easily adapted to for use in defining practice-led research. The second task will be to present a definitional framework for the understanding and operation of practice-led research. The word framework is used deliberately. A solid framework is vitally important for the situation in which it will be applied: the university. However, practice-led research is methodology that permits flexibility in its application. It will be argued that a definition that is too rigid or that provides a strict set of procedures does not allow the methodology to fulfil the purposes for which it has been developed. This, it will be argued, does not affect its academic rigour, but enhances its usefulness. The third and final goal of the chapter will be to distinguish practice-led research from a number of other methodologies that could be considered as bearing some resemblance to it and show where and why they are different. It will be the task of the next chapter to compare it with methodologies used specifically in theology and demonstrate its differences, benefits, and possible weaknesses.

---

2. Thomas, *Blending Qualitative and Quantitative Research Methods*, 7.

Defining Practice-Led Research: The Definition

KNOWLEDGE IN OTHER FORMS

There is an important question to ask in regard to practice-led research, and one that helps to shield against the *mention practice-led research and all will be ok* mentality discussed at the beginning of the previous chapter. The question that must be addressed in the development of a solid understanding of practice-led research has been well phrased by Niedderer and Reilly:

> "[T]hrough the creation of new artefacts, products, services etc., creative practice can be understood to create new experiences. In creating new experience does it thus create new knowledge? How might the creation of new artefacts, products, services etc., create new knowledge, if at all?"[3]

To this end, scholars writing in the area of practice-led research have tried to understand knowledge in different ways to those they argue are dominant. The intent is to expand the concept and make it more flexible. However, authors sometimes present the choice as being either/or with one of the alternatives in loaded and negative language. For example, Graeme Sullivan:

> Notwithstanding the revisionist tendencies of post-positivism in the latter half of the 20th century, the rationality of logical positivism has been the long-term trustee overseeing what is commonly known as the *scientific method*. This approach to knowledge construction is perhaps the most powerful leitmotif of modernism and has high status as the emblem of progress.[4]

Sullivan continues his critique of this approach in the same tone as this quote. After subtly introducing a social constructionist paradigm,[5] he reaches his preferred approach, and the language used makes this clear: "Postmodernism, however, was a sincere attempt to offer a

---

3. Niedderer and Reilly, "New Knowledge in the Creative Disciplines," 83.
4. Sullivan, *Art Practice as Research*, 33 (italics original).
5. Sullivan, *Art Practice as Research*, 38.

critique of the basic assumptions underlying theories and practices of modernity and the invasive constraints of the Western canon."[6]

Despite these sometimes-dichotomous representations there is, using Sullivan's words, a sincere attempt to expand how the university and external funders should understand what it is artists do and that the knowledge they generate is legitimate and of the same standard as produced in other areas.

While the dominant paradigm in the university is a kind of technical rationality as described by Donald Schön and discussed in the previous section, the dominant knowledge paradigm in the practice-led research debate itself is a *social constructionist* model. Although Alvesson and Sköldberg argue that social construction is "central to the social sciences today,"[7] it is not the approach I have adopted in this book (see chapter 2). The reasons this approach is rejected were discussed in chapter 2. There are other consequences from this paradigm for research outputs of the method and the nature of the knowledge it generates.

There is a tendency for some to confuse practice-led research with some type of descriptive personal journey of discovery where the contribution to a wider knowledge base or debate appears to be minimal. One writer recommends this as the focus:

> "The important issue here is where to begin? Where does the emphasis for practitioner-based research lie? As studio practitioners a strong base is in autobiography as a means of linking art and life ... Its methods enable us to explore the variances of artistic decision-making and the diversity of creative experiences."[8]

Beginning from the point that autobiography is "personal investigation of the self: self-research, self-portrait; self-narrative," Stewart argues that autobiography as the ground of practice-led research "enables the studio practitioner to apprehend artistic practice by

---

6. Sullivan, *Art Practice as Research*, 46.
7. Alvesson and Sköldberg, *Reflexive Methodology*, 50.
8. Stewart, "Practice vs Praxis."

Defining Practice-Led Research: The Definition

revealing personal experience, in the context of life stories, as the basis of research."[9]

Research was formulated in the previous chapter as a means to investigate issues of concern to the discipline or issues that might be best answered by a discipline with the aim of increasing the stock of knowledge of humanity. The self-focused mode of research suggested by some writers not only fails at this but also seems to fail the researcher by reducing their engagement with their own community of enquiry and the broader concerns and issues of that intellectual community.

McNamara sums up the concern well (as well as the view of research adopted in this book) when he says that the goal of practice-led research is not to make sense of a practitioners own life or experience—although it may do that—but

> the goal of research—in all its forms—should be to explain something of significance and of broader relevance to a research community; this may be a larger, cross-disciplinary research community, or it may be a wider public audience ... In particular, a PhD research project needs to justify its research contribution in terms that extend past the researcher's subjective experience.[10]

This is an area of the practice-led research methodology that needs to be kept in balance. Firstly, it is not to discount the idea that a higher degree is a part of a personal learning journey and that a researcher grows and develops personally during the process. Further, the things that motivate researchers are often in areas of interest to them. What is being rejected is a narrow isolationist view of the goals of research that primarily focus on personal enhancement. The use of practice-led research can lead an excessive subjectivity, one that lacks a perspective of the wider intellectual community.

This concern is sometimes amplified by the nature of the written component in the standard format of practice-led research, where it tends to be a personal account of the project. This aspect will be

---

9. Stewart, "Practice vs Praxis," 6.

10. McNamara, "Six Rules," who raises other concerns in this paper, some of which will be addressed in chapter 6.

addressed in the next chapter. A crucial caveat to this critique is that a measure of subjectivity is central to the method. Questions for investigation can arise out of the personal experience of the individual's practice: problems encountered, new processes that may need to be developed or unexpected consequences of a particular process as examples. It is the case in practice-led research that this process is overt rather than covert (as may be the case in other methodologies). However, the need to contribute to the stock of knowledge and to the wider intellectual community must be maintained. This tension will be explored in more detail inc hapter 6 of this book. However, the key point for this chapter is that research includes an outcome that contributes to wider debates and the knowledge base of the discipline (at least).

Another issue to be considered here is the question of *meaning* and of *understanding*. It will be argued that these ideas are not in opposition to knowledge or in some way inferior but cover and expand the same areas. It does depend, however, on what is meant by meaning and how to understand understanding.[11]

I noted earlier in this book that if a distinction needs to be made, practice-led research fits broadly under a *qualitative* paradigm.[12] Qualitative, in the words of Denzin and Lincoln, "implies an emphasis on the qualities of entities and on processes and meanings that are not experimentally examined or measured."[13] Among other things, qualitative researchers "seek answers to questions that stress how social experience is created and given meaning."[14] The idea of understanding situations and experiences is the "very aim of [the qualitative] enterprise in all of its current forms."[15] While some writers tend to view qualitative and quantitative approaches as opposites, adopting a very polemical approach to their descriptions,[16] it is the general assumption of this book that the two paradigms are complementary. This understanding

---

11. To paraphrase in part the title of a paper by Schwandt, "On Understanding."
12. See chapter 4.
13. Denzin and Lincoln, "Introduction," 14.
14. Denzin and Lincoln, "Introduction," 14.
15. Schwandt, "On Understanding," 451.
16. For example, this general approach can be seen in the introduction to the Denzin and Lincoln book cited here.

is at least partly grounded in the *critical realist* framework outlined in chapter 2.[17]

A way of conceptualizing knowledge that allows both these *subjective* and *objective* elements to function together, and the one to be adopted in this book, is one based on the concept of *embodied* or *tacit knowledge* and on *multiple intelligences*. It will be argued that these approaches are complementary with other ways of looking at knowledge and are a way of considering knowing that accommodates practice as well as being adaptable to a Christian faith context.

MULTIPLE INTELLIGENCES

Howard Gardner introduced his ideas on multiple intelligences in *Frames of Mind: The Theory of Multiple Intelligences* in 1983 and expanded on them a decade later with *Multiple Intelligences: The Theory in Practice*. His starting point is that in the West at least, there has been a stress on the "existence and the importance of mental powers—capacities that have been variously termed *rationality*, *intelligence*, or the deployment of *mind*."[18] He argues that "as IQ tests measure only logical or logical-linguistic capacities, in this society we are nearly 'brain-washed' to restrict the notion of intelligence to the capacities used in solving logical and linguistic problems."[19] This starting point is confirmed by the discussion on research and knowledge earlier in the previous chapter and by the discussion in chapter 3 relating to the status and position of the artist in society historically and the theologian in contemporary times.

Gardner argues that intelligence has been viewed too narrowly.[20] Therefore, rather than it only being seen in one way—in a logical-linguistic way—Gardner contends that there are "several *relatively autonomous* human intellectual competencies" and that they "can be fashioned and combined in a multiplicity of adaptive ways by individuals and culture."[21] However, according to Gardner, it is not the case that

17. The discussion begins in chapter 1.
18. Gardner, *Frames of Mind*, 5 (italics original).
19. Gardner, *Multiple Intelligences*, 14.
20. Gardner, *Frames of Mind*, 4.
21. Gardner, *Frames of Mind*, 8, 9 (italics original).

any thinking style is an intelligence. A candidate needs to possess two prerequisites. The first requirement is a set of problem solving skills which enables the person to "*resolve genuine problems or difficulties*" and the second is that an intellectual competence must also "entail the potential for *finding or creating problems*—thereby laying the groundwork for the acquisition of new knowledge."[22]

It will be immediately apparent in Gardner's suggestion that intelligence involves the solving as well as the generation of problems, a potential link to the notion of practice-led research. An important goal of practice-led research is to provide a process for finding and solving problems generated by the practice of a specific discipline, the creative arts, and that it is possible to generate new knowledge in and through the practice and the process of investigation. Gardner makes a "rough-and-ready distinction" between *know-how*, that is, "tacit knowledge of how to execute something" and *know-that* described as "propositional knowledge about the actual set of procedures involved in execution."[23] Gardner suggests the intelligences are sets of know-how procedures for doing things.[24]

In his first framing of the theory, seven intelligences were put forward: linguistic, musical, logical-mathematical, spatial, bodily-kinesthetic, and the personal intelligences (interpersonal, and intrapersonal).[25] Gardner suggested that this list may not be exhaustive, but he believed that there were at least these seven.[26] Since these were suggested, numerous other candidates have been put forward. In his own updating of the theory in 1999, Gardner discusses four, of which three are of interest to this discussion: a *naturalist* intelligence, a *spiritual* intelligence and an *existential* intelligence. Partly to demonstrate the process of including a new intelligence, partly to reveal Gardner's own biases in the selection of candidates, and partly as a contrast for the later possible candidates, an outline of the proposed naturalistic intelligence will be presented first.

22. Gardner, *Frames of Mind*, 60, 61 (italics original).
23. Gardner, *Frames of Mind*, 68.
24. Gardner, *Frames of Mind*, 69.
25. Gardner, *Frames of Mind*, 69.
26. Gardner, *Intelligence Reframed*, 47.

Naturalistic Intelligence

At face value, Gardner's naturalistic intelligence is unproblematic. A naturalist is a person who has "demonstrated expertise in the recognition and classification or the numerous species—the flora and fauna—of his or her environment."[27] This person is capable of recognizing the various members of a species, those that are dangerous, which ones to hunt, have a talent for caring or taming animals. He also suggests that this might be possessed by the person that can recognize a car by the sound of the engine or spot artistic styles.[28] It would be a diversion to conduct a full and detailed critical analysis of Gardner's inclusion of a *naturalistic* intelligence, but it is important to note some concerns in preparation for the next two intelligences. Firstly, his description and examination of the intelligence is brief and made over only five pages. It is very specific with few counters or criticisms introduced. Secondly, after this brief analysis, he says he has "acknowledged an eighth intelligence by a simple performative speech act."[29] In this statement Gardner is referring to J. L. Austin's theory of speech acts and his "performative utterances," that is, types of declarative statements that perform some action.[30] They are statements we make to "bring about changes in the world through our utterances, so that the world is changed to match the propositional content of the utterance."[31] In essence, a naturalistic intelligence is one of the multiple intelligences simply because Gardner declares it to be one of them. This admission needs to be kept in mind for the next discussion.

Spiritual or Existential Intelligence

Gardner's second potential addition to the pantheon of intelligences is a *spiritual intelligence,* although he actually considers it to be a "variety" of his third potential candidate, an *existential intelligence.*[32] This

27. Gardner, *Intelligence Reframed*, 48.
28. Gardner, *Intelligence Reframed*, 50.
29. Gardner, *Intelligence Reframed*, 52.
30. Morris, *Introduction*, 232.
31. Searle, "Contemporary Philosophy," 8.
32. Gardner, *Intelligence Reframed*, 60.

section will draw significantly on the writings of others as to what an independent spiritual intelligence may look like. The primary reason for this is that his discussion in *Intelligence Reframed*[33] does not follow his normal pattern: a brief definition and then a comparison with the criteria he set out in his original book from 1983. Instead, he immediately fragments the area and presents rather a discussion of the diverse nature of the spiritual than one considering whether it fits the criteria. Since he believes it to be a subcategory of existential intelligence, the examination will begin there.

The "core ability" possessed by an individual with existential intelligence is:

> the capacity to locate oneself with respect to the further reaches of the cosmos—the infinite and the infinitesimal—and the related capacity to locate oneself with respect to such existential features of the human condition as the significance of life, the meaning of death, the ultimate fate of the physical and psychological worlds, and such profound experiences as love of another person or total immersion in a work of art.[34]

This quote and his following discussion reveal reasons why he rejects spiritual intelligence. His assumption seems to be that there is nothing beyond the physical realm. Further, he groups the religious, mystical and metaphysical together with aesthetic, philosophical and scientific systems designed to address human needs as "culturally devised."[35] Elsewhere, he suggests that the phenomenological states associated with spirituality are best thought of as "external to the intellectual realm."[36] This appears to be an arbitrary distinction based on assumptions not clearly stated and aimed at isolating and so marginalizing spiritual thought. To highlight this, it could equally be said that if Gardner's naturalistic intelligence is to be thought of as anything other than learning facts about plants and animals, the phenomenological experience of caring for and taming animals is external to the intellectual

---

33. Gardner, *Intelligence Reframed*, 53–60.
34. Gardner, *Intelligence Reframed*, 60.
35. Gardner, *Intelligence Reframed*, 61.
36. Gardner, "Case against Spiritual Intelligence," 29.

realm. This distinction seems even more difficult to maintain in the face of an understanding of theology adopted in this book as a close engagement between the intellectual exploration of the faith and one that is believed and experienced.

In an article published in 2000 (to which Gardner's paper mentioned in the previous paragraph was a response), Robert Emmons summarizes a possible case for spiritual intelligence as independent from the others. He firstly presents the eight criteria Gardner insists a candidate must conform to be included as an intelligence. They are:

1. An identifiable core operation or set of operations
2. An evolutionary history and evolutionary plausibility
3. A characteristic pattern of development
4. Potential isolation by brain damage
5. The existence of persons distinguished by the exceptional presence or absence of the ability
6. Susceptibility to encoding in a symbol system
7. Support from experimental psychological investigations
8. Support from psychometric findings[37]

Gardner immediately fragmented the idea of spirituality. Emmons, however, understands it in a broad encompassing way as "the personal expression of ultimate concern," a view he bases on the works of Paul Tillich.[38] It is about having a "passion for the infinite."[39] This expression of an ultimate concern in turn manifests itself in "personal goal strivings" or "what people are typically trying to do, their 'signature' goal pursuits."[40] Spiritual intelligence is formulated in this broad way as it would be possessed by people across the religious spectrum. However, to relate it directly to this book, Christian spirituality generally, and theology specifically, is concerned with a passion for Christ

---

37. Emmons, "Is Spirituality an Intelligence?" 7.
38. Emmons, "Is Spirituality an Intelligence?" 4.
39. Emmons, "Is Spirituality an Intelligence?" 4.
40. Emmons, "Is Spirituality an Intelligence?" 4.

and the variety of "signature goal pursuits" of Christians and the Christian community.

Emmons states that there is little agreement over how intelligence should be defined.[41] To highlight this, he cites a number of examples demonstrating the diversity of views. One is from Walters and Gardner in 1996. Intelligence is "a set of abilities that permits an individual to solve problems or fashion products that are of consequence in a particular cultural setting."[42] His discussion focuses on the adaptive problem-solving nature of intelligence. To this end he suggests a "pragmatic" way of understanding aspects of spirituality as "a set of specific abilities or capacities" and that spirituality "may be then conceptualized in adaptive, cognitive-motivational terms, and, as such, may underlie a variety of problem-solving skills relevant to everyday life situations."[43] However, he does add a caveat that by considering it this way he is not saying that spirituality is nothing but pragmatic problem solving.[44]

Emmons suggests that there are at least five core abilities in a spiritual intelligence:

> At a minimum, spiritually intelligent individuals are characterized by (a) the capacity for transcendence; (b) the ability to enter into heightened spiritual states of consciousness; (c) the ability to invest everyday activities, events, and relationships with a sense of the sacred; (d) the ability to utilize spiritual resources to solve problems in living; and (e) the capacity to engage in virtuous behavi[o]r or to be virtuous (to show forgiveness, to express gratitude, to be humble, to display compassion).[45]

Emmons next proceeds through all the criteria Gardner set out for an intelligence to be included in his list. This process provides evidence that spiritual intelligence fits the criteria. He argues that spiritual intelligence has evolutionary plausibility as a number of mechanisms

---

41. Emmons, "Is Spirituality an Intelligence?" 5.
42. Emmons, "Is Spirituality an Intelligence?" 6.
43. Emmons, "Is Spirituality an Intelligence?" 8.
44. Emmons, "Is Spirituality an Intelligence?" 9.
45. Emmons, "Is Spirituality an Intelligence?" 10.

associated with it enabled our ancestors to solve particular types of problems.[46] He suggests that there is some evidence for the inheritability of religious attitudes and that there is a growing body of evidence on the neurobiological basis of religious belief. The existence of brain systems connected to spirituality[47] fulfils another of Gardner's criteria as an intelligence. Although Emmons questions the ability to measure a *spiritual IQ*—and the wisdom of attempting to do so—it may be possible to develop other more appropriate measures. It also seems clear to Emmons that there is a developmental history for spirituality, "from novitiate to expert, as there are in other systems of knowledge."[48] The criterion that a religious system be coded symbolically "is not likely to be controversial" as he notes that symbol systems "have always played a major role in religious traditions to express truths and insights not reducible to linguistic expression."[49] The final criterion, exemplars of spiritual intelligence, is also uncontroversial as there are numerous examples. He cites the Catholic mystics St. Theresa of Avila and St. John of the Cross, as well as the Sufi master Ibn 'Arabi.[50]

One particular advantage Emmons sees in making a link between spirituality and intelligence is that it will act as an "antidote for antireligious intellectualism" and that instead of "dichotomizing faith and reason" this approach permits an understanding of how spiritual processing can improve cognitive functioning rather than preclude it.[51] This point is especially pertinent to this project as one of its stated aims is to argue that academic research and faith practice sit together appropriately in academic research.

There is one final interesting note on Gardner's discussion of the existence of a spiritual intelligence. At the end of the chapter discussing these new candidates for inclusion, Gardner includes a "personal perspective on spiritual intelligence."[52] It leads him to reject a spiritual

46. Emmons, "Is Spirituality an Intelligence?" 14.
47. Emmons, "Is Spirituality an Intelligence?" 15.
48. Emmons, "Is Spirituality an Intelligence?" 16.
49. Emmons, "Is Spirituality an Intelligence?" 16.
50. Emmons, "Is Spirituality an Intelligence?" 16.
51. Emmons, "Is Spirituality an Intelligence?" 20.
52. Gardner, *Intelligence Reframed*, 64.

intelligence and accept the possibility of an existential intelligence so that he can, at most, "joke about '8½ intelligences.'"[53]

This discussion suggests that on closer inspection, naturalistic intelligence appears to be an increased emphasis on a rationalist scientific paradigm with an accompanying rejection of a spiritual dimension to the human person. While it is important to include in research and the knowledge making enterprise the rational/empirical process, it is the conclusion of this discussion that knowledge is also found and stored in and through an embodied spiritual process. Future discussions in this book therefore accept the notion that there exists a spiritual intelligence.

Gardner's description of intelligences as being a type of *know-how* along with several of the requirements an intelligence has to have to be included, fits them into the broader category of *embodied knowledge*. Embodied knowledge and the related area of *embodied cognition* can further develop the argument presented here that some conceptions of knowledge are artificially narrow and so, to some degree, incomplete.

Michael Polanyi notes at the beginning of his book *Tacit Knowledge* that "*we can know more than we can tell.*"[54] He gives the example of being able to recognize the face of a friend among thousands of even millions yet we cannot say quite how we do this.[55] It is true, he goes on to observe, that it is possible for us to communicate much of this knowledge with the aid of the police system of a large collection of facial features we choose from to compile the face we saw as the witness to a crime.[56] Polanyi notes that we can only do this by knowing how to match the features which is something we may also not be able to fully describe how it is possible.[57] However, it might also be suggested that the knowledge here is a type of visual knowledge (under a rubric of embodied knowledge) and so of a different—but valid—type of knowing.

Polanyi goes on to distinguish two ways of knowing, *explicit* and *tacit*. Explicit knowledge is that which is "capable of being clearly

---

53. Gardner, *Intelligence Reframed*, 66.
54. Polanyi, *Tacit Dimension*, 4 (italics original).
55. Polanyi, *Tacit Dimension*, 4.
56. Polanyi, *Tacit Dimension*, 4.
57. Polanyi, *Tacit Dimension*, 5.

stated."⁵⁸ That is to say, it is the type of knowledge that can be expressed as information and data and can be presented in the form of propositional or statements of the nature of things in the world. Explicit knowledge is not in opposition to tacit knowledge but is complimentary with it and, he argues, tacit knowledge undergirds and makes explicit knowledge possible.⁵⁹ Polanyi's argument for the foundational nature of tacit knowledge is based on the *Meno* paradox from Plato. Polanyi summarizes it this way: "Yet Plato has pointed out this contradiction in the Meno. He says that to search for the solution of a problem is an absurdity; for either you know what you are looking for, and then there is no problem; or you do not know what you are looking for, and then you cannot expect to find anything."⁶⁰ Polanyi argues that if all knowledge is explicit then we cannot know a problem or look for a solution but that "if problems nevertheless exist, and discoveries can be made by solving them, we can know things, and important things, that we cannot tell."⁶¹

It is important to draw out two implications from the argument so far. The first is based on Polanyi's statement that the two forms of knowledge are complimentary and not in opposition or somehow to be separated. Practice-led research will be understood and formulated later in this chapter and in those following as combining these two into a single research process but not favouring one over the other. Both tacit/embodied knowledge *and* explicit/propositional knowledge are a part of the process and the output.

The second implication, and closely related to the first, is that the process of research is a combination of the two styles of knowledge and the legitimacy of knowledge in a wider understanding. Practice-led research may find its research problems in the practice of the individual (tacit/embodied) or in the stated problems and issues of a discipline (explicit/propositional). Further, the research is conducted from this dual base.

---

58. Polanyi, *Tacit Dimension*, 22.
59. Polanyi, *Tacit Dimension*, 24.
60. Polanyi, *Tacit Dimension*, 22.
61. Polanyi, *Tacit Dimension*, 22.

For Polanyi, it is not so much that tacit knowledge is just an additional form of knowledge and you can take it or leave it. Polanyi argues that

> our body is the ultimate instrument of all our external knowledge, whether intellectual or practical. In all our waking moments we are *relying* on our awareness of contacts of our body with things outside for *attending* to these things. Our body is the only thing in the world which we normally never experience as an object, but experience always in terms of the world to which we are attending from our body.[62]

He seems to be saying here that the body is assumed in all the things we do and in all the things we know. He gives the simple example of when we use a probe to feel around a cavern or a blind person uses a stick. Initially, we feel the probe against our hand but after a time, it is the sense of what is at the end of the stick or probe that we feel.[63] The body is then extended into the object "so that we come to dwell in it."[64]

The centrality of the body in our thought, knowledge, and decision making—and importantly, the link between forms of knowledge—is also highlighted by developments in the so-called "cognitive revolution." This section will present supporting arguments from two scholars. The first is based on the work of Lawrence Barsalou on embodiment and religious knowledge and the second is drawn from Antonio Damasio and his work on the link between emotion and reason.[65] The section will begin with Barsalou and colleagues in a paper entitled *Embodiment in Religious Knowledge*[66] and will begin with an overview of the key principles in which he grounds his support of an embodied theory of knowledge.

Barsalou begins by making a distinction between what he thinks is popularly considered knowledge (that which is acquired in formal education or the product of academic enquiry) and what he calls *mundane*

---

62. Polanyi, *Tacit Dimension*, 15.
63. Polanyi, *Tacit Dimension*, 12.
64. Polanyi, *Tacit Dimension*, 16.
65. Damasio, *Descartes' Error*.
66. Barsalou et al., "Embodiment in Religious Knowledge."

knowledge.⁶⁷ Mundane knowledge is the vast array of things we know about physical objects, physical settings, complex events, simple actions and behaviours, mental states, properties, and relations among others.⁶⁸ Although it is possible for individuals to focus on objects and gain more categorical knowledge about things, an individual's mundane knowledge remains largely hidden from view and functions in the main automatically.⁶⁹ Categorical knowledge retains the mundane knowledge connected to the situations in which it is developed.⁷⁰

Importantly for the argument presented here, this mundane knowledge "permeates every aspect of cognitive activity from high to low cognition."⁷¹ To help demonstrate this, Barsalou describes cognition in online and offline terms. As people interact with their environment and are performing various tasks—online cognition—mundane knowledge supports the perception of a scene, the categorization of objects, settings and actions in a scene, and supports these categorizations with "rich inductive inferences that guide interactions with it."⁷² It is not necessary for cognitive processes to start from nothing every time they encounter a scene or engage in an action of some sort.

Mundane knowledge is also important in memory, language and thought activities, that is, offline processing. Barsalou sums up this influence in the following way:

> In memory, mundane knowledge provides elaborative inferences at encoding, organizational structure in storage, and reconstructive inferences at retrieval. In language, mundane knowledge contributes to the meanings of words, phrases, sentences, and texts, and also to the knowledge-based inferences that go beyond them. In thought, mundane knowledge provides representations of the objects and events on which reasoning processes operate.⁷³

---

67. Barsalou et al., "Embodiment in Religious Knowledge," 14.
68. Barsalou et al., "Embodiment in Religious Knowledge," 15.
69. Barsalou et al., "Embodiment in Religious Knowledge," 15.
70. Barsalou et al., "Embodiment in Religious Knowledge," 16.
71. Barsalou et al., "Embodiment in Religious Knowledge," 16.
72. Barsalou et al., "Embodiment in Religious Knowledge," 16.
73. Barsalou et al., "Embodiment in Religious Knowledge," 17.

What is important to note here is that the pervasive nature of mundane knowledge means that thought, memory and language are never entirely separate from the environment in which they are formed, and the experienced environment is intimately connected to the body. It was a failure to recognize this connection that Antonio Damasio describes as *Descartes's Error*. Specifically, he says, "the separation of the most refined operations of mind from the structure and operation of a biological organism."[74] Damasio's own *somatic marker hypothesis* is grounded in similar ideas on how emotions (originating in the body and its experiences) impact on the reasoning of individuals, sometimes for better and sometimes for the worse, but always present.[75]

It would be possible to go even more deeply into this phenomenon and consider its neurological foundations in the modality-specific systems of the brain. However, it is apparent from what has been presented that knowledge and thinking are closely and inseparably linked to the body and experiences. It is reasonable to suggest that those things that rely on knowledge and thinking, for example, research, are also indirectly influenced by latent embodied knowledge. Practice-led research taps into this, employs it and includes it in the research process with the end result of a richer or broader understanding of the question being investigated.

Summary

This section considered ways in which knowledge and intelligence might be understood in expanded ways. It began with an overview of the concept of multiple intelligences as first articulated by Howard Gardner. It outlined the original seven presented by Gardner and then went on to look at three possible new additions. The goal of the discussion in terms of this project is to suggest that there is a spiritual knowledge, and that it is a legitimate area of research pursuit—in the same way that any of the other intelligences are and manifested

---

74. Damasio, *Descartes' Error*, 250. It is beyond the scope of this discussion to consider the debate as to whether Descartes was the hard-nosed Cartesian he is often caricatured as being. A good discussion of this topic is in Baker and Morris, *Descartes' Dualism*.

75. Damasio, *Descartes' Error*. See especially chapter 8 of his book.

Defining Practice-Led Research: The Definition

in an academic environment, be it linguistic, spatial or musical. The conclusion is that there is at least one additional intelligence: *spiritual intelligence*.

It goes on to consider an understanding of tacit and embodied knowledge as central to how humans interact with and understand the world. Mundane knowledge is grounded in our lived experiences in the world and pervades all of thought and action. The conclusion here is that all knowledge is at least partly embodied.

However, it is true to say that in the same way as its musical counterpart, research from a spiritual/faith base—and the knowledge it generates—requires additional tools and approaches; strategies additional for example, those used for propositional approaches. It is into this role that practice-led research falls. The next section will conduct a closer examination of the nature of *practice* in this context.

PRACTICE, PRAXIS, AND PRAXICAL KNOWLEDGE

As suggested at the start of this chapter,[76] what is meant by the term "practice" is, at best, poorly articulated in the relevant literature but more often than not taken as assumed to be understood by everyone. There is a historical level where this approach is understandable. As demonstrated in chapter 3, artists were trained through doing, skills were passed on by the experienced artisan to their apprentice: theory was not important unless it was connected to the execution of a work. It has also been suggested in this chapter that a poor understanding of practice and practice-led research in general has the potential to undermine the methodology being presented in this book.

However, because it is so foundational, a clear understanding of practice is needed. It will be argued in this section that it is more than a list of the activities an artist or other practitioner engages in and is closely connected to purpose and ways of understanding and knowing the world.

It is important at the beginning of this discussion to briefly consider a question of terminology. While the aim of this section is to discuss what it is and how it is best to be understood in terms of this

---

76. See chapter 1.

project, a legitimate question is to ask is it *practice* or *practise*? According to the Oxford English Dictionary, *practice* is the noun and *practise* is the verb.[77] As will be seen in the examination to follow, the discussion revolves both around practices—the skills and actions that can be described—and the doing of those skills—practise. However, no distinction will be made between the two words in terms of meaning other than when it is appropriate in following this grammatical rule. There is an important reason for this: virtually all the scholarly literature uses *practice*. To do otherwise would be introducing unnecessary novelty, unless a substantial reason for doing so is established.

A second reason for maintaining the use of a single term springs from a concern over how practice and research as processes are sometimes understood in the literature. Some writers argue that an artist should avoid writing, that their practice resists explanation and that it gets in the way of the doing of their task. Rebekka Kill argues that this view is prevalent in the literature and reinforced to undergraduates. She cites one author as saying

> how art history is perceived as marginal to "the real job of working in the studios: 'Dangerous, don't get contaminated by all that discourse, or you won't be able to produce'; 'Artists think differently'; 'Words are not important,'" she goes on, "no wonder students hate art history."[78]

The argument is that practice and writing are somehow in opposition. Kill's own research suggests that this is a faulty belief. What is important here is that the term practice-led research can be viewed as a technical term. It reinforces it as a methodology that combines practice in whatever form is relevant to a project as well as reinforcing research in the academic sense involving the written word as a part of the contribution a project makes to the wider intellectual community.

The following discussions will demonstrate that part of the knowing is in the doing. However, an approach that overemphasizes *the doing* runs the parallel risk of minimizing the intellectual engagement

---

77. See "Practice," *OED*.
78. Kill, "Coming in from the Cold," 310.

Defining Practice-Led Research: The Definition

and returning the methodology to one that is vague, unclear and does not make any contribution to the "stock of knowledge."[79]

This view could equally be applied to other activities, including practices relating to faith, but provides potential for insufficiently rigorous intellectual work. In what they described as a "dramatic speech" at the 1995 UK Turner Prize ceremony Gray and Malins cite Brian Eno as saying that

> [t]he Turner prize is justly celebrated for raising all sorts of questions in the public mind about art and its place in our lives. Unfortunately, however, the intellectual climate surrounding the fine arts is so vaporous and self-satisfied that few of these questions are ever actually addressed, let alone answered . . . the arts routinely produce some of the loosest thinking and worst writing known to history . . . Why has the art world been unable to articulate any kind of useful paradigm for what it is doing now?[80]

Further, to deflect scrutiny of the idea with the suggestion that it has multiple meanings may only serve as code for it having no meaning at all. After citing Eno's complaint, Gray and Malins go on to list an unconnected collection of terms and slogans. They say they are attempting to "describe the elephant" of practice-based research (as they prefer to call it)—a large complex thing—by simply throwing out a set of concepts that might be relevant.[81]

More importantly, it may also be argued that an artistic researcher is trying to record and present the results of a project that is conducted *sub-conceptually*—work done at the tacit, embodied level. It is therefore important at this point to establish a firmer foundation for *practice*, one that retains flexibility for the many uses to which it will be put but also allow for the level of rigour and reliability that is needed for the academic context.

In an important way, the lack of engagement with the notion of practice reflects a commonsense view of practice that is, for the most

---

79. See chapter 4.
80. Gray and Malins, *Visualizing Research*, 24.
81. Gray and Malins, *Visualizing Research*, 25.

part, entirely valid. Practice, then, may firstly be described as *the set of skills, abilities,* and *strategies that are characteristic of a particular discipline.* Practice is also, secondly, *what is characteristic of the output or product (in a broad sense) of the discipline.* For example, Edmonds and Candy's understanding has a strong emphasis on the product:

> "Practice is a primary element in the trajectory, providing as it does the motivation for conducting research as well as generating the activities for creating and exhibiting tangible outcomes such as artworks, exhibitions, installations, musical compositions and creative software systems."[82]

While there may be a number of similarities between the skill sets of some creative writers and those of, say, a historian, the output of the research—a piece of creative writing—reflects significant differences in practices. So, when painters talk to painters and dancers talk to dancers and worship leaders talk to worship leaders, there is a very real sense in which they do know what they are talking about and detail on what practice is unnecessary, but only within a particular community.

However, practice-led research is a particular type of practice, one that has a particular goal in mind—the uncovering of new knowledge and meanings—and as research, is intended to have accessibility (potentially at least) outside its own borders. Practice, then, will be formulated in order to try to find a balance between the doing and the end result.

Gray and Malins attempt to define practice in the following way: "Developing and making creative work as an explicit and intentional method for specific research purposes, for example gathering and/or generating data, evaluation, analysis, synthesis, presentation, communication of research findings."[83] Although there is little in this definition that sets practice apart from what might be thought of as standard research activities, there is an important phrase that gives us a clue as to what practice can mean in a research context: *explicit and intentional.*

At the very beginning of his *Nicomachean Ethics*, Aristotle says "Every craft and every inquiry, and likewise every action and decision,

---

82. Edmonds and Candy, "Relating Theory, Practice and Evaluation," 471.
83. Gray and Malins, *Visualizing Research*, 104.

Defining Practice-Led Research: The Definition

seems to aim at some good. For which reason people have rightly concluded that the good is that at which all things aim" (I.1. 1094a1–3).[84] Adapting the idea, what Aristotle argues is true for good action generally is similar to what this section argues is the case for good practice. The section on research in the previous chapter observed a primary aim of research is to contribute to the *stock of knowledge* of humanity in some way. Further, this process is generally guided by a research question or questions.[85] Good research is that which answers or contributes to the answer to a question—in the affirmative or the negative—through a rigorous process. Research, then, has a *teleological* dimension: although the answer is not yet known, it is headed in a particular direction with an aim in mind, with the goal of being of good quality.

An individual's *praxis*, then, is not only rational action, but action that is *preferentially chosen*, the best or the wisest thing for them to do.[86] With this project in mind, it is action that is best suited to the research aim, and this is reflected in the discipline of which the individual is a member. It is important to note here also that "craft (*technē*), inquiry (*methodos*), action (*praxis*), and decision (*prohairesis*) are all rational dispositions and activities."[87]

The choice of these actions is most effectively governed by the appropriate intelligence, be that, a musical or a spiritual intelligence. To rephrase Gardner's original description of the intelligences, it is argued here that the appropriate intelligence—those "*relatively autonomous human intellectual competencies*"—*are* "fashioned and combined in a multiplicity of adaptive ways by individuals" to suit the practice of their discipline.[88]

This framework closely links practice to research. Practice is integral to the aims and goals of the question being investigated—it is not a secondary component but central to the process. Research in the academy is usually presented in a written form, outlining conceptual

---

84. This is cited in Lear, "Happiness and the Structure of Ends," 389.

85. This issue of the *research question* is taken up in relation to practice-led research in greater detail in the next chapter.

86. Lawrence, "Human Good and Human Function," 42.

87. Lear, "Happiness and the Structure of Ends," 389.

88. Gardner, *Frames of Mind*, 8, 9.

and propositional knowledge in the form of structured arguments.[89] Practice-led research, however, affirms an even more foundational role for practice, one that is connected to the generation and presentation of the knowledge uncovered in the research. This is highlighted by the discussion earlier on tacit and embodied knowledge.[90]

One of the underlying arguments of this chapter (and of the next one) is that they are complimentary. Practice-led research as it will be defined in this chapter and how it will be practically developed in the next chapter, demonstrate this complementarity.

A concept well suited to understanding knowledge in terms of practice-led research is one developed by Barbara Bolt drawing on ideas from Martin Heidegger. This idea, *praxical knowledge*, argues that we come to understand the world and the things in it through our involvement with it and our *handling* of it.

Bolt draws four generally applicable key points from an example of a hammer that Heidegger uses. Firstly, there is a difference between observing something and using it. Secondly, our relation to something becomes more original in its use. Thirdly, theoretical observation does not help us to understand the "handiness" of something and fourthly, our use of things has its own kind of seeing or sight.[91]

Points one, two, and three are closely related. The contention is that knowledge of materials and processes comes not (only) from establishing a theoretical understanding of them but using and applying them. Bolt notes that we can read software manuals forever but will not really understand a software program and its operations until we use it.[92] Or, possibly more fundamentally, a sound knowledge of gyroscopic force will have limited use when it comes to learning to ride a bicycle. In terms of practice-led research, new knowing and insight emerges from engaging with the materials.[93]

When we engage with materials and processes it leads to a more original relationship. Here original means more immediate, more

---

89. Such as, it is hoped, this book.
90. See chapter 6.
91. Bolt, *Heidegger Reframed*, 92.
92. Bolt, *Heidegger Reframed*, 92.
93. Bolt, *Heidegger Reframed*, 96.

Defining Practice-Led Research: The Definition

direct. This is illustrated by Heidegger's own example of comparing the use of a hammer with seeing it in a hardware store in the packet.[94] It is only possible to understand *a hammer* in a limited way unless one uses the hammer. Polanyi gives the example of exploring a cave with a probe or the blind person using a stick to find their way around. As the person learns to use the probe or the stick, the feeling of the stick pressing against the hand changes until "we become aware of the feelings in our hand in terms of their meaning located at the tip of the probe or stick to which we are attending."[95]

The fourth point Bolt makes argues that, ultimately, there is only so much we can know about something through theoretical investigation. We may be able to know a considerable amount about some thing (or some person), but it is only through engagement—through relationship—that a full understanding can be achieved. This is achievable through practice.

Praxical knowledge is what emerges from the relationship between the individual and their engagement with the materials and practices of their discipline. Practice, it is argued here, serves to establish a relationship and engagement with the world. Practice bridges a gap between object and subject. The gap it attempts to bridge can also be viewed in terms of the discussion in the previous chapter. It was noted there that theology experienced a time of change after the Thirty Years War, the advent of the Enlightenment and then the influence of Romanticism. The Enlightenment emphasized the object as the aim of investigation while Romanticism emphasized the subject and the subjective experience. The birth of the artist as personality was partly a product of this subjective emphasis. Practice-led research as it is conceived in this book attempts to find a middle ground between important aspects of these two perspectives. It affirms a certain discoverability of knowledge through reason and theory formation as well as the presence of a knowability to the world through engagement with concrete experience.[96]

---

94. Bolt, *Heidegger Reframed*, 91.

95. Polanyi, *Tacit Dimension*, 13.

96. This position is well supported by the critical realist framework adopted for this project (see chapter 2).

By balancing this tension between object and subject, the applicability of practice-led research in a theological context seems clearer. G. E. Ladd notes that knowledge in the Old Testament is neither "the contemplation of [an] object to ascertain its essential qualities" nor is it "a kind of ecstatic mystical vision [and] not rational thought."[97] It is rather characterized by experience; it consists of response, obedience and fellowship.[98] *Knowing* God meant "having an intimate and obedient relationship with him."[99] This is carried over into the New Testament, most notably in the Gospel of John where we know Jesus through our relationship with him.[100] Response, obedience and fellowship involve *preferentially chosen* actions with the goal of a relationship with God.

It is possible, then, to know certain things about God through actions such as reading the Scriptures, studying theology and through the project of natural theology. However, it is only possible to know God in a more complete sense by the process of *handling*, which is to say, through actions that relate the individual directly to God. Examples of this include prayer and worship.

Summary

In terms of practice-led research, practice is the actions, strategies, and processes that are characteristic of a discipline and the means of communication and production of that discipline. They are preferentially chosen and guided by appropriate intelligence with the end goal of answering a research question. Praxical knowledge is generated by the discipline through the engagement of the practice with the materials and modes of the discipline.

A DEFINITION OF PRACTICE-LED RESEARCH

It is now possible to present a definition of practice-led research. The definition attempts to understand practice-led research both generally and specifically. Generally, it provides grounding for any researcher

---

97. Ladd, *Theology of the New Testament*, 296.
98. Ladd, *Theology of the New Testament*, 298.
99. Keener, *IVP Bible Background Commentary*, 290.
100. Ladd, *Theology of the New Testament*, 299.

Defining Practice-Led Research: The Definition

attempting to apply the methodology, and specifically for use in a faith context by Christian researchers. In doing so, the definition also addresses the key concerns raised in this chapter.

This process means it is necessary to detach practice-led research from its grounding in the creative disciplines such that it can be applied elsewhere without losing the benefits it gained from those origins. The definition presented does not aim to be entirely discipline independent. I believe, however, that it can be readily modified to be applied in other areas while still retaining a large degree of precision and so protecting the methodology from a return to vagueness.

Definition

Practice-led research is a methodology that sources its strategies and processes for answering its research questions broadly from those *practices* that are characteristic of the discipline in which they are employed. In a theological context, it is the faith practice of the individual researcher and that of the faith community to which they belong. It answers those questions in and through those practices, producing and disseminating knowledge useful to the community of practitioners of which they are a part.

Practice is the actions, strategies and processes that are characteristic of a discipline and its means of communication and production. They are preferentially chosen and guided by an appropriate mode of thinking—an intelligence—with the end goal of answering a research question. The question or problem of investigation often arises out of the experience of the individual or of the community of practitioners to which they belong. This is not exclusively the case as the methodology can be used to investigate any question. These questions are investigated and answered not from outside that practice but from within. Practice is both a part of the research strategy and the output of the research.

Research is understood as a "systematic process of asking and answering questions," where the answering of a research question is approached in an organized way with the goal of contributing to the "stock of knowledge" of all of humanity. It can then be used and drawn upon by others and can contribute in some way to the whole community (understood as discipline, academic, or broader community) or, at least, has the potential to do so.

Knowledge is understood as both empirical and tacit or praxical. Knowledge is theoretical, quantifiable, formulaic, repeatable, broadly predictive as well as embodied, non-quantifiable, unique, richly descriptive and focused. Practice-led research permits both quantitative, qualitative and hybrid approaches to research and knowledge. Practice-led research disseminates its knowledge in both a written academic form and in a praxis form as appropriate to the discipline. How practice-led research is applied using this definition is developed in the following chapters.

WHAT PRACTICE-LED RESEARCH IS NOT

This section has two aims. Firstly, to distinguish practice-led research from approaches to which it appears to bear some resemblance and, secondly, to separate it from what might be termed *conventional* art practice or *non-academic* art practice. To aid this process, a distinction between three different forms of research proposed by Christopher Frayling in 1993 will be used. Originally writing in an art and design context, Frayling described three types of research in art and design:

- Research into art and design
- Research through art and design
- Research for art and design[101]

The distinctions he makes here are easily transferrable to other areas and will be translated into a practice related frame. The first of his categories, research *into* practice, attends to historical investigation on people and movements as well as theoretical perspectives (social, economic, political among others).[102] This mode examines some aspect of a discipline, is largely of a theoretical nature, and observes practice from the outside. Frayling's second category, research *through* practice, deals with issues relating to the improvement of practice or developing practices for a particular event, task or purpose related to a particular

---

101. Frayling, "Research in Art and Design," 5.
102. Frayling, "Research in Art and Design," 5.

discipline. Examples Frayling gives include material research or developmental work. An example of the second may be "customizing a piece of technology to do something no-one had considered before and communicating the results."[103] His third category is research *for* practice. This is "research where the end product is an artefact–where the thinking is, so to speak, *embodied in the artefact*, where the goal is not primarily communicable knowledge in the sense of verbal communication, but in the sense of visual or iconic or imagistic communication."[104] This chapter (and the one following) argue that both the practice and the written component of the researcher are important. The key idea in *research for art* is not the presence and importance of the artefact as such, but rather practice as it can be more broadly understood, as a communicator of knowledge.

With these distinctions in hand, the next task is to consider methodologies that resemble practice-led research, acknowledge those similarities, while at the same time highlighting their unique features that set them apart from the others. In line with the general tenor of the book, these methodologies are all considered valuable; the purpose is solely to distinguish them from the one proposed in this project.

Practical Theology

Sometimes also called applied theology, the area of practical theology might, at first glance, be thought of as more or less synonymous with practice-led research. This is not quite the case although they certainly have commonalities. In its early form, practical theology drew on the idea from Schleiermacher that "the crown of the theological tree" was an applied discipline consisting of a set of skills and techniques to assist the leadership of the church.[105] It was a "hints and tips for ordinands"[106] approach:

> A teacher with considerable experience of ordained ministry would teach young ordinands how they should conduct

103. Frayling, "Research in Art and Design," 5.
104. Frayling, "Research in Art and Design," 5 (italics original).
105. Dingemans, "Practical Theology in the Academy," 82.
106. Gill, "Practice of Faith," 15.

funeral services, how they should preach, how they should conduct pastoral visiting, or similar related tasks. Having studied biblical and systematic theology in the academy, the applied or practical theologian was the person responsible for teaching ordinands the practicalities of ordained ministry.[107]

The discipline was characterized by a kind of *practicalized* theology taking the conclusions of theological reflection and looking at how they should be lived out and applied in faith communities. However, in more recent years, practical theology has become an academic discipline in its own right with a significantly richer understanding of its role and purpose.

Practical theology is a diverse discipline. Some see the task as a systematic process that separates practice from the reflection on it. For example, practical theology may be understood as "a theory of the epistemological foundation, ethical norms, and general strategies of religious praxis in its various contexts. As a discipline, it should not be confused with the praxis itself, although it is highly relevant to all actual religious practice . . . an empirically descriptive and critically constructive theory of religious practice."[108] The key point to note is the role practice plays in this view of the discipline. While there is a connection to the practices of the church and of believers, their praxis is an object of study. This disjunct is made clearer when practical theology is understood as the "description of and reflection on the 'self-understanding of a particular religious tradition.' This approach moves from practice to theory, then back to practice."[109] In these views, practical theology appears to fit primarily within the first of Frayling's categories in that it engages, for example, in the historical analysis and examines the varieties of practice and ritual in faith communities. As such, there is a significant difference between it and the methodology developed in this book: for practical theology, practice is the part studied rather than a part of the study as it is in practice-led research.

However, there are other ways of understanding practical theology that do bring it closer to practice-led research. Swinton and Mowat

107. Gill, "Practice of Faith," 15.
108. Browning et al., "Series Foreword," xv.
109. Dingemans, "Practical Theology in the Academy," 83.

offer the following as a definition of the discipline: "Practical Theology is critical, theological reflection on the practices of the Church as they interact with the practices of the world, with a view to ensuring and enabling faithful participation in, to and for the world."[110] Before looking at this definition more closely, it is important to examine elements of their framework. Swinton and Mowat argue from the base that all practice is "theory-laden" in the sense all practices contain "their own particular theological meanings, social and theological histories, implicit and explicit norms and moral expectations."[111] This is in agreement with arguments made particularly in hapter 2 that there are always some assumptions implicit in any analysis. This foundation seems at least partially to embed the practices of the church (and the individuals of it) in the lived experience of the faith.

In line with the earlier definition of practical theology, the view of Swinton and Mowat describes it as reflection *on* the practices of the church. However, there are three points that bring their understanding of practical theology closer to how practice-led research has been developed in this chapter. Firstly, they argue the task of the practical theologian to be "the development and maintenance of faithful and transformative practice in the world."[112] Secondly, they argue the discipline works to bring the "practice of the church into the continuing process of theological formulation, clarification and construction."[113] Thirdly, and most relevant, is their view that practical theology aims to "enable personal and communal *phronesis*, a form of practical wisdom which combines theory and practice in the praxis of individuals and communities."[114] This does not aim to gain knowledge for its own sake "but for an embodied, practical knowledge which will enable a particular form of God-oriented lifestyle."[115]

Swinton and Mowat's conception of practical theology is similar to how practice is understood in this book, as being embodied and tacit.

110. Swinton and Mowat, *Practical Theology*, 6.
111. Swinton and Mowat, *Practical Theology*, 19.
112. Swinton and Mowat, *Practical Theology*, 25.
113. Swinton and Mowat, *Practical Theology*, 26.
114. Swinton and Mowat, *Practical Theology*, 26.
115. Swinton and Mowat, *Practical Theology*, 27.

Practice-Led Theology

The goal expressed here is different to that of practice-led research, however. Swinton and Mowat are aiming toward the improvement and faithfulness of practice. This element is true to some extent of practice-led research.

Another view on the nature of practical theology is developed by Terry Veling. Containing some similarities to the views of Swinton and Mowat, Veling's view goes a step further. Veling is particularly concerned with the way theology is divided into highly specialized fields. He sees the role of practical theology as "an attempt to heal this fragmentation of theology."[116] Drawing on the work of Martin Heidegger, Veling argues that it is not possible to "separate knowing from being, thinking from acting, theological reflection from pastoral and practical involvement."[117] He also argues that practical theology is vocational work in that "our purpose for being in the world is related to the purposes of God."[118]

At one level this is in line with part of the way this book conceives the role of practice-led research: it is as a way of combining in one methodology two views or *languages* for how knowledge is expressed and investigated. Particularly in chapters 1–2, a division between a strong rationalism and a naïve experientialism were presented as one of the long-standing swings in theology. Practice-led research has been presented as one way of combining the strengths of each of these positions.

It is important to note that this section is not intended to provide a detailed investigation and analysis of practical theology. For this task, other useful texts such as the *Wiley-Blackwell Companion to Practical Theology* edited by Bonnie Miller-McLemore[119] or Elaine Graham's *Transforming Practice* would be especially helpful.[120] However, it is intended to provide sufficient background in order to distinguish between practice-led theology and practical theology. There is one central way in which I want to complete that task.

---

116. Veling, *Practical Theology*, 3.
117. Veling, *Practical Theology*, 6.
118. Veling, *Practical Theology*, 12.
119. Miller-McLemore, ed., *Wiley-Blackwell Companion to Practical Theology*.
120. Graham, *Transforming Practice*.

Defining Practice-Led Research: The Definition

While this discussion has revealed important similarities, a key difference is one of purpose. Practical theology is a discipline of the intellectual and lived life of the church that is concerned, however it is understood, with the relationship between *thinking the faith* and *being the faith*. Practice-led research is rather a broad-based methodology—not exclusive to the church—that incorporates the lived practice of a believer into the research process. As such it might be conceived as fitting within practical theology, as it may be used as a tool for its researchers. Importantly, however, it also goes beyond practical theology in that it is a methodology that may be used in a wide variety of environments and in places where practical theology as a discipline does not (and maybe cannot) have a presence, such as a secular university.

A further way of clarifying this point is to refer to chapter 2 and the framing of the goals of this book as a *public* and a *private* project. Practical theology is a *private* project as understood in chapter 2, in the sense that it is something the Christian community does for its own benefit, for the integrity of its practice and so on. This does not undermine its powerful drive to engage in and with the world, as Veling has argued.[121] As understood in chapter 2, practice-led research is a public project in the sense that it is a methodology that allows individuals to operate as researchers in the public sphere and legitimately incorporate their faith as a part of that process of engagement.

Action Research

As the definition developed in this chapter indicates, an important feature marking out practice-led research as different to other methodologies is the way in which the process of research is conducted *with and within* an individual's practice; it is not secondary nor does it only play a support role. Another methodology where practice is a central theme is *action research*. Action research refers to "ways of investigating professional experience which link practice and the analysis of practice into a single productive and continuously developing sequence, and which link researchers and research participants into a single community of interested colleagues."[122] Another understanding of action research is

---

121. Veling, *Practical Theology*, 6.
122. Winter, "Some Principles and Procedures," 14.

the following: "Action research aims at changing three things: practitioners' *practices*, their *understandings* of their practices, and the *conditions* in which they practice. These three things—practices, how we understand them, and the conditions that shape them—are inevitably and incessantly bound together with each other."[123]

These two definitions indicate that the core characteristic of action research is the investigation of practice in order to improve it—to transform it—as well as aiming to improve the impact that practice has on those who are affected by it. It investigates issues that may be ongoing concerns of a discipline, problems that might normally be investigated by the analysis, and development of theories characteristic of the discipline. When the research is conducted by a discipline's practitioners in the environment they normally operate in, it is possible to find new approaches that will lead to different types of answers.

Action research and practice-led research both share a focus on a particular practice and investigation is conducted with a close connection to a practice. However, a first and key difference in the practice of the individual or group is the *subject* of the investigation rather than the means of the investigation. This might seem a subtle difference, but it is an important one. Practice-led research uses its particular practice as a component of the research output, and, importantly, *it forms a part of the knowledge contribution made by the research*. This is not the case for action research and while it is not essential that an action research report follow a standard form, the outcomes of the research are presented in a written form.[124]

Action research fits more closely with Frayling's second category, research *through* practice. That is, research that aims to understand practice and to improve it and those that use it or are influenced by the practice. One of Frayling's own examples is a type of what he calls action research: "where a research diary tells, in a step-by-step way, of a practical experiment in the studios, and the resulting report aims to contextualize it. Both the diary and the report are there to communicate the results, which is what separates research from the gathering of

---

123. Kemmis, "Action Research," 1 (italics original).
124. Winter, "Some Principles and Procedures," 25.

Defining Practice-Led Research: The Definition

reference materials."[125] Despite this close connection to practice and the desire to improve it, the research process is still separated from practice. Practice-led research integrates it into a project as a part of the knowledge produced in the research.

Conventional or *Non-academic* Art Practice

This chapter has attempted to show practice-led research as a methodology that generates new knowledge and understandings, one that stands up to the rigour and expectations of academic scrutiny. The primary goal of the next part of this book (chapter 6) is to seek to apply the methodology in a different area, that of theological research. Yet, it is still useful to further distinguish the method by looking at the question as to what makes practice-led research different from what an artist, performer, or religious believer may do outside of an academic environment.

There is both a broad and a narrow issue here. The broad issue is to what extent practice—frequently creative practice—may be considered a form of research and knowledge. This is a broad question indeed and a complete answer is well beyond the scope of this book. The narrower issue relates to how practice may be considered research generating knowledge as understood in the academic environment. Practice-led research is a method that specifically addresses this question.

It is certainly true that practitioners can and do engage in many levels of research and it is not the intention of this section to deny the skills and intellect needed to undertake the creative process and the production of a final work. Practice-led research, however, combines the practice of the artist with a systematic research strategy, the requirements for conceptual rigour characteristic of the academic environment, and the obligation of a researcher to disseminate the results of the process. It might be thought of as different to, but a specialized subcategory of what is carried out by practitioners in various disciplines.

The important point is that not all creative practice is research in an academic sense. Green expresses the key issue here:

---

125. Frayling, "Research in Art and Design," 5.

> Instead, we need some way to differentiate the researcher who explores research questions through practice-led methodologies and creates new knowledge that might take artistic form and the artist who creates a new work without a conscious engagement with research. If no such distinction is made then every published novelist might claim a Masters in Creative Writing, and every exhibited painter a Doctorate.[126]

Green is saying that unless there are certain academic requirements made of the practice-led researcher, anyone can be awarded a postgraduate qualification for any creative output, although there may be a need for it to be of a certain standard of practice. This practice would make the research process and the associated degree meaningless. It is necessary, therefore, to disagree with Haseman when he argues that a characteristic of practice-led researchers "lies in their insistence that research outputs and claims to knowing must be made through the symbolic language and forms of their practice. They have little interest in trying to translate the findings and understandings of practice into the numbers (quantitative) and words (qualitative) preferred by traditional research paradigms;"[127] and that "the material outcomes of practice [are] all-important representations of research findings in their own right."[128]

In its strong form, this means that the performance or creative work is all that is required for research output. There are a number of issues with this discussed in this and the following two chapters that relate to dissemination of research and questions of rigour and contribution to a discipline. The view of this project is that describing the methodology as qualitative is the preferred option. This decision is based on a broad understanding of the meaning of qualitative but in addition, important reasons for this choice flow out of implications of the alternative.

There is general agreement that practice-led research does not fall under the umbrella of a *quantitative* paradigm; however, there is no clear agreement that it should then be placed under a *qualitative*

---

126. Green, "Recognising Practice-Led Research," 2.
127. Haseman, "Manifesto," 100.
128. Haseman, "Manifesto," 103.

paradigm. Haseman has argued for the emergence of a "third methodological distinction," one that is "aligned with many of the values of qualitative research but is nonetheless distinct from it."[129] It is a view he calls *performative*.[130]

However, in order to make room for his third space, Haseman relies on a very narrow (and quite abbreviated) understanding of qualitative research, as well as a bifurcated view of the motivation of researchers. The first concern will be addressed here, but the second reserved for the next chapter.

Quoting another writer, Haseman states that "qualitative research has a primary aim of 'understanding the meaning of human action,'"[131] it deals primarily with *texts* which Haseman restricts further to "non-numeric data in the form of words" and appears to mean the written word (as distinct from the spoken word or the sung word).[132] The narrow way in which he has defined qualitative research means that his performative paradigm (into which would fit a version of practice-led research) cannot be qualitative, and manifestly so. This concern can be easily addressed with a fuller definition of what qualitative research is (presented in the next section).

While the centrality of practice to the research process is affirmed by Haseman, the first significant problem with this approach is the issue of accessibility of the research to the wider research community. To build on the research it is legitimate to ask what was the research investigating or attempting to answer. What did the researcher conclude? What was the process or what theoretical framework was the research grounded in? As discussed in chapter 2, all research has some philosophical and theoretical underpinnings.

The second concern, and one that further distinguishes practice-led research from conventional art practice, is expressed by what Biggs and Büchler call the *Isolationist Position*.[133] They identify it in a dis-

129. Haseman, "Manifesto," 102.
130. Haseman, "Manifesto," 102.
131. Haseman, "Manifesto," 99.
132. Haseman, "Manifesto," 99.
133. Biggs and Büchler, "Eight Criteria," 6.

cussion of the broader discipline, the creative and cultural industries (CCI):

> To claim that CCI is an independent subject in which we can define for ourselves what research means, and we will do so without reference to anything else, is equally unhelpful and results in poor scholarship . . . Academics exist in a comparative competitive environment and must therefore find and place themselves in relation to their peers. They are members of the academic community as a whole and not just a community of kindred colleagues from similar creative disciplines.[134]

Therefore, when a creative practitioner or a faith practitioner enters the academy for research, they bring with them their practice but add to it certain approaches to research that are broadly common to all and including methodologies, definitions, processes of dissemination and rigour.

However, Haseman is correct in saying that ". . . people who wish to evaluate the research outcomes also need to experience them in direct (co-presence) or indirect (asynchronous, recorded) form."[135] The practice is central, but the obligation to record and disseminate that research is also vital. The next chapter addresses the mechanics of this distinction.

CONCLUSION

This chapter has attempted a number of tasks centred on forming a definition of practice-led research. The definition sought was one that was comprehensive yet flexible to allow the application of the method in areas outside the creative disciplines.

For this purpose, the nature of research was considered in an academic setting, how knowledge could be understood as a multifaceted concept but particularly from an embodied position, how the notion of multiple intelligences could be used to enhance the conceptualization of knowledge for practice-led research, and finally how understandings

---

134. Biggs and Büchler, "Eight Criteria," 6.
135. Haseman, "Manifesto," 101.

Defining Practice-Led Research: The Definition

of praxis could be used to provide a sound theoretical understanding of the nature of practice.

After examining these concepts, a definition incorporating the conclusions of each of those discussions was presented. The definition remains faithful to the underlying principles of practice-led research but frees it from any necessary connections to the creative areas from which it came.

This completes the theoretical phase of the project. The next chapter will discuss the structure of a practice-led research project and consider its application to Christian theological research projects. After that discussion is completed, some important technical issues will also be considered relating to practice-led projects.

Chapter 6

Application

Principles

INTRODUCTION

Up to this point, practice-led research has been approached rather like a newly discovered, but yet unexplored, continent. The first two chapters represent the exploratory brief, outlining the starting point of the explorer. Several of the issues dealt with there are sometimes ignored or only considered in a cursory way. However, they are important for a cross-disciplinary study such as this since certain assumptions of one or another area—such as those of an epistemological and ontological nature—cannot be taken for granted. Chapter 3 began with a consideration of what the relationship was between the peoples of the two existing well explored lands of creative arts and theology and found that this relationship was not always amicable, and often not a relationship at all. That chapter provided some additional rationale for looking at ways to deepen and strengthen the relationship between theory and practice. Chapter 4 began to map out the terrain beginning with the general borders and framework of the concept. The chapter also described key features that need to be taken into consideration in developing a full understanding of the area. Chapter 5 followed this work by expanding the concepts, detailing important areas and developing a clear definition. Now that these tasks have been completed, it is possible to consider how practice-led research looks in application, how the theory can be put into practice but also how it has been applied and used by universities to date and how it might be employed practically in theological contexts.

Firstly, the typical structure of a practice-led research project will be considered. This usually consists of two components: a creative component and a written component. The examination will be done mainly by considering a number of guidelines for practice-led researchers issued by a selection of Australian universities. These will demonstrate the general procedures and expectations of practice-led research by universities.

Secondly, the written component of a practice-led project will be considered in detail. This is most frequently called *exegesis*. The way exegesis is understood in theology and in practice-led research will be compared. A number of models for the exegesis will be considered and how they relate to the creative component. The models will be critiqued, and a preferred model will be presented. This model will be based on the discussions on structure in this chapter and be grounded in the conclusions of previous chapters. The aim will be to present a model that draws on the strengths of practice and has a rigorous understanding of the nature and goals of research.

Thirdly, the creative component will be surveyed. Options for the presentation of a creative component will be considered and the nature and role of the written component will be examined. General principles for the presentation and preservation of the creative element will be sketched.

Various suggestions will be made in the chapter on how practice-led research may look in a theological context. However, the goal of this task will not be to give a definitive list of situations where a faith-based practice-led research project might be conducted but rather to illustrate contexts that might benefit from its application.

FORMAT OF A PRACTICE-LED THESIS: GENERAL PRINCIPLES

It is in the examinable material produced in a practice-led research degree where the blend of two complementary ways of knowing can be seen clearly. The typical format consists of a creative component and a written component. The creative component is the product of whatever is the practice of the individual researcher. For a visual artist, it may be an exhibition or series of exhibitions containing a group of works produced in the project. For a choreographer/dancer, it may be a performance piece as would also be the case for a musician and a composer. A creative writer may present a short novel, a set of short stories or a collection of poetry. A discussion of the presentation of the creative piece will be outlined later in this section.

THE EXEGESIS

The written component is frequently termed an *exegesis*, and although the term differs from the way it is understood in theology, it will be argued that elements of significant commonality can be found. While the exegesis is usually shorter in length when compared to the traditional thesis format, actual word counts vary from institution to institution (see later in this section). As was the case with defining practice-led research itself, understandings of the nature and function of the *exegesis* vary considerably.

The first part of this section will consider how universities understand the exegesis through their regulations and guidelines. Secondly, an overview of how the exegesis has been implemented in completed projects. Thirdly, a definition of what exegesis is and means will be worked out and some guidelines on structure will be suggested.

Regulatory Structure

Regulations provided by institutions are very general in nature. They generally present the practice-led research degree in the standard format and provide broad guidelines on size and presentation of the exegesis. They do not proscribe how the exegesis will look or what it will contain, as is the case for the traditional format. For example, at Curtin University in Western Australia, Rule Number 10 which applies to research doctorates states:

Application: Principles

The thesis shall be based on research conducted during the period of enrolment and shall be presented in one of the following forms:

(i) a typescript, or

(ii) a creative or literary work or series of works in any approved medium accompanied by an exegesis, or

(iii) a published book or series of published papers presented in accordance with Section 11(e).[1]

The Rule goes on to state that a thesis in the form of a typescript must not be longer than 100,000 words excluding features such as appendices. An exegesis must not exceed 40,000 words excluding appendices, tables, and so on.[2] More detail is provided on the role and function of the exegesis by Curtin University in their *Guidelines for Creative Production Theses*. These will be examined in a later section.

The University of Canberra provides more detail on the role and function of the exegesis in "Higher Degrees by Research: Thesis Submission and Examination Guidelines" as follows:

The following principles apply with regard to the PhD thesis incorporating creative production:

(a) the creative component must be prepared during the period of candidature;

(b) where a creative thesis is produced, the candidate will also provide an exegetical component of at least 30,000 words that operates in a symbiotic relationship with the creative work;

(c) the exegesis and creative work may be integrated; and

(d) the academic rigor of the exegesis is critical to determining whether the thesis meets the requirements of the research degree.[3]

1. "Rule No. 10," 13.
2. "Rule No. 10," 13.
3. "Higher Degrees by Research," 1–2. These guidelines were particularly easy to locate. For many of the other institutions, a considerable amount of digging was needed to locate the appropriate regulations.

An interesting note on these two guidelines is that the first restricts the upper limit of the exegesis, while the second requires a minimum. This is already in contrast to conventional theses; for example, a PhD thesis is usually within a narrow band of between 80,000 to 100,000 words.

A third example comes from the Queensland University of Technology. Section 8.11 of their "Doctor of Philosophy Regulations" states:

> A PhD may be awarded on the basis of the submission by Creative Works which has been indicated in the Stage 2 submission. In the case of a thesis submitted in the area of artistic practice, presentation may be in one of two forms: a theoretical thesis or artwork and exegesis. Guidelines have been approved by the Research Degrees Committee which governs the format and presentation requirements of the PhD by Creative Works.[4]

The guidelines this paragraph points to are "Thesis by Creative Works Guidelines":

> Key points regarding the exegesis are:
>
> - The examiners will attend the exhibition/performance, at which time they will be given a copy of the exegesis in temporary binding. A final copy of the exegesis will be provided to the examiners within three months of their viewing the artwork.
> - The exegesis is required to describe the research process and elaborate, elucidate and place in context the artistic practice undertaken.
> - The exegesis can be up to 50,000 words.[5]

University regulations, then, recognize the validity of practice-led research and award degrees on the basis of research done in this mode. However, in general, they do not provide specific guidelines on what the exegesis should contain or lay out. They do go into some detail on general formatting issues (page size, margins, line spacing, binding,

---

4. "Doctor of Philosophy Regulations," 12.
5. "Thesis by Creative Works Guildelines," 1.

Application: Principles

number of copies for example) but not into content. This is in line with the *text only* thesis as there are many different patterns and expectations across the many disciplines on a university campus. Individual schools do provide some additional advice to students which will be considered in later sections.

The definitions of what the term means in relation to practice-led research degrees provided only a general *administrative* understanding of the nature of an exegesis. The next step is to consider how the exegesis has been implemented by HDR candidates in universities.

OVERVIEW OF COMPLETED EXEGESES

There have been a number of studies conducted examining the nature of the exegesis as it is used and applied by students in higher degrees. This section will draw on two of these, one by Barbara Milech and Ann Schilo published in 2004[6] and another by Jillian Hamilton and Luke Jaaniste from 2010.[7]

Milech and Schilo suggest that the exegesis broadly falls into two types, a *context* model and a *commentary* model.[8] Hamilton and Jaaniste suggest a third type, the *connective model* which is a hybrid that attempts to combine the two other models.[9]. Milech and Schilo also propose a model of their own, one that will be adopted for this project. The model will be discussed later in this chapter.

Context Model

In this model, the thrust of the exegesis is to provide the general context of the creative component and the circumstances that gave rise to it: "In this format the student submits a written document that rehearses the historical, social and/or disciplinary context(s) within which the student developed the creative or production component of her or his thesis."[10] The context model uses the exegesis as a type of position

---

6. Milech and Schilo, "'Exit Jesus.'"
7. Hamilton and Jaaniste, "Connective Model," 31–44.
8. Milech and Schilo, "'Exit Jesus.'"
9. Hamilton and Jaaniste, "Connective Model," 39.
10. Milech and Schilo, "'Exit Jesus.'"

statement, locating the student and their work in the broader realm of the discipline and looking for links between the work of the student and the debates in the field. The exegesis in this model "encourages research students to think about connections between practice and institutional, social or disciplinary contexts."[11]

In a paper from 2012, Josie Arnold describes her understanding of the role and function of exegesis in the following way: "The exegesis model enables the weaving throughout of relevant debates and references. It may well be advisable for examination purposes, however, also to have a section that establishes how this work sits within the academic debate and contributes new aspects to it."[12] This comment suggests the exegesis to be little more than a record of the contemporary discussions of a discipline. Milech and Shilo believe that this is "probably the dominant model across Australian universities."[13]

Commentary Model

This model views the exegesis as an "explication of, or comment on, the creative production" and comes in "strong" and "weak" versions.[14] The weak version is represented by a university guideline that describes the exegesis for a Master's program as "a brief explanatory annotation may be submitted as a support to the creative work submission."[15] While the strong version is a "research report" resembling a conventional research document except that it is to "describe the research process, and elaborate, elucidate and contextualize the work."[16]

In another review, Brian Paltridge describes the exegesis in creative projects as "descriptive, evaluative and reflective."[17] Many exegeses, at least in part, "documented the creation of the student's visual project" and included a section on methodology of the project.[18] The

---

11. Milech and Schilo, "'Exit Jesus.'"
12. Arnold, "Practice Led Research," 16.
13. Milech and Schilo, "'Exit Jesus.'"
14. Milech and Schilo, "'Exit Jesus.'"
15. Fletcher and Mann, "Illuminating the Exegesis."
16. Fletcher and Mann, "Illuminating the Exegesis."
17. Paltridge, "Exegesis as a Genre," 91.
18. Paltridge, "Exegesis as a Genre," 92.

Application: Principles

commentary model allows for a clear link between the creative component and the exegesis, and, Milech and Schilo suggest, is closer to the meaning of the word "exegesis"[19] (this question of the meaning of exegesis will be taken up in a later section of this chapter).

Hybrid Model

The contextual model and the commentary model appear to be the two main models in use in Australian universities. They are not always clearly delineated, however, and blended versions are not uncommon. Hamilton and Jaaniste have observed and support a "connective model," one that aims to combine the strengths of the commentary and contextual models.[20] They describe their model in the following way:

> The contents and approaches of the context model are adapted within the "situating concepts" and "precedents of practice" sections for the purposes of reviewing the existing field (established ideas and practices), and the contents and approaches of the commentary model are adapted for the "researcher's creative practice" section (the researcher's own ideas, processes and creative works).[21]

The model essentially attempts to incorporate what are seen as the strengths of the commentary and context models by attempting to situate and describe the project. They argue that the connective model calls for a "dual orientation" on the part of the researcher.[22] The researcher looks outward to the context of their field, what comes before their work, as well as looking inward to the "internally situated intimate relationship with the practice."[23]

The content analysis study Hamilton and Jaaniste conducted at their own institution reflected this form. They found theses followed a general form:

> Introduction

---

19. Milech and Schilo, "'Exit Jesus.'"
20. Hamilton and Jaaniste, "Connective Model."
21. Hamilton and Jaaniste, "Connective Model," 39.
22. Hamilton and Jaaniste, "Connective Model," 39.
23. Hamilton and Jaaniste, "Connective Model," 39.

First main section: Situating Concepts
Second main section: Precedents of Practice
Third main section: Researcher's Creative Practice
Conclusion

The "situating concepts" section "frames the research through an explanation of the key concepts that situate the research and practice."[24] Here are found definitions of key terms, important issues in the field, as well as a theoretical framework for understanding the practice.[25] The "precedents of practice" section situates the project in relation to the work of others and the broader discipline, and how key examples relate to the practice of the researcher.[26] Finally the "researcher's creative practice" section describes the creative process, methods, and may include discussions of exhibition or performance as well linking back to earlier discussions considering how the practice relates to the wider field.[27]

Although they argue that these sections combine to "illustrate how the creative practice extends and makes a contribution to the field" it is not clear how this or the other approaches constitute *research* as understood in the university context (see previous chapter) or make a *knowledge* contribution to the field. The following section will present a broader critique of these models.

CRITIQUE OF THE MODELS

A significant weakness of the context model is that in its focus on the place of the work in relation to the past and present state of the discipline, it has a tendency to ignore the creative component.[28] The artefact is taken as a given and examined from the outside, and a (new) niche is found for it. The commentary model, on the other hand, is "internally oriented and introspective" and "it might create the impression that the practice is of peculiar interest to, and therefore of value only to, the

---

24. Hamilton and Jaaniste, "Connective Model," 34.
25. Hamilton and Jaaniste, "Connective Model," 34.
26. Hamilton and Jaaniste, "Connective Model," 35.
27. Hamilton and Jaaniste, "Connective Model," 35.
28. Hamilton and Jaaniste, "Connective Model," 37.

Application: Principles

researcher."[29] In the context model the writer "rehearses the historical, social and/or disciplinary context(s) within which the student developed the creative or production component of her or his thesis."[30]

There are potential issues with this model for practice-led research within theology. Exegesis maybe little more than a way to compare and contrast the researcher's creative piece with its historical precedents. Although it may prove to be an interesting exercise as religious art is rich and diverse, the contribution of such a task to research and the stock of knowledge would be limited.

There is also scope in this model for the inclusion of Christian theorists on the motivations for the production of particular art works and theoretical frameworks. However, this may become an extended literature review on current debates on the topic of interest in a theological context and the actual theological research could be left undeveloped and limited. It also has little to do with the practice that is central to the process.

In the commentary model where the exegesis is reporting on the creation of the creative work, it is secondary to the creative work as it only comments on and describes the process of creation and the ideas and theories that may have been used in the development of the concepts. Practice is granted a central role only in as much as it is the focus of a discussion. The exegesis plays a descriptive, supportive function.

For example, despite the claim that the exegesis and the creative component "must 'speak to' one another and form a whole together" the exegesis for one writer appears to fit into a hybrid of the commentary/context model, holding an inferior secondary role.[31] The exegesis is described as a "privileged space for the candidate/practitioner to work in," and acts to show "wonder, creativity and surprise as it reviews and revalues the work undertaken in the artefact and in entering the academic debates that are relevant."[32] Headings for the exegesis come from issues that arise in practice as recorded in the journal.[33] Finally,

---

29. Hamilton and Jaaniste, "Connective Model," 38.
30. Milech and Schilo, "'Exit Jesus.'"
31. Arnold, "Practice Led Research," 11.
32. Arnold, "Practice Led Research," 13.
33. Arnold, "Practice Led Research," 14.

this is made clearer still when the writer states: "The exegesis model enables the weaving throughout of relevant debates and references. It may well be advisable for examination purposes, however, also to have a section that establishes how this work sits within the academic debate and contributes new aspects to it."[34] This would appear to be a reluctant concession, perhaps, to the academic process.

The tendency in this approach is for the exegesis to become a personal account of the research process and how it impacts the individual. For example, one author emphasizes autobiography as a starting point for practice-led research and states that its "methods enable us to explore the variances of artistic decision-making and the diversity of creative experiences" and allows for "a personal investigation of the self: self-research, self-portrait; self-narrative."[35] Further, it permits artists "to attend to issues which give meaning to our thoughts and actions as artists . . . by ordering and presenting personal experience as a way of understanding aspects of reality."[36]

In line with the argument in earlier chapters of this book, Linda Candy and Ernest Edmonds observe that research ends in new knowledge or new understandings.[37] These results must be in a form that can be shared, and this must be considered new "in the world rather than to the researcher."[38] It is certainly true that research results that are new to the world will also be new to the researcher. However, the point to be emphasized is the research "must contain knowledge that is new, in the world, that can be shared with others and that can be challenged, tested, or evaluated in some way."[39]

There are significant potential weaknesses with this model when applied to theological research. Since there is a tendency in this model to focus on the creative process of the individual artist/researcher, an exegesis in theological practice-led research may become only an account of the individual's faith walk as they worked on the creative piece,

34. Arnold, "Practice Led Research," 16.
35. Stewart, "Practice vs Praxis."
36. Stewart, "Practice vs Praxis."
37. Candy and Edmonds, "Role of the Artefact," 124.
38. Candy and Edmonds, "Role of the Artefact," 124.
39. Candy and Edmonds, "Role of the Artefact," 124.

or an account of the charismatic experience of worship, or prayer, or other creative process. It is certainly the case that aspects of the individual faith experience are central to the practice-led idea (expanded on later in this chapter). However, as it is for the exegesis in practice-led research normally, in theological applications, if the exegesis is *only* an account of this experience, then the research contribution of a project will be significantly weakened or absent entirely. McNamara summarizes the concern when he notes, "The primary criterion is not that the researcher makes sense of his or her own experience. The research project may do this, but this does not justify it as research. In particular, a PhD research project needs to justify its research contribution in terms that extend past the researcher's subjective experience."[40]

These issues are not solved by the connective model proposed by Hamilton and Jaaniste:

> [T]he context model orientates the researcher to look out at what precedes, contextualizes or frames the practice, while the commentary model orientates the researcher to look inwards and to assume the perspective of an internally situated intimate relationship with the practice. In the connective exegesis, the researcher adopts a dual orientation—looking both outwards and inwards.[41]

However, as it only attempts to combine the two orientations of the other two models, practice still seems to have little to do with the research of the project.

SUMMARY

Broadly, each model "preserves the theory-practice divide."[42] In the commentary model, the exegesis is about the researcher and the creation of the artefact and in the context model it is about the artefact and its place in the wider situation. The practice of the researcher is not well integrated into the research; they are, to a degree, silent to each other—that is, they are not actively communicating with each

---

40. McNamara, "Six Rules," 6.
41. Hamilton and Jaaniste, "Connective Model," 39.
42. Milech and Schilo, "'Exit Jesus.'"

other. It is certainly true that practice-led research by its very nature requires the presence of the researcher in a visible way as their practice is integral to the process. However, the main issue with both models and the hybrid version is the almost exclusive focus on the researcher. The context model asks *Where am I?* in relation to the field, while the commentary model asks *Who am I?* as a practitioner.

THE EXEGESIS: EXPANDED AND DEFINED

The aim of this section is to reconsider the aim and purpose of *the exegesis*. It will first consider what the term can mean, the purpose of the exegesis (and whether it is actually needed at all) and then consider making suggestions on a structure. Generally, it will be argued that the format of a creative component and a written exegesis is a useful and helpful structure but is not to be taken as prescriptive. It will be the characteristics of the exegesis that will be important rather than a format, per se.

What Is *Exegesis*?

A closer examination of the term will be helpful for developing an understanding of this project. While many writers in the field gloss over or do not at all address the use, meaning, or origins of the term exegesis, it certainly did not originate with practice-led research and so it is necessary to look elsewhere.

At the outset, it will be worth noting the presence of two related terms: *hermeneutics* and *exegesis*. The term hermeneutics did not appear until the seventeenth century. However, methods for interpretation date back far longer, at least as far as when Stoic philosophers first systematized methods for understanding the mythic tradition of the time.[43] The term will be understood here within the framework established in chapter 2. While recognizing that there might be divisions of hermeneutics—theological hermeneutics and philosophical hermeneutics for example[44]—the term will be taken to be the overarching

---

43. Grondin, *Introduction*, 1, 24.
44. Grondin, *Introduction*, 1.

Application: Principles

disciplinary term of which exegesis is a part.[45] The terms do not seem to be confused in any way in the practice-led research where hermeneutics is understood as philosophical hermeneutics. However, this distinction is worth making given the nature of this project of applying the methodology to theology where the two terms can sometimes be indistinct.[46] Millard Erickson, for example, talks of hermeneutics being understood in at least three senses: "Perhaps the most common refers to the actual techniques of biblical interpretation. A second sense has to do with the application of these techniques with the results of that endeavour or the interpretation of the passage. A third sense refers to the whole conception of the nature of the interpretational task."[47] The focus of this section is on the second of these terms, *exegesis*, and will mainly be drawn from writing in theology and biblical studies. Later it will be then necessary to return to the idea of hermeneutics. It will be helpful to begin with some definitions of exegesis. "*Exegesis*," states Grant Osborne, "means to 'draw out of' a text what it means, in contrast to *eisegesis*, to 'read into' a text what one wants it to mean."[48] There are, according to Osborne, a number of components in the process of interpretation which include historical and biblical context, grammar, semantics, syntax and the historical and cultural background.[49]

Gordon Fee defines exegesis in the following way:

> The term "exegesis" is used . . . in a consciously limited sense to refer to the historical investigation into the meaning of the Biblical text. Exegesis, therefore, answers the question, What *did* the Biblical author *mean*? It has to do with *what* he said (the content itself) and *why* he said it at any given point (the literary context). Furthermore, exegesis is primarily

---

45. Osborne, *Hermeneutical Spiral*, 21.

46. See, for example, Osborne, *Hermeneutical Spiral*, 21, who highlights these differences in making his own use clear.

47. Erickson, *Evangelical Interpretation*, 9.

48. Osborne, *Hermeneutical Spiral*, 57 (italics original).

49. Osborne, *Hermeneutical Spiral*, 57 (italics original). These points are discussed in various chapters of the book. These steps can be seen outlined in the contents pages.

concerned with intentionality: What did the author *intend* his original readers to understand?[50]

Writing only for New Testament exegesis, Fee provides fifteen steps needed to properly analyze any New Testament passage. All the steps have multiple components, and several have sub-categories according to whether the passage is from the Gospels, Acts, and other genres present in the New Testament.

Another understanding comes from the *Dictionary for the Theological Interpretation of the Bible*. After some brief historical notes, Snodgrass argues that "'Exegesis' then means 'explanation,' nearly always intended as explanation after careful consideration and usually with regard to Scripture or founding documents. It is the process we go through in explaining any communication, whether written or oral."[51] Further, Snodgrass says, "Valid exegesis will always involve an attempt to understand the historical and cultural context in which the communication arose, and by necessity it leans more toward an author-oriented hermeneutic. Exegesis is rightly assumed to be a *foundational* task for doing theology."[52]

There are several points common to these views. Firstly, it involves *meaning*, and revealing or obtaining the meaning that is in the text (in this case). Secondly, exegesis, at least in the sense used in theology, seems to be connected to intent—what it is the author was attempting to convey in the passage. A goal is to recover, as best is possible, the message and intent of the author. Thirdly, context is important in the following sense: a particular text was written at a particular time, in a particular historical context, within a particular culture. All these factors will have some impact on the text as it stands. Fourthly, the process is somewhat involved, requiring the engagement with background texts, social, cultural and political studies, languages, historical data, and so on.

---

50. Fee, *New Testament Exegesis*, 21 (italics original).
51. Snodgrass, "Exegesis," 203.
52. Snodgrass, "Exegesis," 203(italics original).

Application: Principles

PURPOSE OF THE EXEGESIS

With this background information in place, it is now possible to consider what the purpose and goals of the exegesis might be. However, first it is necessary to ask the question—so far largely assumed—is an exegesis in any form needed? The following discussion is a reframing of views outlined at the end of the previous chapter, but it is worth reviewing the points as some of these scholars are frequently cited in the literature, and importantly, recommended to higher degree candidates.

There are a number of scholars that entirely reject the need for a written component in practice-led research. For example, to reiterate what Brad Haseman has claimed, practice-led researchers "have little interest in trying to translate the findings and understandings of practice into the numbers (quantitative) and words (qualitative) preferred by traditional research paradigms."[53] Graeme Sullivan only mentions the thesis or exegesis in passing as a possible option for the visual arts researcher.[54]

There is a certain irony in these claims and similar ones from other authors: the production of detailed written arguments to refute the need for a detailed written argument. However, what is being discussed here is a particular form of research grounded in practice, not just practice and creativity and performance. As highlighted at the end of the previous chapter on what practice-led research is not,[55] it is practice with an intentional research goal. A more generous reading, then, of those that reject the need of an exegesis (or anything like it) is that not all creative practice projects require an exegesis. Lelia Green sums up this point well:

> [W]e need some way to differentiate the researcher who explores research questions through practice-led methodologies and creates new knowledge that might take artistic form and the artist who creates a new work without a conscious engagement with research. If no such distinction is made then every

---

53. Haseman, "Manifesto," 101.
54. Sullivan, *Art Practice as Research*, 221.
55. See chapter 4.

published novelist might claim a Masters in Creative Writing, and every exhibited painter a Doctorate.[56]

Another perspective is expressed by Biggs and Büchler:

> We believe that rather than being a distinct category of research that should be guided by special concepts, PbR is a subcategory of academic research that can and should attend to and observe conventional research criteria.[57]

One reason for this requirement is a question about the validity of curators or art critics being a part of the peer review process. The motivations of the commercial world may be quite different to those of the academy, but there certainly are "distinct models of patronage and finance that underpin success and reputation development."[58] This issue was discussed in some detail throughout chapter 3.

It is the (obvious) view of this book that some form of exegesis is needed in order to *draw out* the meaning of a project in terms of its contribution to the human *stock of knowledge* and for reasons of rigour and dissemination discussed elsewhere in this book. However, what form should this document take? In order to answer this question, it is necessary to first outline a proposed model for structuring practice-led research projects.

RESEARCH QUESTION MODEL

The review of the common models of the exegesis earlier in this chapter argued that the practice element in a project is either over-emphasized or, alternatively, marginalized in the research process. It was also argued that while a hybrid model may address this imbalance, it does not solve the issue of demonstrating a project as *research*.

The aim of this section is to use the *research-question model* suggested by Milech and Schilo as a framework for developing a model of the exegesis suitable for this project. They state the foundational aim of their proposal is that "[b]oth the written and the creative component

---

56. Green, "Recognising Practice-Led Research," 2.

57. Biggs and Büchler, "Rigor and Practice-Based Research," 64 ("PbR" refers to practice-based research).

58. Mottram and Rust, "Pedestal and the Pendulum," 136.

of the thesis are conceptualized as independent answers to the same research question—independent because each component of the thesis is conducted through the 'language' of a particular discourse, related because each 'answers' a single research question."[59]

It will be the contention of this section to argue firstly that the two components are separate in the sense that they do attempt to answer a single question in and through two different languages but secondly, that they are not entirely independent of each other, but must interact. It is important at the outset to address a concern sometimes expressed by writers in the field.

Is a Research Question Needed?

Practice-researchers sometimes voice worries for anything that might impact serendipitous moments in their creative practice; that they need to be free to follow leads. Drawing from Carole Gray's definition, Haseman argues that the problem or problems of research "emerge over time according to the needs of the practice and practitioner's evolving purposes."[60] Evans and Le Grice take a similar but more moderate position when they argue that for practice-led research projects, "The project process is largely iterative based on partial definition of the issues, followed by practical exploration or experiment, followed by a refinement of the issues or problems. In the arts, definition of the problems is an integral part of the exploratory process."[61]

Firstly, there seems to be no unique reason why it is only the practice within a research program that is relevant to the development of a research question. Practitioners entering a higher degree program will usually have a history of practice and can draw on this history for the initial stages of developing the project.

Secondly, these writers and others with similar views seem to be confusing the idea of research with the methodologies that are used for it. Practice-led research may indeed have some of these characteristics, but it does not follow that this is unique to practice. Research is, by its very nature, about discovery and it tends to be an iterative process. This

---

59. Milech and Schilo, "'Exit Jesus.'"
60. Haseman and Mafe, "Acquiring Know-How," 214.
61. Evans and Le Grice, "State of the Art," 4.

means that research questions are frequently refined as the research progresses.

Therefore, a research question does not proscribe the answer to that question. Therefore the model presents no impediment to creative freedom or those moments of inspiration. This model provides instead the stability for the research to allow that freedom and by providing a firm foundation for the work to flourish. To reiterate discussions of earlier chapters, practice-led research is about academically valid and rigorous research or which practice is a key component in the research process.

A secondary—and possibly temporary—advantage of this initial understanding is that it demonstrates continuity with *traditional* research models, those familiar to disciplines other than creative arts, specifically for this book, theology.

The Research Question

In this model, the process is guided by a clearly defined research question. However, in this context, *clearly defined* does not mean proscriptive. A research question is understood here as one David Silverman calls "workable."[62] Adapting the work of Keith Punch, Silverman states that a workable research question gives a project clarity and focus. Punch suggests a research question:

- organizes the project and gives it direction and coherence;
- delimits the project, showing its boundaries;
- keeps the researcher focused;
- provides a framework when you write up your research;
- points to the methods and data that will be needed.[63]

In these points significant help to practice-led researchers can be found. For example, if there is a lack of experience in writing up research, then the framework a question provides would be beneficial. Some clues to areas of exploration and development of practice may be

---

62. Silverman, *Doing Qualitative Research*, 83.
63. Silverman, *Doing Qualitative Research*, 84.

Application: Principles

gained from the direction a question will provide. What is clear from these points is that none of them are constraining on what the research will find or on the freedom to follow leads in the research.

While Punch's (and Silverman's) audience is mainly beginning student researchers, though not specifically to any particular discipline, Estelle Barrett gives some suggestions specifically aimed at practice-led researchers. Barrett refers to the initial part of a project as "staging the research" and goes on to contribute to the introduction. It answers these questions:

- What is the subject or topic to be investigated?
- What are the specific areas of interest and what ideas and positions have other studio practitioners taken in relation to theses?
- How does the project relate to previous practice and theory in the field?
- What is the research question or hypothesis?
- What is the research objective or aim—what will be achieved at the end of the process?
- What is the thesis or main argument?
- How will this be developed in the research paper?[64]

As with Punch's guidelines, none of these are proscriptive to the outcomes of the research and Barrett is herself aware that designing practice as a research project at the outset can be "daunting, since the outcomes of creative practice cannot be pre-determined."[65]

The use of a research question, then, assists practice-led projects to find direction and structure. As raised in earlier chapters, many practice-led research projects lack clarity, direction, and any clear idea of what the project is contributing to the "stock of knowledge."[66] It also assists in meeting the expectations of research that all disciplines must meet as argued in the previous chapter, such as the contribution to knowledge, dissemination and review.

---

64. Barrett and Bolt, *Practice as Research*, 186.
65. Barrett and Bolt, *Practice as Research*, 186.
66. OECD, *Frascati Manual 2012*, 30.

Punch and Silverman are addressing researchers whose project generally fits into the 'traditional' mode, that is, a written thesis. Barrett's main focus appears to be in the write up of a project that would consist of an exegesis/creative component combination.

However, the model being proposed in this section argues that *the research question applies to both the exegesis and the practice component.*

In their original proposal, Milech and Schilo stated the relationship between the two elements in the following way: "Both the written and the creative component of the thesis are conceptualized as *independent answers to the same research question*—independent because each component of the thesis is conducted through the 'language' of a particular discourse, related because each 'answers' a single research question."[67] Each aspect of the project—the written and the practice—directly addresses the research question and attempts to answer it through its own methods. Guidelines produced by Curtin University in Western Australia for students doing practice-led style projects express it similarly "The two components of the thesis form two complementary outcomes of a singular research program. Both components must address the same central research question through articulating, in differing modes or languages, ideas or meanings which *address* that question."[68]

Some of the strengths of this approach have already been mentioned, such as providing direction and coherence to a project, as well as situating practice-led projects within the wider research culture of the academy. In terms of the practice itself, this model also serves to respect that practice by allowing it to speak on its own terms and in its own language. Milech and Schilo note that "this model resists the theory/practice, artist/scholar, studio/library divide" and "respects the authority, autonomy, languages and conventions of the disciplines that produce creative works and production pieces."[69]

Speaking specifically about the visual arts, the research of Rebekka Kill, for example, argues that the idea that creativity and formal writing do not mix is a misconception: "That is, that art students are not very

---

67. Milech and Schilo, "'Exit Jesus.'"
68. "Guidelines for Thesis Preparation and Submission," 5 (emphasis mine).
69. Milech and Schilo, "'Exit Jesus.'"

good at writing, that they don't want to write, and furthermore, that writing gets in the way of the real business of making art."[70] One of the reasons for this is historical. Maziar Raein argues that the "methods of teaching art and design history have been adapted unquestioningly from traditional academia, and in essence these teaching methods were and are at odds with traditional studio teaching activities."[71] This is not surprising considering the long-standing divide between the practitioners and the theorist identified in chapter 3. However, as with the practical/theoretical divide, the making/writing divide is artificial. Kill's own work argues that when students are encouraged to explore forms of writing, "resistance to writing appeared to have been dramatically reduced."[72]

One of the individuals interviewed for this project, an established visual artist, completed a practice-led PhD in 2008. Barbara's examinable work consisted of a final exhibition (there had been several throughout her candidature) and an exegesis.[73] She expressed no conflict between the written component and creative work, but rather was looking for a "way of saying what I do in the studio." For this artist, rather than seeing a conflict between her creative work and the written exegesis, she draws on Paul Carter's ideas on "material thinking" as "another term that allows us to write about what happens in the studio or in the field when you're gathering this visual stuff." The exegesis also played a role in describing the nature of practice-led research in her case as "embodied subjectivity" drawing on writers such as Merleau-Ponty. It is worth noting that her exegesis contained many visual elements (photographs, drawings, and graphics).

THE PRACTICE COMPONENT OF PRACTICE-LED RESEARCH

It will be necessary to explore the relationship between the exegesis and the practice component in more detail. Before that is possible, however, it is necessary to look more closely at how practice might be employed

70. Kill, "Coming in from the Cold," 309.
71. Raein, "Where Is the 'I'?" 1–4.
72. Kill, "Coming in from the Cold," 315.
73. Barbara, interview by Neil K. Ferguson.

in a practice-led project. One issue is immediately evident: practice can be very diverse. For this reason, it was defined in the previous chapter in a way that made it clear what practice was but allowed for this diversity. Two approaches were suggested: "Practice, then, may firstly be described as the set of skills, abilities, strategies that are characteristic of a particular discipline. Practice is also, secondly, what is characteristic of the output or product (in a broad sense) of the discipline."[74] It is necessary to be somewhat resistant to a *strong* definition of what constitutes the practice or creative component. To state that a creative component consists of certain forms, no matter how broadly stated, potentially excludes yet to be developed procedures or those that the writers of the definition had not thought of, or, did not wish to include. It is also, in a sense, incoherent: is it possible to say that creativity looks like any proposed list of things?

The aim of this section, then, is to offer examples of what practice might look like in its native environment and then offer some suggestions on what might constitute the practice or creative component in a theological context. These are intended to be illustrative and not exhaustive. It is important to note that practice is only constrained by the goal of the research project in answering the question. *How* practice does this and *what* practice can do are aspects of what a particular research project is attempting to uncover or develop.

Practice-led projects have included all the various disciplines that creative faculties engage in. Some of the edited works cited in this book contain examples of practice-led projects. Estelle Barrett and Barbara Bolt's *Practice as Research: Approaches to Creative Arts Enquiry* contains examples mainly from dance and performance.[75] *The Routledge Companion to Research in the Arts* edited by Michael Biggs and Henrik Karlsson contains a number of examples mainly from the visual arts area.[76]

Visual arts examples include representatives from painting, sculpture, film, photo-media and print making. The performance arts

---

74. See discussion in chapter 4.
75. Barrett and Bolt, *Practice as Research*.
76. Biggs and Karlsson, eds., *Routledge Companion to Research in the Arts*.

include projects from theatre, dance and music. Creative writing disciplines are also represented and include, for example, poetry and short novels.

There are examples of all these creative forms throughout Christian faith contexts in the past and present. Some of these forms have been used to communicate Christian messages or address issues from a Christian perspective, while some have been refined to suit the faith context developing their own visual language and symbols.

While there may be certain content, techniques, or strategies that faith based researchers may choose not to use, none of these various creative modes of production are excluded. However, faith is rich with practice and ritual. Christian faith-based researchers, therefore, have additional areas that may be explored.

EXAMPLES OF PRACTICE-LED RESEARCH IN THEOLOGY

The purpose of this section is to present a series of brief outlines of how practice-led research may be adopted in a theological context. The examples suggested here are only developed in a rudimentary way and intended to explore possibilities and to illustrate the general concept. chapter 8 presents a more fully worked example presented as a research proposal.

A first example is the case of prayer. Formal prayers are akin to poetry and so can be recorded in writing in a similar way. However, prayer is different to poetry in the sense that prayer is part of a conversation between an individual and God. Prayer may be in the form of poetry, but is ultimately about relationship as God is not "some*thing* but some*one*—and primarily someone that is spoken *to*, rather than spoken *about*."[77] Prayer is centred on God.

Prayer has many components as the classic introductory model suggested to new Christians illustrates: A (Adoration); C (Confession); T (Thanksgiving); S (Supplication).

Believers have reason to expect a result of some kind (for example, James 4:2).[78] There is, further, a sense in which prayer is a type of speech-acts, attempting to bring about a particular state of affairs in

---

77. Migliore, *Faith Seeking Understanding*, 242 (italics original).
78. Grudem, *Systematic Theology*, 377.

the world through prayer and God's action. Prayer contains speech that is declarative—sentences that make some truth claim about a state of affairs in the world[79]—but also language that contains what J. L. Austin called *performatives*. These sentences "seem not to describe anything in the world at all, and so seem not to be true or false. Instead, they seem to *get something done* . . . performatives [are] sentences we can *do* things with."[80] It may be possible in a practice-led research project centred on prayer to explore the performative nature of the language of prayer along with the performative nature of prayer itself. Prayer is often associated with the physical: posture (standing, kneeling, laying prostrate), ritual (prayer formats, times) as well as location and environment (venue such as a church and its spatial and lighting characteristics, a *quiet corner*, the use of incense).

Importantly, there is a long and diverse history of prayer in the church. The Psalms, for example, contain a variety of forms including hymns, prayers, complaints of the people and songs of praise.[81] Many of these are intended to be performed by choirs[82] and were the expectation in Hebrew worship. They are rich in musical and performance descriptions.[83] The example given here is only one of a multitude of possible frameworks that could be explored through the methodology.

Practice-led projects might be developed in which theological conceptions of prayer are explored through writing and/or the performance of prayer. A multidisciplinary approach could be adopted, incorporating ethnographic studies and historical investigations. It must be remembered that this is not about studying prayer, nor is it about the question of its possible divine response. Prayer is rather a key part of the process of answering a particular research question by using its own language, motifs and processes.

---

79. Morris, *Introduction*, 231.
80. Morris, *Introduction*, 232 (italics in original).
81. LaSor et al., *Old Testament Survey*, 431–40.
82. LaSor et al., *Old Testament Survey*, 431.
83. Walton et al., *IVP Bible Background Commentary*, 516.

Application: Principles

A second example is worship. Worship can be described as the primary function of the church[84], it is a foundational ministry.[85] In the words of the *Sacrosanctum Concilium* from the Second Vatican Council, worship, as expressed in liturgy, is "an exercise of the priestly office of Jesus Christ" (7) and in the "earthly liturgy we take part in a foretaste of that heavenly liturgy which is celebrated in the holy city of Jerusalem toward which we journey as pilgrims" (8).[86]

Due to the central position worship, in its many forms, plays in the church and the community of faith, it may present particularly diverse options as it includes within the rubric a wide range of practices. Song, for example, which implies the possible use of poetry in the lyrics, music, dance, gesture and prayer. It may be highly structured, unstructured, or a combination of these.

Hughes suggests three criteria for establishing meaning in worship: "The event has to *make sense* in some degree or another (i.e., some level of rationality is demanded); the meanings have to be *multisensory*, transmitted and apprehended as much along nonverbal as verbal channels of signification; and they have to be *theologically competent* (make sense in terms of a theistic reading of the world)."[87] Hughes takes a broadly semiotic approach to worship, that is, understanding it as a system of symbols. This is one way of understanding meaning in worship that might be applied in a practice-led research project. An exegesis on a project grounded in worship may include examinations of the symbols and the meaning they have for a practice.

Both the examples reflect the close relationship seen between prayer and worship and the beliefs and doctrine of the individual and of the church. The phrase *lex orandi, lex credendi* is usually translated as the *law of prayer is the law of belief*, or *as we pray so we believe*. Williams argues that this is a two way relationship: "If we take seriously the notion of *lex orandi, lex credendi*, then we must realize that the relation between theology and prayer runs in two directions: our prayer is the form and sign of our belief, but prayer also teaches belief and forms us

---

84. Williams, *Renewal Theology*, 3:87.
85. Grenz, *Theology for the Community of God*, 490.
86. Pope Paul VI, "Sacrosanctum Concilium."
87. Hughes, *Worship as Meaning*, 31.

in faith."[88] The practice and action of prayer and worship, our engagement with God within a community of faith influences the things we believe and how we understand God. Practice-led research is able to explore this in different ways by being driven by the practice of prayer and worship and accessing this knowledge process.

A third example is set in a charismatic context. Charismatics (and Pentecostals) argue that revelation from God is continuous; that it did not cease with, for example, the closing of the New Testament canon. They argue that revelation is ongoing and remains relevant through all ages of the church.[89] It appears, for example, in two of the nine spiritual gifts—the *word of wisdom* and *word of knowledge*—discussed by Paul in his letters to the Corinthians. A word of wisdom is "in some way an explication of the mystery of God that centres on Jesus Christ" and is where "the Holy Spirit may so move upon a person as to impart depth-understanding to a truth of the gospel."[90] A word of knowledge is "essentially an inspired word of teaching or instruction that occurs within the context of the gathered community" and comes from the inspiration of the Holy Spirit.[91]

Charismatics also understand that any revelation that comes through these two gifts, to be legitimate, will never contradict Scripture, but rather is grounded within it and is in accord with its message.[92] It might be possible to envision a practice-led project conducted by a person with either or both of these two gifts who investigates the nature of revelation as understood by charismatics. It may investigate questions relating to community relationships with each other, with God or the broader community they live in. The exercise of these gifts is usually centred on deep worship and prayer and is often exercised publicly and performatively.[93] Investigation of historical records of the exercise of these gifts may also be included.

88. Williams, "Mystical Theology Redux," 54.
89. Williams, *Renewal Theology*, 2:327.
90. Williams, *Renewal Theology*, 2:350, 354.
91. Williams, *Renewal Theology*, 2:356.
92. Williams, *Renewal Theology*, 2:351.
93. It is important to note that *performance* here is not to be understood that the exercise of the gifts is a "mere" performance, but rather they are often ties to music and prayer and ritual.

Application: Principles

A fourth example centres on mysticism and mystics. The common approach to study in this area would be to examine the ideas, history and ways of the mystic and mysticism, to study an individual mystic or a mystic and their contemporaries or to consider the significance and theology of their writings. However, by adopting the model and definition developed in this book, rather than researching only *about* mystics, a researcher may choose to *directly explore elements of mystical experience in practice*.

To explore this idea, a working definition on the nature of Christian mysticism is useful. According to Martin, Christian mysticism "seeks to describe an experiential, direct, nonabstract, unmediated, loving knowing of God, a knowing or seeing so direct as to be called union with God."[94] A second understanding is from a classic work in the field, *Mysticism* by Evelyn Underhill. Mysticism is the "expression of the innate tendency of the human spirit towards complete harmony with transcendental order whatever be the theological formula under which that order is understood."[95]

At least two elements are clear from these generalized definitions. Firstly, that *practice* and the *experiential life* of the mystic are essential to the nature of what it means to be a mystic. Secondly, mystics make attempts to express or describe their experience in a written or other form. In these two ways, mystics are a prototype of the practice-led researcher.

A simple summary of the practice-led research model developed in this book, a researcher begins (approximately) with a research question and seeks to find answers to that question through the language of their practice and through written language. From this base, it can be imagined that a variety of questions raised by the faith community could be explored this way.

For example, questions relating to ritual practice and how it might be made more immanent or intimate for a faith community. A researcher might be able to explore deeper understandings of certain doctrinal elements through mystical approaches and both write what they find as well as answer in other creative modes such as painting or poetry.

---

94. Martin, "Mysticism," 806.
95. Underhill is cited in McGinn, *Foundation of Mysticism*, 274.

McGinn writes on the language of inner experience in mysticism[96] and explorations within a practice-led structure—from within the mystical process—are opportunities to explore this language academically.

Scholars have debated the epistemic status of the mystical experience as well as what category of knowledge within which it might be described.[97] A practice-led research project might explore this from two perspectives, philosophically and 'mystically;' that is, from without and within. This exploration might be extended by exploring the Christian notion of the inner witness or inward testimony of the Holy Spirit. This in part relates to the Holy Spirit granting, in addition to the conviction of faith, "further assurance of the reality of God."[98] This has been developed in other ways, however. Alvin Plantinga includes it in his development of reformed epistemology. Plantinga understands belief in God as properly basic; that is, not depending on other beliefs for its truth.[99] He employs Calvin's concept of the *sensus divinitatis* which he understands as "a disposition or set of dispositions to from theistic beliefs in various circumstances or stimuli that trigger the working of this sense of divinity."[100] He further employs the inner witness or instigation of the Holy Spirit as "a source of belief, a cognitive process that produces in us belief in the main lines of the Christian story."[101] This can be understood as a non-propositional type of knowledge but may be strengthened, supported, and understood by propositional knowledge. A practice-led project might explore these ideas and express them through a multi-practice approach (for example, performance and visual arts expression) or be an integrated project having no separate creative component but include creative writing or poetry and songs.

A fifth example might be grounded in the life of a monastic. For example, *The Rule of Saint Benedict*, named after Benedict of Nursia who was born about 480, exchanges the extreme asceticism that had been the norm until Benedict's time with a "wise ordering of the

---

96. McGinn, "Language of Inner Experience."
97. For example, Levine, "Mystical Experience."
98. Williams, *Renewal Theology*, 48.
99. Moreland and Craig, *Philosophical Foundations*, 164.
100. Moreland and Craig, *Philosophical Foundations*, 164.
101. Moreland and Craig, *Philosophical Foundations*, 165.

Application: Principles

monastic life, with strict discipline, but without undue hardship."[102] The life of the monk revolved around a cycle of prayer, work, study and rest. A kind of *ritual-led research* project might involve the investigation of the linkages between each element of this cycle in and through its action across weeks or seasons. This could be by an individual monk, a researcher who adopts the *Rule* or even the lay person who follows a monastic rule in everyday life. A thesis submission could include a theoretical investigation of the relevant section of the rule, historical context, various alternatives across Christianity or in other faiths, its intent and outworking. The practice component might entail a creative component such as poetry, fiction, or a performance. Another option might be a photographic record of the passing of the seasons linked to parts of the *Rule*. With this last suggestion in mind, a practice component may also incorporate biblical ideas on time. One aspect of this relationship, for example, might be between *chronos* time—duration or a point in linear time—and *kairos* time—a point manifesting suitable circumstances or a fitting season.[103]

A sixth example begins with an argument made by Sandra Harding that there is no such thing as a *feminist research method*. The reason is, she notes, feminist researchers "use just about any and all of the methods . . . that traditional androcentric researchers have used."[104] What is distinctive about feminist research lies elsewhere and is not merely a case of "adding women" to existing approaches.[105] Rather, it is that women's "characteristic social experiences" provide a different basis for reliable knowledge claims.[106] This idea falls broadly under the terms *standpoint epistemology* or *standpoint research* and fits loosely with the first element of the critical realist approach adopted in this book, *epistemic relativism*. Standpoint research "starts with a focus on experience."[107] Specifically, feminist standpoint theories "claim to represent the world from a particular socially situated perspective that can

---

102. González, *Story of Christianity*, 1:239.
103. Mounce, *Analytical Lexicon*, 259, 484.
104. Harding, "Introduction," 2.
105. Harding, "Introduction," 4.
106. Harding, "Introduction," 10.
107. Letherby, "Standpoint Research," 288.

lay a claim to epistemic privilege or authority."[108] While it is certainly true—almost obviously so—that there is no single place that can claim to be a "women's standpoint," practice-led research as formulated in this book permits the development of a researcher's perspective as a part of the research foundation.[109]

With this groundwork in place, a researcher's project may begin from her experience as a Christian woman in relationship to the church, the roles she plays in it, the roles she plays in the community, is expected to play in the community, and the positions and tasks she is not permitted to access (e.g., priest). In this case, a practice-led research methodology might operate as an overarching approach. It would allow the legitimization of the experience and practice of the researcher; it would begin from a standpoint epistemological base and draw on appropriate tools such as autoethnography to explore their position within the structure of the faith community. Practice-led research would also provide an appropriate structure for the researcher to present their findings in whatever experiential or practical approach was relevant to their knowledge discoveries.

A seventh example begins with what might be called "experiential symbolism." By this term I mean not so much symbolism we see and recognize—although that is certainly important—but rather symbolism we participate in, enact and re-enact. A framework could start in the Sacred Paschal Triduum that begins with the evening Mass on Thursday and continues through to the Easter Vigil on Saturday evening and the following day, the Sunday, begins the season of Easter. This time in the Catholic calendar is rich in symbolism that is *enacted* by the faith community. The Washing of the Feet is conducted by the priest, a reminder of Jesus's washing of the disciple's feet in John 13 and the Roman Missal links it closely to this biblical event.[110] Other examples include the silence at the close of the Friday of the Passion service[111] and the lighting and passing of the flame at the Easter Vigil

---

108. Anderson, "Feminist Epistemology."

109. It is important to bear in mind certain caveats to this idea discussed in chapter 7.

110. Goonan et al., *St Pauls Sunday Missal*, 236–37.

111. Goonan et al., *St Pauls Sunday Missal*, 265.

Application: Principles

on Saturday night.¹¹² These events—or any others in the Christian calendar—provide a practice base for a research project into aspects of faith. For example, a research project might explore the events of the Triduum in small or isolated communities who lack a regular priest and how they might the richest experience might be conveyed. A key difference of such a project when explored through practice-led research would be that rather than only making suggestions, plans and outlines, the project might include photos, film, and creative written experiences (poetry, short stories) that fully embody the research exploration.

These examples are presented to help demonstrate that practice-led research working with faith practices has rich potential, may require some innovative thought on the part of the researchers, but is restricted only by the limitations of the researcher's resourcefulness and exploratory imagination.

KNOWLEDGE AND MEANING IN PRACTICE-LED RESEARCH

The original description of the research-question model and the statement in the guidelines produced by Curtin University reveal a potential criticism of the model. In both quotes reproduced earlier, *answers* is highlighted with quotation marks.

There are two possible explanations for the highlighting of *answer*. Firstly, it can be explained in part by remembering that the project speaks in more than one language and so the answers need to be understood in this way also. This may be a way of highlighting that the outcomes of a project will include more than an answer in the traditional style as well as being presented in ways other than solely in the traditional format. A second and related possibility concerns how the answer to the research question provided by the practice component is comprehended, especially by those that do not *speak* the language of the researcher's practice. In this view, *answers* is highlighted to point out that there are multiple ways of reaching an answer to a question, ways broader than using language in a conventional sense. Part of this issue could be addressed in the framing of the research question itself.

---

112. Goonan et al., *St Pauls Sunday Missal*, 267.

While not pre-empting any particular outcome, the question may flag what an answer to the question may look like in terms of the researcher's individual practice.

The third possibility raised by the isolating *answers* may reflect an underlying skepticism of the possibility of answers to questions. This does not relate to an understanding of the provisional nature of research conclusions, results that can be changed or expanded or developed by later research, but rather what might be a strong version of a constructivist position. Put simply, this view argues that answers are not really answers, but rather only a reflection of the cultural and historical context of the researcher.

The remaining section of this chapter will address this concern from three angles. The first approach will be to argue for the possibility of answers by building on *critical realism* as first presented in chapter 2. The second approach will be to further develop the exegesis with the concept of *narrative hermeneutics*. The third approach will be to present a provisional (and somewhat speculative) understanding of the knowledge outputs of the methodology that will illustrate the multiple levels available. Each of these approaches will be developed with the view to how they might be best applied to practice-led projects and the answering of the research question. One of the key concerns seems to centre on the nature of research itself and so a brief review is valuable.

At the start of chapter 4, a number of definitions on the nature of *research* were presented.[113] One was from Clough and Nutbrown who suggested that "all research, necessarily, is about asking questions, exploring problems and reflecting on what emerges in order to make meaning from the data and tell the research story."[114] A second succinct definition came from one of the interviewees who described research as the "systematic process of asking and answering questions." The most important understanding of research developed in that chapter, however, was from the OECD's Frascati Manual: "Research and experimental development (R&D) comprise creative work undertaken on a systematic basis in order to increase the stock of knowledge, including knowledge of man, culture and society, and the use of this stock of

---

113. See chapter 4.
114. Clough and Nutbrown, *Student's Guide to Methodology*, 4.

Application: Principles

knowledge to devise new applications."[115] This definition was explored in some detail due to its wide influence: it is often cited directly when a definition of research is sought, and it forms the basis of other definitions on the nature of research. Not only does the definition encompass the key elements of what research is, but its incorporation of the Frascati Manual's definition allows it to form a key basis for the assessment of research by government agencies, whether researchers themselves are aware of it. For these reasons, it was also explored in detail so it might be incorporated at some level into the conceptual framework of practice-led research outlined in chapter 5.

One issue of importance to this section arises from these definitions of research and needs to be considered in a more detailed way. The Frascati Manual requires the outcomes of research to make a contribution, in some way, to the stock of knowledge of humanity. It was noted in chapter 4 that, at face value, the authors of the Manual seem to understand knowledge in what was described as a "common sense" way, that is, as information about an object or situation. While this is true in part, on closer examination it was seen that the Manual frames the understanding of knowledge within a certain set of parameters, that is, in a *quantitative* sense. Garwood defines quantitative research as

> research involving the collection of data in numerical form for quantitative analysis. The numerical data can be durations, scores, counts of incidents, ratings, or scales ... The defining factor is that numbers result from the process, whether the initial data collection produced numerical values, or whether non-numerical values were subsequently converted to numbers as part of the analysis process ...[116]

However, although they may include quantitative elements, as a discussion in chapter 5 suggested, practice-led research projects fit more closely within a *qualitative paradigm*. Qualitative research may be understood as using "a range of methods to focus on the meanings and interpretations of social phenomena and social processes in the

---

115. OECD, *Frascati Manual 2012*, 30.
116. Garwood, "Quantitative Research," 250.

particular contexts in which they occur."[117] Qualitative research focuses on questions and situations that are not as amenable to quantitative methods, which may not possess the same generalizability beyond specified situations but which still add to the stock of knowledge when understood as a contribution to, for example, particular disciplines, times, cultural milieus, or groups. While it is certainly true that both qualitative and quantitative approaches conduct research into social phenomena and social processes, the key difference in qualitative approaches is the attention to meanings and interpretations. There are a number of other issues as well that will not be directly addressed. For example, Sumner mentions concerns such as rigour and small sample sizes. However, these arguments are frequently phrased as if quantitative research is the benchmark to which other forms of research must aspire, but this is a matter of debate and arguments and evidence in support of that contention would need to be presented and defended.[118]

Nevertheless, how knowledge is understood in terms of practice-led research needs to take these distinctions into account. The definitions also imply that there is some form of an answer or outcome from the research, one that represents some contribution to the knowledge base of humanity and that it is disseminated in some way. The possibility of answers in practice-led research projects will now be addressed.

Critical Realism

It was argued in chapter 2 that critical realism fits well with the Christian perspective of this book. According to Andrew Wright, critical realism

> seeks to map a path beyond the extremes of modern certainty and postmodern skepticism via a triumvirate of core philosophical principles: ontological realism, epistemic relativism and judgmental rationality. Ontological realism asserts that reality exists for the most part independently of human perception, epistemic relativism asserts that our knowledge of reality is limited and contingent, and jjudgmental rationality

---

117. Sumner, "Qualitative Research," 249.
118. Sumner, "Qualitative Research," 249.

asserts that it is nevertheless possible to judge between conflicting truth claims while recogni[z]ing that all such jud[g]ments necessarily remain open to further adjudication.[119]

Ontological realism was supported by the Christian notion of a material world created by God but separate from God and humans, there is a material, physical world in which we live and move.[120] For practice-led research projects, this means that it is possible to study and draw conclusions about this world and the people encountered, along with experiences, emotions and ideas and their expression. A practice-led project has the potential at least of drawing conclusions and uncovering real understandings about the question or questions under investigation. This *potential* is no different from other projects and in part hinges on the quality of the research, the framing of a question and the collection of data in whatever form that may take.

However, this position must be tempered with the second element, *epistemic relativism*. It was further suggested in chapter 2 that human reason is fallible. Since the Fall, our cognitive functions are not totally reliable and, as a result, their conclusions are also potentially fallible, they are, as Wright suggests, contingent. Further to this, we develop our ideas in a particular historical time period, a particular culture, from the perspective of a particular gender, using a particular language. The implication for practice-led research projects from this element of critical realism is that it is crucial to remember that that the outcomes of research are provisional and always open to review.

The third element of Wright's triumvirate is *judgmental rationality*. This element argues that given the contingent nature of conclusions about the world, it is possible to make assessments between conflicting truth claims but that these are always open to reassessment. A research project founded on one or more research questions can present conclusions and implications based on assessments of the strength of the position while being aware of the provisional and contingent nature of their conclusions. Further, given that various judgments or assessments are made consciously or unconsciously during the research process,

---

119. Wright, *Christianity and Critical Realism*, 9.
120. See chapter 2.

some form of statement of a researcher's position—that is to say, their context—would be appropriate in the exegesis. This will assist in the full assessment of a research project. In terms of a practice-led research project, judgments are made in the exegesis and in the practice that are thought to best express or encapsulate the question, phenomenon, experience or idea under investigation. It would be recognized, however, that another practitioner in the same or different discipline may reach a different conclusion. This, however, does not automatically mean that different answers render the whole process meaningless as no *agreement* is reached but rather that additional elements have been revealed.

These arguments, which are drawn from the work of Andrew Wright, are enhanced by the work of a namesake, N. T. Wright in his book *The New Testament and the People of God*.[121] Wright walks a middle ground and his model, which is also grounded in a version of critical realism, is compatible with the conclusions I have outlined up to this point.

Wright begins with the idea that "we can affirm both that the text does have a particular viewpoint from which everything is seen and at the same time the reader's reading is not mere 'neutral observation.'"[122] Wright's first point is specifically related to the text itself. A text will make a certain claim from a particular viewpoint, but that view will be impacted by the presuppositions and perspective of the reader. This was particularly evident, for example, from the beginning of this project. There are many examples in the literature on practice-led research where the researcher spends considerable time recounting their investigations and is written largely by and for those in the creative industries for their own use. Much seemed to be assumed and this had the tendency to obscure the nature and processes involved. There appeared to be no thought or interest among these writers of how the outcomes of their practice-led research might be accessed outside their own disciplines let alone anywhere outside the creative arts. In terms of practice-led research projects, a project includes—in part—the practice of an individual researcher who engages a particular question through that practice. However, that practice is conducted within the

---

121. Wright, *New Testament and the People of God*.
122. Wright, *New Testament and the People of God*, 64 (italics original).

individual's worldview, experience, skill, and cultural and historical situation. Further, when an individual comes to that project, as an examiner or as someone wishing to draw on the ideas presented, they too have a particular view that will have an impact on how they understand the ideas and outcomes presented.

Secondly, Wright states that "we can affirm *both* that the text has a certain life of its own, *and* that the author had intentions of which we can in principle gain at least some knowledge."[123] When an author sets out to produce a written work, they have an aim in doing so—for example, they may wish to say something particular about an event or person or present their view on some issue. There is a goal the writer wishes to achieve. A text is not entirely separate from its source. Yet, a reader is limited in what they can know about the writer and their goals in writing. Therefore, an excessive focus on these intentions is misplaced and a reader must often work with the text alone.

In the model developed in this book, the practice-led researcher begins with a research question, one that may be recognized as provisional and modified as the research progresses. The research moves toward the aim of reaching an answer to this question through the practice and the exegesis. At its completion, the project is *released* from the researcher and must, to a degree, stand on its own. One of the goals of the models presented throughout this book is to provide the foundation for a practice-led project to contribute to the debates of a discipline in a way that is more independent of the individual than has often been the case. However, Wright is saying that the context of the researcher has a bearing on the project and its outcomes and knowledge of these aspects provide a richer understanding.

Finally, Wright argues that "we can affirm *both* that the actions or objects described may well be, in principle, actions and objects in the public world, *and* that the author was looking at them from a particular, and perhaps distorting, point of view."[124] In line with the critical realist position outlined earlier, reality is not solely a construct of the observer, but is always grounded in the world. However, it is also the case that

---

123. Wright, *New Testament and the People of God*, 64 (italics original).
124. Wright, *New Testament and the People of God*, 64 (italics original).

the views of those events are always influenced by the perspective of the observer.

This process is rich in complex interactions. Andrew McNamara argues that "good PLR," that is, practice-led research "is a complicated affair necessitating a complex, back-and-forth interaction between the practice and its conceptual framework or articulation. It forces one to consider how each component—the creative practice and exegetical research framework—is capable of producing knowledge, and thus of furnishing unique understanding and insights."[125] Not only is practice-led research an interaction between practice and the exegesis (as formulated here) in order to reach some conclusions about the question under investigation, but any outcomes also need to be expressed in multiple languages.

Narrative Hermeneutics

One approach to explore and encourage the tension between practice and its articulation as well as the tension in the differing languages of practice and exegesis is to use an approach termed *narrative hermeneutics*. Critical realism supports the possibility of conclusions to research while a narrative hermeneutic will assist in the ways answers may be reached.

Although possibly more visible in the exegesis, the hermeneutical and interpretive task are a function of both the exegesis and the practice of the research. Many of the faith practice examples in the previous section are rich in symbolism and many of these symbols have ancient origins. Further, many of these symbols are unfamiliar to contemporary audiences, often even to those of the same faith community. The model advocated in this chapter contends that the exegesis and the creative piece are answering the same research question but using different languages and often producing different types of knowledge. In order to maintain a link between the two components, the exegesis may provide support by incorporating the symbolism from the practice into the exegesis or applying discussions in the exegesis into the practice; the two work in complementary ways. So, the exegesis need not be

---

125. McNamara, "Six Rules," 8.

only text, but can be integrated or combined with other elements of the project, such as images or sound. The exegesis provides the additional function of supporting any creative component in providing explanations and background information to assist the examiner and others in fully grasping the answers and conclusions of the project as a whole.

This can be achieved, according to Wright, by thinking of how humans understand the world as a process of telling stories. By *story* Wright does not mean "once upon a time . . . and they researched happily ever after" but rather as a process that brings "worldviews into articulation."[126] Wright defines hermeneutics as "the whole activity of understanding, including the historical reading of texts."[127] A text is neither "the 'neutral' description of the world," nor is it merely "a collection of subjective feelings."[128] According to Wright: "There is no such things as 'neutral' or 'objective' proof; only the claim that the story we are now telling about the world as a whole makes more sense, in its outline and detail, than other potential or actual stories that may be on offer."[129]

These conclusions have an important consequence for the practice-led projects. All such research projects may be considered as "texts" in a broad sense and are narratives *expressing, articulating and describing individual understanding and knowledge* ultimately grounded in a worldview. A practice-led research project is a narrative—a story—of a research process and offers an account of a particular aspect of the world through a written text (the exegesis) and a practice (visual arts, performance, etc.). It is also worth noting that all research—qualitative or quantitative—does to varying degrees describe individual understanding of the world grounded in a world view whether it is individually or corporately held.

This has important implications for the knowledge outcomes of practice-led research projects. There is only limited discussion on the literature on this aspect of the methodology and could prove to be a weakness particularly when practice-led research projects are viewed

---

126. Wright, *New Testament and the People of God*, 65 (italics removed).
127. Wright, *New Testament and the People of God*, 19n32.
128. Wright, *New Testament and the People of God*, 65.
129. Wright, *New Testament and the People of God*, 42.

from the outside. Further, as was the case with the search for a definition, the discussion is fragmentary with useful elements located across the field. The following framework, then, is suggested as a starting point for developing a broad and flexible, but still coherent understanding of the specific knowledge outputs in practice-led projects. The discussion presented here is complementary to the outline of explicit and tacit knowledge developed in chapter 5 as preparation for the definition presented in that chapter.

The practice-led research methodology may be understood as generating knowledge in a triangulated way, that is, in three forms: *propositional*, *non-propositional* and *pre-propositional* knowledge.

The first point of the proposed triangle is *propositional knowledge*. This is "knowledge of truths"; that is, "knowledge that involves a belief or judgment in some true claim or proposition."[130] In the words of another author, propositional knowledge is knowledge "*that* something is so"[131] and most closely linked to the explicit knowledge as discussed in chapter 5. This style of knowledge is theoretical, analytical, and easily expressible in statements and assessments of states of affairs in the world, now or in the past. Knowledge in this form is most characteristic of the traditional thesis.

The second element is *non-propositional knowledge*. This form is closely linked to the tacit and embodied knowledge discussed in chapter 5. Non-propositional knowledge is characterized by knowledge *of* something, such as by acquaintance,[132] knowledge how, such as how to ride a bicycle,[133] as well as the praxical knowledge, the knowledge in the handling and use of items in the world as also outlined in chapter 5. Knowledge in this form is symbolic, interpretive and representational. The intelligences, such as the spiritual intelligence discussed in chapter 5, fit largely in here. This knowledge is knowledge we can be aware of but is not always amenable to translation into a propositional form or easily applied from propositions. A simple example is learning to ride a bicycle. It is possible to study the principles of bicycle riding and

---

130. Hasan and Fumerton, "Knowledge by Acquaintance vs. Description."
131. Moser, "Epistemology," 273 (italics original).
132. Moser, "Epistemology," 273.
133. Fantl, "Knowledge How."

Application: Principles

develop an understanding of the physics involved. However, this will only provide a limited level of preparation for the ability to remain upright on a two wheeled vehicle. This form of knowledge is most closely linked to the skills, methods and techniques of a practitioner.

The third element in the triangle is *pre-propositional knowledge*. Although sometimes combined with non-propositional knowledge, the pre-propositional variety is more accurately described in what Panksepp calls the "experientially rich emotional systems" in the sub-neocortical regions of the brain.[134] Panksepp goes on to say:

> The varieties of affective feelings are enormous, and many humans are skilled in talking about the meaning of such feelings in their lives. However, at their core, raw affective experiences appear to be pre-propositional gifts of nature—cognitively impenetrable tools for living that inform us about the states of our body, the sensory aspects of the world that support or detract from our survival, and various distinct types of emotional arousal that can inundate our minds.

Their influence appears to be, for the most part, one way. They have an impact on an individual's emotional states and thinking, but are not influenced, at least directly, by the cognitive processes of that individual. While Panksepp suggests that this is "cognitively impenetrable" it may be possible to access this knowledge—the processes a person is using in approaching the world through reflection or contemplation and meditation as, for example, practiced by mystics. This in itself would constitute an interesting element of a practice-led research project.

The relationship between these three versions of knowledge has been represented in Figure 4.

---

134. Panksepp, "On the Embodied Neural Nature," 168.

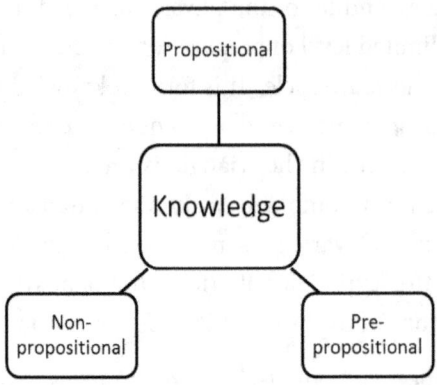

Figure 4. Relationship between Knowledge Styles

Each element in this relationship is important and neither takes precedence over the other. However, some are more visible than others and each may have a greater emphasis at different stages of the process and may be more characteristic of a different component of a completed project.

Propositional knowledge would normally be more apparent in the exegesis component. The exegesis addresses the research question, in part, in a way that is more characteristic of the traditional thesis. Sentences have propositional content, facts and data about the world, as revealed in the research process. The exegesis also attempts to provide some translation of the other aspects of the research to clarify and interpret elements in the practice component.

Non-propositional knowledge would normally be more apparent in the practice/creative component of a practice-led research project. Practice was described as embodied and tacit in nature, often described as "know how" rather than the "know that" of propositional knowledge. Non-propositional knowledge is conveyed in the same way it is formed, that is to say, at an embodied level: it is understood by individuals in a physical, bodily way.

Pre-propositional knowledge is present at two stages. Firstly, for the practitioner/researcher, it can be found at the root of their practice, in the emotional—visceral—drivers and motivators or the practice and research. Secondly, these emotional reactions may be received by viewers or participants through their reactions and engagement to the

Application: Principles

creative/practice work. All of these three knowledge varieties can be supported with the unifying tool of Wright's story approach bringing all three of these elements into a clearer articulation.

CONCLUSION

This chapter considered a number of principles that relate to how a practice-led research project would be practically developed. Firstly, it considered the *typical* structure of a practice-led project, a creative/practice component and a written component, usually referred to as an exegesis. This process demonstrated the general acceptance of practice-led research as a methodology but also reflected what might be described as a *hands-off* approach, providing only general format and size guidelines, leaving the details to the school and supervisors. The next section presented the main existing models that characterize the exegesis. These were the commentary model, the context model, and a less common hybrid model which is broadly a combination of the other two. A number of criticisms were presented; mainly that each tends to favour one component of the research project to the detriment of the other. Following a discussion on what the term *exegesis* can mean, a model was developed based on the work of Milech and Schilo which grounds the research process in a research question. A number of important advantages were suggested: it provides a coherent framework for the entire research project and resists divisions between practice and exegesis.

The chapter proposed a number of heuristic illustrations of what practice-led research projects may look like in theology. These were intended to show the combination of faith practice and theoretical understandings in a number of areas. The final section expanded on the discussions in earlier chapters relating to the nature of knowledge outputs from practice-led projects. The section suggested these could be understood through propositional knowledge, non-propositional knowledge and pre-propositional knowledge. The next chapter deals with a number of important issues related to the practical application and presentation of practice-led research projects.

Chapter 7

Application

Preparation and Assessment

INTRODUCTION

GROUNDED IN THE DEFINITIONAL work of chapters 4–5, chapter 6 laid out the theoretical structure of a practice-led research project. The chapter developed a model for practice-led research based on a research question or questions and centred on both the form of the researcher's practice and an exegesis. Each of these components answers the question(s) in their characteristic language.

This chapter builds on this formulation by considering a number of important practical concerns in the life of a practice-led research project. Once a practice-led project is completed—like all research projects—it needs to be assessed, recorded, and preserved as well as have its findings disseminated. There are also several issues that are more characteristic of these projects that need to be examined. It will be the task, then, of chapter 7 to bring all these elements together and present a worked example of how a practice-led project might look in a theological context.

REVIEW

A brief review of points relevant to this chapter from preceding ones will be helpful. Chapter 2 made the important point that the researcher

Application: Preparation and Assessment

and their research are closely connected to their *worldview*. The chapter grounded this project in a Christian view of the world, one broadly describable by the traditional creedal formulations of the church. This project is also framed within a critical realist theoretical perspective. Critical realism holds that that there is a world "out there" independent of us, but our understanding of it is filtered being understood through our cultural context; we cannot know the world as it is.

A distinguishing feature of the practice-led researcher is their manifest *presence* in their research. The practice of the researcher is fundamentally central to the process which leads to the personal facet of the research and the personal component in the reporting of that research is clearly apparent. Drawing on the earlier discussions of worldview and theoretical perspective, the first section addresses a number of concerns raised by practice-led researchers and those in more traditional modes. The section deals with stylistic issues related to the writing of the exegesis that come out of the very nature of the methodology's grounding in a researcher's practice and the closer link the project has to the researcher that is not always the case in other approaches (although present nonetheless) and what might be termed the red herring of objectivity.

It was also argued in chapter 2 that faith discourse has a legitimate place in the public sphere. The public sphere, however, was narrowed to mean essentially the university environment. While not discussed in a separate section, this will be raised at various points in the discussions that follow. Chapter 2 argued that it is alien to conceive of theology as an intellectual discipline separated from faith or the absence of faith. It outlined the close connection between the artist and the theologian with their economic, political and social context. All these are issues practice-led research has the ability to address.

Chapter 4 defined practice-led research in the following way: "Practice-led research is a methodology that sources its strategies and processes for answering its research questions broadly from those practices that are characteristic of the discipline in which it is being employed." The skills, strategies and abilities of a researcher—collectively their *practice*—are the means of the research process. One of the goals of the first section of this chapter will be to examine the positives and potential negatives of this situation.

The discussion in chapter 4 understood knowledge in a broad way as empirical and propositional as well as tacit and praxical. The key feature of a practice-led research project is the centrality of the practice of the researcher. While this may seem like a tautology, it is important to highlight because the practice is not only a part of the research process, it is also a component of *the final assessable material*. This means that the knowledge revealed in a practice-led research project is presented in ways additional to the written word. A later section of this chapter will look at the ways this has been and could be carried out. This also raises questions of examination and assessment and the related area of the preservation of the project. Ways this has been and can be done will also be considered as well as broader issues relating to the dissemination of the content of a practice-led project.

RESEARCHER VISIBILITY

At several points in this book, attention has been drawn to the central role the practice of the researcher plays in the research process. Although not exclusively so, the researcher is both the source and the means of the research. However, it has also been argued that the knowledge produced in the research is not wholly contingent on the researcher and has an independence making it available to others in the research community. Fundamentally, these are issues concerning the relationship of subjectivity and objectivity in research. While it is clear that the researcher is always present in their research, a key question here asks to what degree the presence of the researcher should be made manifest in the description and writing up of the research.

The arguments of this section will contend that it is necessary for the integrity of the research for the researcher to be visible, that is impossible for practice-led research to be described entirely separately from the experience of the researcher and that it is academically legitimate and permissible for this to take place. Three steps will be given to make this case.

Firstly, researcher visibility is epistemologically appropriate especially given the theoretical assumptions of this book outlined in chapter

Application: Preparation and Assessment

2. The status of research as knowledge demands an awareness of the situation of the researcher. Secondly, first person authorship is currently widespread across disciplines. This might be viewed as merely a stylistic issue but goes deeper to the perceived nature of research outputs as well as the purpose and the goal of academic writing. A series of corpus studies will be presented to demonstrate this to be the case. Thirdly, a socio-cultural argument based on the observation that faith is both an objective and a subjective reality, that the Christian life—Christian praxis—is relational, social, communal, interactive, and contains an important personal component. All theology contains and draws upon personal experience and that of the community of believers.

The Situation of the Researcher

Michael Crotty suggests two questions should be the starting point for research: "[I]n developing a research proposal, we need to put considerable effort into answering two questions in particular. First, what methodologies and methods will we be employing in the research we propose to do? Second, how do we justify this choice and use of methodologies and methods?"[1] Chapter 2 of this book went into some detail to answer these questions. These discussions are often at the start of a thesis and there is good reason for this: all the decisions that follow in the research flow out of the positions a researcher takes at this point. While it might be tempting to think that this is simply a requirement of the process that needs to be completed before the *real research* begins, this is a misunderstanding. As Jonathan Grix notes, "if we are to present clear, precise and logical work, and engage and debate with others' work, then we need to know the core assumptions that underlie their work and inform their choice of research questions, methodology, methods and even sources."[2] A researcher makes decisions to include or exclude information based on these assumptions, and sources are selected or excluded based on their assumptions of what is considered to be a good or reliable source.

There is a clear conclusion from these points: the researcher is always present in the research whether they inform their audience of

1. Crotty, *Foundations of Social Research*, 2.
2. Grix, *Foundations of Research*, 57.

their positions or not. As the definition in chapter 4 made clear, the practice of the research is integral to the research process. It is a part of the toolkit for answering the research questions proposed (and may have been a part of how those questions were arrived at in the first place). In the case of practice-led research then, the presence of the researcher is a matter of degree, rather than something that is the case here and not the case in other forms of research.

The Use of the First Person in Academic Writing

The previous section argued that the researcher is always present in their research to some degree and that absolute objectivity is not possible. There is an important implication of this for academic writing generally and practice-led research writing particularly. There is a view that the use of personal reference in academic writing—such as *I* or *We*—is not appropriate. Harwood surveyed a number of English for Academic Purposes textbooks and found this to be standard advice, quoting one as saying that "personal pronouns are to be avoided."[3] Hyland is much stronger: "The convention of impersonal reporting remans a hallowed concept for many, a cornerstone of the positivist assumption that academic research is purely empirical and objective, and therefore best presents as if human agency was not part of the process."[4] This type of advice, however, does not reflect the actual practices of academic disciplines. Rather, a range of corpus studies have demonstrated that *all* disciplines use them to one degree or another.

Before giving some examples, a brief consideration of the nature of a corpus study will be helpful. Essentially, in a study of this type, a range of texts are selected, entered into concordance software to search for word appearance and context. In one study, Hyland analyzed 240 published journal articles, 30 each from eight disciplines.[5] In another study, also from Hyland, he analyzed a collection of 64 student reports across a range of disciplines totalling 630,100 words and a selection of 240 research articles published in journals totalling 1,323,000 words.[6]

---

3. Harwood, "'We Do Not Seem to Have a Theory,'" 366–67.
4. Hyland, "Humble Servants," 208.
5. Hyland, "Options of Identity," 352.
6. Hyland, "Authority and Invisibility," 1097.

Application: Preparation and Assessment

In a third study from Hyland, three research articles each were selected from 10 journals that represented eight disciplines: 240 articles totalling 1,400,000 words[7]. In a study by Harwood, a selection of leading journals in four professions were nominated by lecturers at universities in the UK. Ten articles were selected totalling 325,000 words.[8]

Although a number of studies have been conducted looking at MA and PhD theses, much of the work has looked at journal articles. It might be argued that there is enough of a difference between the two writing styles to make theses exempt from the conclusions the corpus studies suggest. This is a false distinction. Hyland suggests that "articles are sites of disciplinary engagement, where writers interact with specialist audiences rather than with general readers" and that "research writing involves writers in a process of both textualizing their work as a contribution to the field, and in constructing themselves as plausible members of the discipline, competent to make such a contribution."[9] This is manifestly a part of the goals of a research degree.

In a 2001 study, Hyland selected a range of disciplines for analysis. They were mechanical engineering, electrical engineering, marketing, philosophy, sociology, applied linguistics, physics, and microbiology.[10] Self-mention was present across all the disciplines in the study, leading Hyland to observe that "academic writing is not the faceless, formal prose it is often depicted to be."[11] Further, in philosophy, the discipline that can be considered closest to theology, had the second highest use of "I" when considered across the corpus, but the highest use when considered as cases per paper.[12]

Two important points can be drawn out of studies of this nature. The first is that statements suggesting academic writing is of a particular nature—impersonal and objective—are false, but rather that there are differences across disciplines. Generally, "humanities and social

---

7. Hyland, "Humble Servants," 211.
8. Harwood, "'We Do Not Seem to Have a Theory,'" 349–50.
9. Hyland, "Humble Servants," 209.
10. Hyland, "Humble Servants," 211.
11. Hyland, "Humble Servants," 212.
12. Hyland, "Humble Servants," 212 (see esp. Tables 1 and 2 on page 212; see also Table 4 [214]).

sciences feature *I* more frequently than the sciences, which feature heavier use of *we*."¹³ Academic writing, according to Hyland, "displays considerable differences between disciplines."¹⁴

The second is that pronouns perform an important *academic function*. Harwood observes:

> These studies have shown that pronouns can help the writer organize the text and guide the reader through the argument (e.g., "First, I will argue that . . ."), define terms (e.g., "In this paper, I understand this term to mean..."), state personal opinions, arguments, and knowledge claims (e.g., "As a result of these calculations, we believe . . ."), recount research procedure and methodology (e.g., "We distributed questionnaires to 80 informants"), and acknowledge funding bodies, institutions, and individuals that contributed to the research in some way (e.g., "I thank X for checking the algorithm").¹⁵

Academic writing, in all its forms, is a site of disciplinary engagement.¹⁶ These various elements are forms of *metadiscourse*, that is, "various kinds of linguistic tokens that an author employs in her text to guide or direct her reader as to how to understand her, her text, and her stance toward it."¹⁷ These forms of discourse are instrumental in

> a tenacious desire inculcated in the author to secure the illocutionary outcome and to control the perlocutionary effect of her primarily ideational discourse. Such a desire is being fed and fueled, continuously, by an external rhetorical imperative to mark individuality and craft originality. To the extent this desire is appropriately displayed in discourse, the author succeeds in projecting and maintaining her own credible *ethos*.¹⁸

Their use "is a powerful means by which writers express an identity by asserting their claim to speak as an authority, and this is a

---

13. Harwood, "(In)Appropriate Personal Pronoun Use," 426.
14. Hyland, "Options of Identity," 352.
15. Harwood, "(In)Appropriate Personal Pronoun Use," 426.
16. Hyland, "Humble Servants," 209.
17. Mao, "I Conclude Not," 265.
18. Mao, "I Conclude Not," 272 (italics original).

key element of successful academic writing."[19] Hyland points out that "while impersonality may often be institutionally sanctified, it is constantly transgressed."[20]

The Grounding of Christian Praxis

Chapter 2 presented an argument on the integral nature of Christian faith to the believer. This came from a Christian believer, Alvin Plantinga, and from a non-believer, Jürgen Habermas. I suggest in chapter 2 that Plantinga's advice, although aimed at philosophers, can also be applied to other disciplines where Christians operate. Plantinga argues (in part) that Christian philosophers are "the philosophers of the Christian community" and it is a part of their task to serve the Christian community which "has its own questions, its own concerns, its own topics for investigation, its own agenda and its own research program."[21] He acknowledges that it is important to be engaged in the wider debates of the discipline, but those that only focus on these will be neglecting a "crucial and central part of their task."[22]

In a similar vein, Jürgen Habermas recognizes that religious belief is more than the and acceptance of a set of doctrines and concepts but rather a "source of energy that the person who has a faith taps performativity and thus nurtures his or her entire life."[23] Religious belief—specifically here, Christian belief—influences, drives, and motivates their thought and action in all aspects of their life. While it is certainly *not* the case that an atheist or agnostic is therefore more objective than a believer, it is only the case of the believer that is being presented here. The belief in Christianity, then, pervades the lived life of the Christian believer. It is not an outer garment, but rather a part of the body.

---

19. Hyland, "Authority and Invisibility," 1093.
20. Hyland, "Humble Servants," 209.
21. Plantinga, "Advice to Christian Philosophers," 255.
22. Plantinga, "Advice to Christian Philosophers," 255.
23. Habermas, "Religion in the Public Sphere," 8. See also discussion in chapter 2.

Implications for Practice-led Research

There are important conclusions to be drawn from this discussion for practice-led researchers. Firstly, the practice of the Christian researcher is influenced by their belief. While this is certainly true of anyone that actively believes or disbelieves anything, the concern here is for the Christian researcher. As such, positional statements of the researcher are important. Secondly, it is clear that there is a close connection between the practice of the researcher and the investigative process. The research question may have arisen out of issues noticed in the researcher's practice, and further, may be a question that is only seen in practice. For these reasons, it should be expected that their presence be manifest in their reporting. Attempts to remove their presence are artificial and, to a degree, deceptive.

However, there is an important balance to be maintained: the research is not only focused on the personal aspects, but neither should the researcher attempt to return to a wholly objective point-of-view, one that is ultimately unachievable. McNamara suggests a number of rules that should guide practice-led researchers:

> *Rule 1: Eliminate—or at the very least, limit—the use of the first person pronoun, "I," as a centrepiece of a research formulation.*
>
> When writing an exegesis or thesis, practice-led researchers should monitor whether whole passages are becoming over-reliant on the use of "I." Whenever this occurs, it is more than likely that the research topic is becoming blurred or lost entirely.[24]

McNamara's caution that personal experience should be avoided in the research formulation is certainly wise. The research question, as argued in chapter 5, should be one that is answerable in multiple languages—through written language and that of the researcher's practice. A useful extension to the nature of the research question would be that it should be formulated in a way that might allow another researcher to pursue the question through their own practice, or potentially, through a different practice. This would help to address McNamara's concern.

---

24. McNamara, "Six Rules," 5.

Application: Preparation and Assessment

McNamara is also concerned with the over-reliance on the use of "I." It is worth noting that *over-reliance* is not an empirical term but a subjective one and may largely depend only on the reader. However, his concern is legitimate when considered in light of what he sees as artists shifting from the "quasi-confessional mode of the artist statement to a research model that requires a critical reflection involving the communication of the contribution to knowledge and its findings."[25] These are indeed two different styles with quite different purposes, and McNamara is correct in distinguishing them. However, it is not therefore a requirement to limit all use of personal pronouns. The corpus studies discussed earlier indicate that this is not actually the case in academic disciplines. McNamara's second rule is as follows:

> *Rule 2: Avoid recourse to one's own experience as the basis or justification of the research ambition.*
>
> Should the goal of PLR be to make sense of a practitioner's own life or experience? (I've actually seen this written as a goal and outcome of PLR.) Sorry, but the answer is "no"![26]

This issue was touched on in chapter 4 where it was suggested that practice-led research should not be merely a record of a personal journey. It must make some contribution to knowledge for the benefit of the wider discipline. This is in line with McNamara's concern that research "should be to explain something of significance and of broader relevance to a research community; this may be a larger, cross-disciplinary research community, or it may be a wider public audience."[27]

A balance must be maintained and there is a fine line between practice and personal experience. McNamara is concerned with "candidates who do not have an established body of practice to draw and reflect upon" and complains of the "recourse to the experiential."[28] However, practice is a part of the research process and the output—this point was outlined in detail in chapter 4. Certainly, this problem would be aggravated by the lack of a solid definition of practice-led research.

25. McNamara, "Six Rules," 5.
26. McNamara, "Six Rules," 6.
27. McNamara, "Six Rules," 6.
28. McNamara, "Six Rules," 6.

This is not to say that an individual's personal situation should somehow be ignored in the research process as it can be appropriate to draw on the personal experience of the individual practice as a part of the research process.

Students are often encouraged to include "process traces or ephemera" in their final submission material.[29] These documents include journal entries, preliminary notes, sketches, drafts and so on. The purpose for the inclusion of this material is to "indicate the directions/decision-making of the research journey."[30] This idea is especially characteristic of the *commentary model* discussed in the previous chapter. In this model, the "exegesis is conceived as an explication of, or comment on, the creative production."[31] However, the model adopted in this book is the research-question model where a question is formulated and answered in multiple languages—text and one related to the researcher's practice. Does this sort of material still have a role? In answering this question, it is valuable to tie it to the idea of the literature review.

In his general introduction to qualitative research, David Silverman draws on the work of others and offers two tables summarizing what a methodology chapter should contain. The first describes ways research should be documented transparently:

> Give an honest account of the conduct of the research;
>
> Provide full descriptions of what was actually done in regard to choosing case(s) to study, choosing your method(s), collecting and analyzing data;
>
> Explain and justify each of your decisions;
>
> Discuss the strengths and weaknesses of what you did;
>
> Be open about what helped you and held you back.[32]

The second table suggests that a methodology chapter answer four questions:

29. Phillips et al., *Dancing between Diversity and Consistency*, 6.
30. Phillips et al., *Dancing between Diversity and Consistency*, 6.
31. Milech and Schilo, "'Exit Jesus,'" 5.
32. Silverman, *Doing Qualitative Research*, 333.

Application: Preparation and Assessment

> How did you go about your research?
>
> What overall strategy did you adopt, and why?
>
> What design and techniques did you use?
>
> Why these and not others?[33]

Silverman suggests that student researchers do keep a diary or field notes of their ideas, hopes and worries to use in an edited form for a "natural history chapter," a section he places within the methodology chapter.[34] This section addresses aspects of the objects of the methodology chapter expressed in the two tables and addresses issues such as the following:

> the personal context of their research topic;
>
> the reasons for their research design;
>
> how they developed their research through trial and error;
>
> the methodological lessons they learned.[35]

This approach allows readers to engage with the researcher's thinking during the process and "are in a far better position to assess the degree to which you were self-critical."[36] This approach helps make visible key decisions in the research process.

In a practice-led research project, this process includes more than the review of printed literature—books, journal articles and theses. It "extends beyond the reading of texts to the engagement with the work of other practitioners."[37] One approach highlighted by Haseman is the "artistic audit."[38] This approach highlights the need of the researcher to "reach beyond their own labors to connect with both earlier and contemporaneous productions which contribute to the overall research context for their work."[39] This linking of past practice with the

---

33. Silverman, *Doing Qualitative Research*, 334.
34. Silverman, *Doing Qualitative Research*, 40, 334.
35. Silverman, *Doing Qualitative Research*, 335.
36. Silverman, *Doing Qualitative Research*, 336.
37. Barrett and Bolt, *Practice as Research*, 188.
38. Haseman, "Manifesto," 105.
39. Haseman, "Manifesto," 105.

researcher's current approach requires some self-awareness and this data may be appropriate to include, again, only where it is in support of the research question.

In a comment in the same vein as McNamara, Silverman makes clear that this does not mean "anything goes" and that readers will "not want to hear needlessly and endlessly about how your personal life impinged upon the process of obtaining your degree!"[40] In the context of the model adopted in this book, the volume of this type of material needs to be monitored and should be included insofar as it supports and enhances the answering and clarification of the research question. While Silverman restricts this information largely to the methodology chapter, in the case of practice-led research projects, it would certainly be appropriate to include this information at other key points in the exegesis, but again, only insofar as it supports and enhances the answering and clarification of the research question.

THE DOCUMENTATION OF PRACTICE-LED RESEARCH

It was argued in chapter 4 that a key element of all research is the need to document and disseminate the conclusions of the research process. This need presents some particular challenges for some types of practice-led projects.

The traditional thesis is bound and laid out in a particular way as set by the institution. Guidelines typically describe page size, border, line spacing, font size and/or type, the style of binding for examination and then for archiving, order of sections (title page, contents, abstract and so on) and various other stipulations. The institution of my PhD,, University of Notre Dame, Australia, lays out their requirements in "Guideline: Thesis by Publication."[41] The Guideline document states the candidate should make sure that high-quality white bond paper of international A4 size be used for all pages of your work with the following format:

- Print on one side of the paper only
- Left margin must be 4.0 cm wide

---

40. Silverman, *Doing Qualitative Research*, 336.
41. "Guideline."

Application: Preparation and Assessment

- Right, top and bottom must be 2.5 cm wide . . .
- Page numbers should appear at the bottom of each page . . .[42]

Importantly, the traditional thesis is presented in its entirety to the examiners and can be read at any time, chapter by chapter, indexed, paged forward and back, and previous sections read again.

The exegesis in practice-led research often also conforms to these sorts of requirements. For example, the University of Canberra's *Gold Book* makes no distinction between the formatting requirements of a thesis that does or does not have a creative component.[43] Curtin University also has one document that applies to all theses, *Preparing and Presenting a Research Thesis for Examination*.[44] What is broadly true of the traditional thesis is also true of the exegesis: it can be read at any time, paged through and re-read.

However, in addition to the exegesis, the practice-led research project will usually be accompanied by a creative component of some form. The two institutions mentioned in the previous paragraph have additional guidelines that apply to these situations. University of Canberra's Gold Book has an additional section while Curtin has a separate document for creative production theses, *Guidelines for Creative Production Theses*.[45]

Creative works are generally presented in the form that is most characteristic of them. So, for example, paintings and sculptures are shown in galleries and other presentation spaces, and often have a public exhibition also. A play or dance piece might be held in a theatre, or playhouse. While creative writing is usually presented as a part of the printed thesis, poetry may also include a recital in front of an audience. The general principle applies to all forms, however: the final examinable material is presented in a way that is usual for its display/performance.

The consequence is that those tasked with examining the work "need to experience them in direct (copresence) or indirect

---

42. "Guideline." Having cited this document, there is now no excuse for me not to get it right.
43. "Higher Degrees by Research," 14.
44. "Preparing and Presenting a Research Thesis."
45. "Guidelines for Thesis Preparation and Submission."

(asynchronous, recorded) form."[46] This means that the examiner ideally would attend the performance or exhibition and engage as the researcher intended for participants.

However, as with all research, a permanent record needs to be made so that the research is available to others for analysis, use, and reference and the personal attendance of the examiner may not always be possible. Therefore, other means must be found:

> Where a written thesis is accompanied by supplementary non-print material such as three dimensional objects, sound/video recordings, computer disks, paintings, maps, plans, etc., the supplementary material will need to be reproduced in a form suitable for storage and retrieval purposes and must be suitably packaged. Photographic representation, photo reduction, microforms, etc. should be used where appropriate.[47]

Curtin University makes a number of recommendations for the thesis (although there seems to be a clear expectation that the examiner will attend any performance or exhibition personally). For the permanent record of the production thesis, the university states that it "should use technologies appropriate to the field of study. Such material must be presented in a stable and commonly accepted format."[48] The guidelines say that "[p]ermanent records of a performance/exhibition element of a creative production thesis should be comprised of a CD/DVD compilation of a video, audio or digital recording of a performance or exhibition, or a combination of these; in some instances a professional exhibition catalogue may be an alternative." This is also done in a way that is most characteristic of the form. A musical performance would have an audio recording made (video may also be appropriate). Photographs of 2D and 3D works would be made and possibly a video recording of the exhibition. Video recordings would also be made of other performance arts such as dance.

Some of these methods could be adapted directly to faith-led pieces. Religious music, poetry, plays as well as 2D and 3D art forms

---

46. Haseman, "Manifesto," 101.
47. "Higher Degrees by Research," 15.
48. "Guidelines for Thesis Preparation and Submission," 3.

could all be performed and recorded in the same way. Differences may arise in the location of performances. For example, in the case of iconography, the most relevant place of display may be in a church instead of a gallery. Research centred on worship may need multiple methods for archival. Since worship contains visual and audio elements and involves (often) both performers and the congregation, audio-video recordings may need to be supplemented with photographs of individual elements.

It is important that the process of preservation is not seen as secondary or a merely an administrative burden. Two reasons are readily apparent. The first is that research is intended to be available to others to build on, critique, analyze and so on. Therefore, all parts of the research need to be available to future researchers. The second reason flows from this. The model developed in the previous chapters argues that a research question is answered in multiple ways. If the performance or artefact is not preserved or done so poorly, the result will be that only a part of the answer will be readily available—the exegesis—and so the project will be incomplete.

ASSESSMENT OF PRACTICE-LED RESEARCH PROJECTS

Webb, Brien, and Burr observe how it is "widely acknowledged that not much is known about the actual process of examination of doctoral dissertations."[49] They observe that "the variation across programs and universities is potentially damaging to scholarly rigor and consistency in the field, and yet the differences between art forms and disciplines areas should be preserved" and that "there is insufficient support given to examiners, training in examination, or awareness of standards in examination practice."[50]

However, they also found that there was some resistance to the idea of standards for the practice doctorate: "This idea of a criteria rubric for the examination of doctoral theses was perhaps the most contentious issue we raised with participants of the project. The first response of virtually all those involved was that 'standards equals standardization,'

---

49. Webb et al., "Examination of Doctoral Degrees," 30.
50. Webb et al., "Examination of Doctoral Degrees," 6.

and standardization is the death of art."⁵¹ This raises a number of issues; some have been dealt with elsewhere in this book. Firstly, that art is somehow exempt from scrutiny and accountability. One obvious concern is the conflation of *standards* with *standardization*—they are not the same concept. Standards do not automatically proscribe a format for all art. It is *not* the case that all art is the subject of standards nor is it that art in the context of practice-led research is to be the subject of a standard rubric.⁵² Rather it is that the project as a whole is to be guided by certain criteria as is the case with all postgraduate research in all disciplines.

It is true that the very nature of a practice-led research project present additional challenges in the area of examination. Part of this challenge relates to the poorly defined nature of the methodology: it is difficult to give guidance to an examiner when it is not clear what form a project should take and what it is supposed to achieve.

This is reflected in some of the guidelines offered to examiners by institutions supporting practice-led research degrees. From the two institutions used as examples earlier in this chapter, University of Canberra offers the following information in their general guidelines on a creative production thesis:

a. the creative component must be prepared during the period of candidature;

b. where a creative thesis is produced, the candidate will also provide an exegetical component of at least 30,000 words that operates in a symbiotic relationship with the creative work;

c. the exegesis and creative work may be integrated; and

d. the academic rigor of the exegesis is critical to determining whether the thesis meets the requirements of the research degree.⁵³

---

51. Webb et al., "Examination of Doctoral Degrees," 44.

52. See the discussion on the difference between creative practice and creative practice as a part of practice-led research in chapter 4.

53. "Higher Degrees by Research," 30.

Application: Preparation and Assessment

While these guidelines suggest that academic rigour of the exegesis is critical, what this exegesis is supposed to achieve or say is unclear. That the guidelines comment on the importance of the exegesis suggests examiners have been overemphasizing the creative component, something Webb, Brien, and Burr found to be characteristic of less experienced examiners.[54]

Curtin University has a research question model[55] and provides the following advice to examiners: "In some disciplines, such as the creative arts, the thesis may instead take the form of a literary work (or works), or exhibition or performance accompanied by an exegesis which addresses and elucidates the research question that motivates the thesis as a whole. The creative work(s) and exegesis will be examined as an integrated whole."[56] While this guideline provides some information on the project as a whole, there is still little real guidance to an examiner.

In their report, *Examination of Doctoral Degrees in Creative Arts: Process, Practice and Standards* Webb, Brien and Burr compiled a list of questions examiners ask of a thesis. This list was based on discussions and focus groups with examiners.[57] These questions were presented as recommendations to examiners in a booklet published as a result of their research:[58]

1. Does it offer an original contribution to knowledge in the field?
2. Does the thesis as a whole satisfy external needs as well as personal outcomes (that is, advances knowledge and not just practice)?
3. Is the work as a whole scholarly, coherent and rigorous? Is there a thorough literature review that engages key and seminal works, and traces the line of thought across the topic area?

---

54. Webb et al., "Examination of Doctoral Degrees," 35.
55. This book draws on the same research that provided the basis for Curtin's model: Milech and Schilo, "'Exit Jesus.'"
56. "Advice for Examiners," 1.
57. Webb et al., "Examination of Doctoral Degrees," 34.
58. Webb et al., "Examining Doctorates in the Creative Arts," 6.

4. Is there a contextual review that accounts for key works in the same art form and topic area?
5. Does the artwork show innovation, a line of argument, technical expertise?
6. Is there a synthesis between the artwork and the essay?
7. Does the essay use a vocabulary appropriate to the art form?
8. Is the written work free of typographical and grammatical errors?

Due to the usefulness of this set of questions to examiners, they will be adapted for the model proposed in this book. There are two issues with the questions that need to be addressed. The first relates to their specific focus on the presence of an *artwork*. This concern can be addressed by adjusting the wording of some of the questions (attempted in the following section). The second issue relates to the apparent assumption that students will be using a primarily contextual/commentary model. This is especially apparent in the wording of questions (2), (4), and (5).

With these notes in mind, the following is a suggested set of revised questions:

1. Does it offer an original contribution to knowledge in the field?
2. Is the work as a whole scholarly, coherent and rigorous?
3. Does the practice component show innovation, a line of argument, technical expertise?
4. Is there a thorough literature review that engages key and seminal works, from both the published literature and the researcher's practice?
5. Do the practice and the exegesis both address the research question(s)? Is there a synthesis between the practice and the essay?
6. Is the written work free of typographical and grammatical errors?

Application: Preparation and Assessment

Question 1 is unchanged from the initial questions as it is an expectation of all doctorates that they make some original contribution to the field they are in, that they advance their topic area in some way.

Question 2 relates to issues of the clarity of the argument, soundness of the logic and careful analysis. The question is intended to apply to the project as a whole, but as there is a separate question relating to the practice component (question 3) it may also be used to apply to the written exegesis as well. Mullins and Kiley interviewed a range of experienced examiners in 2002 and found that the "development of a well-structured argument was highly valued in a thesis" by examiners.[59] When examiners ask this question of a thesis, what they were looking for included "argument, conceptualization, conclusion, design, logic and structure."[60] Examiners also used the term "scholarship" which was "described by interviewees from all disciplines as originality, coherence, and a sense of student autonomy or independence."[61] This question also incorporates the vocabulary question from the initial set: does the thesis use language appropriate to the discipline in which the researcher works. This is a part of the researcher's *scholarship*.

In a sense, question 3 might be thought of as a subset of question 2. However, due to the centrality of practice in this mode of research, it is essential that the practice of the individual and the output of that practice be assessed in its own right and not as a secondary aspect.

Question 4 has been separated from its initial inclusion in question 3. The reason for this is to emphasize that a review contains two separate tasks. Firstly, there is the standard literature review. In a review of examiners' expectations of the literature review, Holbrook et al. suggest there are four aspects: coverage, demonstrating a working understanding, critical appraisal of the literature and the connection made to the researcher's findings and argument.[62] Silverman offers four pieces of advice: show respect for the literature, be focused and critical, avoid mere description and write it up after your other

---

59. Mullins and Kiley, "It's a PhD, Not a Nobel Prize," 379.
60. Mullins and Kiley, "It's a PhD, Not a Nobel Prize," 379.
61. Mullins and Kiley, "It's a PhD, Not a Nobel Prize," 379.
62. Holbrook et al., "Examiner Comment," 353.

chapters.⁶³ More information on the literature review and alternatives was discussed earlier in this chapter.

Question 5 is one that is central to the model proposed in chapter 5 and is related to question 2. Both the exegesis/written component and the creative/practice components need to address the research question. However, they are not independent of each other and must relate. This was discussed at length in chapter 5.

Although the selection of examiners is an issue between the candidate, the supervisor and the institution, one suggestion in this area is that as the practice-led project is an exercise in research and practice, an examiner should ideally be both an academic and a practitioner in the relevant discipline. This was noted in the Webb, Brien and Burr report. Experienced examiners suggested that it be required for "all examiners to be practitioners in the art field being examined, and also to be academics, and not solely commercial/practice-based."⁶⁴

CONCLUSION

The goal of this chapter has been to attend to issues of a practical nature related to practice-led research projects. These have ranged from the difficult issue of researcher presence in projects and the documentation and preservation of these projects to suggestions on the process of examination, especially where it may differ from the traditional thesis.

Chapters 5–6 have dealt with theoretical and practical issues relating to the implementation of a successful practice-led research project in theology (and, it is hoped, other disciplines as well). The following chapter combines these principles along with the definitional work of chapter 4 into an example proposal for an imagined prospective candidate in theology.

---

63. Silverman, *Doing Qualitative Research*, 323.
64. Webb et al., "Examination of Doctoral Degrees," 47.

Chapter 8

Application

A Project Proposal

INTRODUCTION

THE BROAD OBJECTIVE OF the book up to this point has been to provide the theoretical and historical underpinnings of practice-led research. It has also attempted to present how and why it can and should be used as a method for theological research. A brief review of the key points of the previous chapters will prove helpful.

Chapter 3 presented the historical triggers that led to the development of practice-led research in the academy. It argued that it presents the art practitioner and the faith practitioner with an opportunity to do academic research without abandoning or somehow ignoring their art or faith practice. The chapter also argued that there has long been a close relationship between theology and the creative disciplines—sometimes one of engagement and sometimes one of proscription.

Chapter 4 then presented an understanding of what research means in the academic environment. It also outlined the regulatory frameworks from the government and universities that guide research. It demonstrated that the methodology fits the criteria as academic research and is therefore a legitimate avenue of research. The institutional examples indicated that many institutions have already come to this conclusion. The chapter developed a comprehensive definition of practice-led research that incorporated the key elements of research, aimed to be rigorous while also trying to maintain the flexibility of the methodology.

Chapter 5 then outlined a model for doing practice-led research. The model is based on a research question guiding and integrating theoretical and practice-based answers to that question. It argued that a practice-led project answers the research questions in the different languages of the research, one text-based and the other in the language of the individual's practice.

The aim of this chapter is to combine all the theoretical discussions from previous chapters and present an extended worked example or case study of a practice-led research project undertaken in a theological context. It is important to note that this example was invented. However, it attempts to combine the existing processes and outcomes of practice-led researchers and then imagines in a theological context what is possible based on what has been examined in previous chapters of this book.

In order to explore in a theological context as many elements of how practice-led research might be conducted, the example will take the form of an abbreviated *research proposal* and will be presented with the typical headings that such proposals would have.[1] It will consist of an abstract, an overview containing the topic, research questions, potential significance, possible limitations and important literature that might be considered. This will follow with a discussion of how the methodology might work in the situation and any ethical considerations as appropriate. The study will conclude with any additional considerations, such a budget or timeline issues.

Two important points need to be highlighted. Firstly, the proposal is intended to be self-contained, that is, how a proposal might be seen in the field. Therefore, while the proposal is grounded in and draws on the conclusions of the thesis, it will not refer directly to it. Secondly, the proposal format requires the discussion and review of various theological debates as well as ideas and processes related to the particular practice under examination. Therefore, what is presented in the case

---

1. For convenience, the format I have selected is from my my original study institution, The University of Notre Dame, Australia.

Application: A Project Proposal

study is meant to be accurate and is intended to consider key aspects of the issue in question. Further, it has been constructed within the philosophical and theological framework outlined in chapter 2.

It is important to note, then, that the chief purpose of the theological and other discussions in the following example is to provide grounding and context for the framing of a practice-led research project so that the model and process may become clear. Those discussions are not to be understood as comprehensive or definitive; other views are certainly possible and a full research project would bring those out. They have been consciously constructed to frame a practice-led project.

Practice-Led Theology

VISUALIZING THE DIVINE: CONTEMPORARY TRINITARIAN LANGUAGE AND THE PRACTICE OF ICONOGRAPHY

Abstract

This project will explore the ways in which iconography reflects, informs and/or influences Trinitarian discussions in modern Christian theology. The project will begin with an investigation of the 1410 icon by Andrei Rublev, *Trinity*. The project will further develop this idea by creating a series of new icons that visually interrogate contemporary Trinitarian discussions.

Introduction

Christian icons are more than stylized representations of God and saints. The Second Council of Nicaea in 787 concluded that the contemplation of icons leads the "beholders to be aroused to recollect the originals and to long after them, and to pay to the images the tribute of an embrace and a reverence of honor, not to pay to them the actual worship"—which is proper only to the divine nature—for "the honor paid to the image passes to its original, and he that adores an image adores in it the person depicted thereby."[2] In the same vein, Cornelia Tsakiridou writes of a type of Orthodox image that "embodies and realizes deified existence aesthetically."[3] These icons bring the image they depict in to "a state of temporal realization, as if in showing it they are bringing it into existence and keeping it alive and present in time" and that looking at them, "we have the sense that we are in the presence of something actual and alive."[4] Icons, then, are not a focus of worship, but rather a conduit of worship, a way of focusing contemplation.

Topic and Purpose

Many considered the Trinity to be "beyond all depiction" in any way through art even to the point that Augustine of Hippo "forbade any

---

2. Bettenson and Maunder, *Documents*, 103.
3. Tsakiridou, *Icons in Time*, 8.
4. Tsakiridou, *Icons in Time*, 4.

Application: A Project Proposal

attempts to picture the Trinity, symbolic or anthropomorphic."[5] However, artists still attempted to visualize the Trinity and numerous styles have been developed (discussed in a later section).

It is the argument of this project that how the Trinity is understood in the popular mind as well as in theological discussions will have some impact on the way the Trinity or individual persons of the Trinity will be portrayed in the creative arts. Many of the theological approaches discussed produce art that is grounded in that understanding of the world.

Through a practice-led research methodology, this project will explore some implications of contemporary Trinitarian discussions and their impact on iconography. It will investigate how theological debates have influenced the writing of icons in the past and, through the writing of new icons, how the contemporary theological discussions on the language used to describe the Trinity, might be employed in the creation of contemporary Christian icons.

Potential Significance

A potential area significance of this research lies in is how the contemporary language used when discussing the Trinity influences the understanding of the Trinity when the language is translated into visual images. Although this project is only exploring iconography, it will attempt to reveal some ways in which these views may restrict or enable images of the Trinity, whether they might be understood as better or richer or fuller, or additional and expansive of how the Trinity might be understood.

Another area of significance will be in the visual exploration of contemporary Trinitarian language as a type of both the church and human relationships through the particular formalized processes of icon making. Aspects of the project may also contribute to discussion on the changing depiction of the Trinity in art reflecting the discussions of the nature of the Trinity in theology. As well as a link to contemporary discussions on the nature of the church as *ekklesia*, as a relational community, the Trinity can be seen as a kind of prototype, or model.

---

5. McGinn, "Theologians as Trinitarian Iconographers," 186.

Practice-Led Theology

Research Questions

The following three research questions will be explored in this project:

- To what extent and in what ways might contemporary theological conceptions of the Trinity be portrayed in Christian iconography?
- In what ways can the terms used to describe the members of the Trinity in contemporary theological discussions be portrayed visually in the modes of iconography?
- What impact do visual interpretations of contemporary Trinitarian conceptions have on a believer's understanding of the Trinity?

Limitations

As the literature review below will reveal, there is a large and rich debate on the nature and description of the Trinity. Only a very limited number of contemporary Trinitarian conceptualizations will be able to be explored within the limits of this project. Early research will need to determine what may prove to be the most fruitful. The probable approach will be to restrict the work to the most contemporary Trinitarian formulations. Suggestions for further research may be able to investigate other images or use other creative approaches.

Theoretical Perspective

There are two foundational components to this project. The first is that it is *Christian*. What is meant here is not generic Christianity but one that firstly holds to early creedal affirmations such as the Nicene-Constantinopolitan creed and secondly of a liturgical nature, accepting the importance and role of icons in worship.[6]

This project is theoretically grounded in *critical realism*. According to Andrew Wright, there are three components to this view. He writes, critical realism

---

6. It is not necessary in this proposal to go into detail on the debates surrounding the use of icons or their role as objects of veneration. These issues can be examined as appropriate in the thesis itself. This is also the case for other issues mentioned in the following such as the *filioque* controversy.

Application: A Project Proposal

seeks to map a path beyond the extremes of modern certainty and postmodern s[k]epticism via a triumvirate of core philosophical principles: ontological realism, epistemic relativism and jud[g]mental rationality. Ontological realism asserts that reality exists for the most part independently of human perception, epistemic relativism asserts that our knowledge of reality is limited and contingent, and jud[g]mental rationality asserts that it is nevertheless possible to judge between conflicting truth claims while recognizing that all such judgments necessarily remain open to further adjudication.[7]

Wright's "triumvirate" has specific implications for this project. Firstly, God and the universe are ultimately independent of humanity. "The reality of God," according to Williams, "is the fundamental fact. *God is.* This is the basis of everything else."[8] The reality of the *material* world would be obviously true in this view, but the Christian perspective of this project also holds it to be true of the *spiritual* world.

Secondly, while the ability of the individual to know God and the world is impacted in varying degrees by our cultural, historical and many other circumstances as well as our sin and human imperfection, it is still possible to draw probable conclusions on truth claims, recognizing they are, to a degree, provisional. Icons are conscious stylized representations of ontological spiritual realities.

Literature Review

This section will first look at some theological issues relating to the Trinity and then will look at the depiction of the Trinity in icons.

Theological Issues

Although the doctrine of the Trinity was largely worked out in the early centuries of the church, it was largely the case that after the *filioque* controversy of the Eleventh Century, other issues occupied the mind of the church resulting in limited discussion of the Trinity.[9] Discussion

---

7. Wright, *Christianity and Critical Realism*, 9.
8. Williams, *Renewal Theology*, 1:47 (italics original).
9. Grenz, *Theology for the Community of God*, 63.

of the Trinity receded from the arena of academic focus. This neglect reached its culmination in the work of Schleiermacher, the father of liberal theology, who relegated discussion of the Trinity to the conclusion of *The Christian Faith*. He claimed the doctrine was in need of a complete review and needed only be dealt with after other points of doctrine.[10]

However, the Twentieth Century saw a resurgence of theological interest in the Trinity, most notably with the work of Karl Barth.[11] Grenz argues that in Barth's *Church Dogmatics*, the doctrine of the Trinity acts as a "type of prolegomenon" and forms the basis "from which his systematic theology flows."[12] Revelation is a Trinitarian event and consists of three "moments," namely, *Revealer*, *Revelation*, and *Revealedness*, corresponding to Father, Son and Holy Spirit.[13] Already in Barth, there is alternative language for the three persons of the Trinity.

Later, other theologians have done important work on the Trinity including Karl Rahner, Jürgen Moltmann, and Wolfhart Pannenburg.[14] For example, McGrath notes the contribution provided by the thought of Rahner on the relationship between the "economic Trinity" and the "immanent Trinity." The economic Trinity describes the "way in which we experience the diversity and unity of God's self-disclosure in history" while the immanent Trinity describes "God's diversity and unity as it is in God." [15] McGrath describes this as a corrective to an overemphasis on the immanent Trinity to the disregard of the relationship between God and humans. Icons stand at the interface of this relationship and may be able to contribute to both aspects of this view of the Trinity.

As a reformulation of the liberal tradition[16], process theology has tried to respond to some of the issues present in modern theology. Daniel Migliore summarizes some of these relating to the doctrine of God. A longstanding criticism since the Enlightenment is the idea that "God

---

10. Schleiermacher, *Christian Faith*, 2:749.
11. Grenz, *Theology for the Community of God*, 64.
12. Grenz, *Theology for the Community of God*, 64.
13. Grenz, *Theology for the Community of God*, 65.
14. Grenz, *Theology for the Community of God*, 65.
15. McGrath, *Christian Theology*, 336.
16. Grenz and Olson, *20th-Century Theology*, 113.

Application: A Project Proposal

and human freedom are incompatible."[17] An extension of this idea is the notion that religious belief and the very idea of God is somehow irrational.[18] According to Migliore, in a post-holocaust age, questions are raised about the presence of God in history and seem to encourage the idea that God is indeed dead,[19] or at the very least, irrelevant.

Originally based on the process philosophy of Alfred North Whitehead, process theologians have argued that traditional doctrines view God as unaffected by events and sees God as treating the world unilaterally and coercively.[20] The traditional view is thought by these thinkers as "utterly incompatible with the modern experience of reality as dynamic, processive, and relational."[21] The approach of these thinkers is to view God as a "participant in the temporal process."[22] That is, God is "continually adding to himself all the experiences that happen anywhere in the universe, and thus God is continually changing;" God is "truly affected by these actions and the being of God changes."[23]

What is of particular interest to this project is the nature of the language used by process theologians. For example, Grenz and Olsen cite process theologians saying that "antiquated concepts of God" include the Cosmic Moralist, the Unchanging and Passionate Absolute, the Controlling Power, and the Sanctioner of the Status Quo.[24] By rejecting these terms and emphasizing God as "persuasive, not coercive" and as "Lover God ... the fellow-sufferer who understands" in Whitehead's words humans may become "co-creators" and "fellow-workers" (a term borrowed from St. Paul) in "the great cosmic adventure."[25]

---

17. Migliore, *Faith Seeking Understanding*, 64.

18. There are numerous Christian theologians and philosophers arguing for the coherence of the concepts involved. An excellent and concise article on the topic is Taliaferro and Marty, "Coherence of Theism."

19. Migliore, *Faith Seeking Understanding*, 65.

20. Migliore, *Faith Seeking Understanding*, 65.

21. Migliore, *Faith Seeking Understanding*, 65.

22. Grenz and Olson, *20th-Century Theology*, 131.

23. Grudem, *Systematic Theology*, 166.

24. Grenz and Olson, *20th-Century Theology*, 131.

25. Pittenger, "Process Thought," 116.

While the so-called "antiquated" language is a caricature of the position the process theologians reject,[26] and the modern alternative is over-reliant on philosophical formulations, it is clear that both views lend themselves to creative visual symbolism. Further, process theology generally rejects the authority of the Bible as revelation and suggests that there are "universally experienced prereflective elements" that, according to Whitehead, "constitute the ultimate religious experience."[27] It may be only through the creative arts that these experiences can be expressed.

A collection of theological views developed in the late 1960s broadly fit under the rubric of liberation theologies. These views reject the intellectualism of theological debates and argue that if God is real "then this God must be involved in the struggles of the present to bring about liberation from oppression."[28] For example, Black theology was not so much concerned with how God could be made "palatable to the modern mindset" as this was not seen as an issue in their community, but rather "to harness the biblical imagery for the goal of the advancement of the Black community."[29]

In a liberation theology "one commits oneself to the transformation of society on behalf of and along with the oppressed."[30] It is the experience of the oppressed people that is the starting point and focus of theological action and reflection and, as a result, there exist multiple liberation theologies. Of particular relevance to this project is the work of feminist theology. Here, the experience of women is the starting point. Hannah Bacon describes the problem this way: "'Father-Son' language, it has been suggested, presents an exclusively male view of God which leads to an understanding of the Trinity as two males and a bird ('bird' here referring to the winged animal, usually a dove, or the token presence of a stereotypically 'feminine' dimension), or as

---

26. See for example critiques in Grenz and Olson, *20th-Century Theology*, 142–44. See also Grudem, *Systematic Theology*, 166–67. The remainder of Grudem's chapter addresses some of the issues of process thought indirectly.

27. Smith, *Handbook of Contemporary Theology*, 155.

28. Grenz and Olson, *20th-Century Theology*, 201.

29. Grenz and Olson, *20th-Century Theology*, 202.

30. Smith, *Handbook of Contemporary Theology*, 204.

Application: A Project Proposal

two males and an amorphous third."[31] There have been a number of suggested alternative formulations for Trinitarian language. Elizabeth Johnson uses "Spirit-Sophia, Jesus-Sophia, and Mother-Sophia" and moves to "She Who Is."[32] Kathryn Greene-McCreight summarizes a number of other possibilities: "Others use Creator, Redeemer, Sustainer, still others Source, Offspring, Wellspring; Abba Servant Paraclete; Mother, Lover, Friend; and Father, Son, Holy Spirit: One God, Mother of Us All." The adoption of any of these formulas will have an impact on how an icon might be rendered and the symbolism used as well as the connection to the divine an individual might make through it.

Another question that may need closer examination is raised by Sallie McFague. Her suggestion of Mother, Lover, Friend raises the issue of whether personal metaphors are needed at all. Her conclusion is that they are valuable and offers a number of reasons including the observation that personal models are the only ones we know "from the inside" and that they allow for a recognition of personal agency and so "reflect a view of God's activity in the world."[33] Questions of the personal nature of an icon will need to be investigated.

Further to these discussions on language used to describe the Trinity is a growing understanding of the relational and communal nature of the Trinity internally and with the church especially. For example Graham Buxton uses the Greek term *perichoresis* to describe the Trinity as a "relationship of mutual indwelling."[34] This relationship is dynamic: "Just as the three persons of the Trinity interact with creative and recreative energy, ever gracious in their perichoretic dance of life, so all who are caught up in this life engage in the same liberating dance in the power of the Spirit."[35] The Trinity is dynamic and relational and this aspect might be effectively expressed in icons.

---

31. Bacon, *What's Right with the Trinity?* 1.
32. Greene-McCreight, "Feminist Theology," 104.
33. McFague, *Models of God*, 82, 83.
34. Buxton, *Dancing in the Dark*, 19.
35. Buxton, *Dancing in the Dark*, 57.

The Trinity in Icons

Christians have long attempted to render visible things in order that the "invisible attributes—and the saving design—of God" are shown forth.[36] This has been through visual interpretations of the members of the Trinity or through other ways such as geometric or other abstract means. McGinn notes that some scriptural support exists as Jesus took on flesh (and so became visible) in the Incarnation and the Holy Spirit is depicted in the form of fire and a dove.[37] Indeed, Christ is the *image of the invisible God* as Paul puts in in Col 1:15. Another style is the *Ancient of Days* from Dan 7. It includes God the Father represented as a hand in the sky or as an old man, with Jesus and the Holy Spirit as a dove flying above.

Another version, appearing in the fourth century is the *Philoxenia*, or the *Hospitality of Abraham*.[38] It is from the scene in Gen 18 where Abraham and Sarah host the three angels who visited them near the great trees of Mamre. These images clearly show a divine connection for the three figures (angels wings or the inclusion of the nimbus) and Abraham and Sarah frequently appear as well.

Although the project will contain some historical discussion on iconography, existing icons and the patterns of the past serve as inspiration and guidance for the project; they are a type of graphical reference point for the project. The discussion in the final exegesis may touch on the *acheropoietoi*, icons that were miraculously created. The existence of these icons seems to highlight the special nature of icons as somehow more than *just a painting* but reinforces the idea that they are a conduit to the divine.

---

36. Nichols, *Redeeming Beauty Soundings*, 18.
37. McGinn, "Theologians as Trinitarian Iconographers," 186.
38. McGinn, "Theologians as Trinitarian Iconographers," 186.

Application: A Project Proposal

Figure 5. *The Holy Trinity* or *Hospitality of Abraham*. Andrei Rublev (ca. 1410)

This style reached its apogee somewhere around 1410, when Nikon of Radonezh asked Andrei Rublev to paint icons for the Monastery of the Holy Trinity (Figure 5). The monastery had been rebuilt after its destruction by the Tatars in 1408. One of Rublev's works for this project is entitled *Trinity*. Although Rublev's teacher, Theophanes the Greek, had rendered the Trinity as three figures before (Figure 2), it is still very much linked to the original Genesis account with Sarah in the lower right, and Abraham in the left (now missing).[39] Rublev's icon was unique in that the three images were now not accompanied by Abraham or Sarah (Figure 6). It draws on the image of the Hospitality of Abraham but seems to be a more conscious depiction of the Trinity as three persons.

---

39. Tsakifidou, *Icons in Time*, 262.

Practice-Led Theology

Figure 6. *The Hospitality of Abraham.* Theophanes the Greek (ca. 1378)

Underlying Rublev's work was monastic *hesychasm*.[40] Hesychia, meaning stillness or silence, is a practice where one "arrests the passions and trains the senses to wait patiently for God to enter and awaken the heart."[41] Hesychasts' prayer technique consisted of "concentrating mind and body in silence."[42] The process involves concentrated breathing techniques as well as reciting internally or vocally *The Jesus Prayer*: "*Lord Jesus Christ, Son of God, have mercy on me, a sinner.*"

After long periods of deep prayer, hesychast's would report experiences of uncreated light and fire. For example the biographer of Sergius of Radonezh, the teacher and predecessor of Nikon of Radonezh, reports him having the following experience during one of his prayer vigils: "Responding to a voice calling him by name, Sergius opened the window of his cell whereupon 'a great light appeared from heaven and

---

40. Tsakifidou, *Icons in Time*, 258.
41. Tsakifidou, *Icons in Time*, 58.
42. Rojek, "Logic of Palamism," 4.

Application: A Project Proposal

drove away all darkness of the night, and the night was illuminated by this light which excelled by its brightness the light of day."[43]

St. Gregory Palamas (1296–1359) was a central figure in the debates and formulation of hesychasm. Palamas has been seen as equivalent in status as Aquinas is in the West.[44] One of his main opponents was Barlaam of Calabria. Some of these criticisms centred around the integral role of the body. It was argued by Barlaam "that since God remains essentially unknowable and inexperienceable, the reported light could not be divine."[45] He also ridiculed their particular breathing technique by describing them as the "people having their soul in their navel."[46] Eventually, Palamas's teachings were confirmed as official.[47]

In contemporary language, hesychastic practices are *embodied*. The truth of this is in part revealed by some of the criticisms brought against hesychasm. This approach to prayer and contemplation involves a profound link between the mind and the body. The process of writing of an icon also involves the deep spiritual engagement of the mind and the body in one prayerful and contemplative whole. It is not possible to separate the two and still create an icon–prayer and contemplation are integral to the process. To investigate the research questions, it will be necessary to adopt a methodology that permits these two elements to be present and still carries out academic research.

Design and Methodology

The construction of an icon is significantly more than the use of distinctive materials such as specially prepared boards and the use of gold leaf or following a set of proscribed patterns. The iconographer is intimately involved in the process. Icons cannot be created "by the sheer force of the will" of the iconographer, but rather by becoming "an instrument through which God can create something wonderful."[48]

---

43. Tsakifidou, *Icons in Time*, 259.
44. Rojek, "Logic of Palamism," 3.
45. Rojek, "Logic of Palamism," 4.
46. Meyendorff, "Is 'Hesychasm' the Right Word?" 448.
47. Rojek, "Logic of Palamism," 5.
48. Pearson, *Brush with God*, xiii.

The icon process is about learning "how to work in a way that carries you toward God."[49]

For these reasons, this research will be grounded in a *practice-led* methodology. I describe the methodology as one that "sources its strategies and processes for answering its research questions broadly from those *practices* that are characteristic of the discipline in which it is being employed."[50]

This approach is well suited to a project of this type as it provides a way for a single set of research questions to be answered through the language of the icons as well as in *conventional* written academic material. I understand practice in two ways as both what is "characteristic of the means of communication and production" of, in this case, icons, as well as actions that are "preferentially chosen and guided by an appropriate mode of thinking—an intelligence—with the end goal of answering a research question."[51] Iconography has a well-structured and standardized language of its own; a language that it uses to convey the gospel and the teachings of the church, one of an icon's key functions.[52] However, there are related—but equally important—practices such as prayer and fasting that are a part of the iconographer's broader practice. The specific skills of an iconographer can also be understood as being guided by a *spiritual* intelligence. Based on the work of Howard Gardner who argued that intelligence had been too narrowly viewed and that there are rather "several *relatively autonomous* human intellectual competencies" each of which is a part of the way individuals and cultures think and adapt.[53]

Emmons understands spiritual intelligence in a broad encompassing way as "the personal expression of ultimate concern," a view he bases on the works of Paul Tillich.[54] In Christian terms, this would equate to a passion for Christ and the concerns of the Christian community. One particular advantage Emmons sees in making a link

---

49. Pearson, *Brush with God*, 11.
50. This is from the definition presented in chapter 5.
51. See definition in chapter 5.
52. Nes, *Mystical Language*, 13.
53. Gardner, *Frames of Mind*, 8. Italics in original.
54. Emmons, "Is Spirituality an Intelligence?" 4.

between spirituality and intelligence—and one that sits well with this project—is that it acts as an "antidote for antireligious intellectualism" and that instead of "dichotomizing faith and reason" this approach permits an understanding of how spiritual processing can improve cognitive functioning rather than preclude it."[55] This project attempts to allow room for other ways of knowing in addition to conventional linguistic conceptions.

Barbara Bolt argues that practice-led research "introduces the possibility of the visual argument" which may enable "a shift in thought itself."[56] The project is already investigating shifts in how the Trinity is understood in language and how this might be depicted. However, is there the possibility of contemporary icons leading to a shift in thought and possibly spiritual practice? As a single individual, it is only possible to measure this in a limited way. For this reason, two components will be included to examine this aspect. The first will be a number of artist talks during the period of the exhibition. The aim of these events will firstly be to allow visitors to the exhibition to ask questions about the icons, the process and the thought behind them. However, it will also be an opportunity for me to find out from people how the icons impacted them both intellectually and their faith, understanding, and experience. As the research progresses, a small set of general questions will be formulated for me to include in the discussions with visitors to garner some of these views.

The second way of assessing how the project does, or has the potential to, shift thinking will be through an iconography workshop. The aim of the workshop will be to explore in and through practice the experiences and understandings of the Trinity in a collaborative way. A small group of approximately four to six Christian practitioners will be invited. In this context, *Christian practitioners* means believing Christians involved in a faith community as well as engaged in a practice of some kind, but may not necessarily be, or have been, iconographers. Their practice may be the visual arts, performance, creative writing, in addition to specific Christian practices such as worship and liturgy,

---

55. Emmons, "Is Spirituality an Intelligence?" 20.
56. Bolt, "The Magic Is in the Handling," 29.

leading prayer groups and meditation. Participants may have multiple practices.

Broadly, it is envisioned that the workshop will follow roughly the following format. It will begin with focused reflection, prayer, and discussion on a contemporary phrasing of Trinitarian language. The aim is to reach an understanding of the language used and possibly the intent and assumptions of the approach.

As this session progresses participants will be encouraged to explore their understanding of the Trinitarian approach by means of their own practice. This may mean developing prayers, songs, dance movements, sketches and so on. It is obviously impossible to predict what will happen in this process, but my role is to facilitate this and to draw on and record the ideas, motifs, themes and metaphors the practitioners are using in their explorations.

The third stage is to return to a "round table" and to discuss with the participants how they understood the language, ways they interpreted it, and in what ways it—if it did—impacted or changed or strengthened their existing understanding of the Trinity.

Finally, I discuss my own practice as an iconographer and seek input from the participants on the translation of their experiences into a visual theological language that might be employed in the creation of icons. One possible way of progressing this stage would be the development of some preliminary sketches for discussion, criticism and suggestions from those present.

It is clear that there are multiple layers and perspectives in a project of this nature. There is, firstly, the theoretical work relating to the theology of Trinitarian descriptions and how they might be understood. Secondly, there are the icons themselves, the process of creation and the way in which they carry a Trinitarian understanding. Thirdly, there is also the data from feedback from discussions and workshop on how people have been affected by the icons and their various understandings. Finally, there is my own engagement with the process and my own practice. The project presents a challenge in coordinating the multiple voices into a coherent whole.

In order to achieve equal voice for the components, I will adopt a strategy developed by Alvesson and Sköldberg. Broadly, their approach

Application: A Project Proposal

is *reflexive interpretation* but their approach contains for levels or components. For this reason they call it "quadruple hermeneutics" or *quadri-hermeneutics*. They describe it as *qualitative, interpretive* and *reflexive* representing "the open play of reflection across various levels of interpretation."[57] It is a "framework for drawing attention to and mediating between core dimensions in reflection, for initiating acts of reflection and maintaining movement between reflective themes."[58]

The first layer is *interaction with empirical material*.[59] In terms of this project, this material includes the icons themselves, theological information from literature as well as the data from interviews and the workshops. Their second layer is described as *interpretation*.[60] Here, the concern is with uncovering the underlying meanings in the material and what happens in the interrelation between elements. The third layer they term *critical interpretation*.[61] What they describe here relates to "ideology, power [and] social reproduction."[62] One area this will be particularly helpful will be in relation to the backgrounds and contexts of the various views of the Trinity: what motivates them and what are their political and social drivers? Finally, Alvesson and Sköldberg describe a fourth layer they term the *reflection on text production and language use*.[63] Here they talk about reflection on my own text, and an awareness of both any claims to authority made and selectivity made in the voices represented in the text.[64] This will be particularly relevant, for example, in whatever conclusions are reached as to effectiveness of the icons in representing Trinitarian understandings.

In adopting this approach, it will be possible to coordinate the varying elements of a project of this nature and attempt to ensure broad range of coverage. This will be especially true as the project has two

---

57. Alvesson and Sköldberg, *Reflexive Methodology*, 271.
58. Alvesson and Sköldberg, *Reflexive Methodology*, 270.
59. Alvesson and Sköldberg, *Reflexive Methodology*, 273.
60. Alvesson and Sköldberg, *Reflexive Methodology*, 273.
61. Alvesson and Sköldberg, *Reflexive Methodology*, 273.
62. Alvesson and Sköldberg, *Reflexive Methodology*, 273.
63. Alvesson and Sköldberg, *Reflexive Methodology*, 273.
64. Alvesson and Sköldberg, *Reflexive Methodology*, 273.

Format

One of the unique features of a practice-led research project is that it "disseminates its knowledge in both a written academic form and in a praxis form as appropriate to the discipline."[65] A typical form of a practice-led project is that, firstly, the question or questions are addressed through written language in an *exegesis,* and secondly answers to the research question are found through a creative component, in this case, the creation of a series of icons. While both parts answer the research question on their own terms, they are not independent of each other and must interact—the exegesis expands on the creative component while the creative component works out some of the material developed in the exegesis. The final submission for this project will consist of two parts: a creative component and an exegesis.

Creative component

The creative component will consist of a series of icons painted over the period of research. The first will be a benchmark or reference piece, executed in the style of the Rublev icon, broadly following the structure of the work and using the traditional descriptive terms of the Trinity. This icon will represent a visual reference point for the other icons to be written but will also be a reference in terms of my practice as an iconographer.

As discussed earlier, the process of icon making is one that engages the technical skill of the iconographer but also their spiritual practice. Prayer and fasting is a part of this practice for many iconographers (although not all in the contemporary milieu). During the making of each icon, my prayer and spiritual reflection will be centred on the same language being used for the icon. This will do justice to the language being explored as well as allow me to engage fully with the language and reflect personally and theologically on it. I will maintain journal entries for each icon, tracking the development of each icon, any areas

---

65. See definition in chapter 5.

Application: A Project Proposal

that were particularly difficult or easy, as well as any areas where a specific theological issue or disjunct occurred—that is, situations where the theology underlying the icon and the symbolism might not have aligned. This material will be used in the preparation of the exegesis.

Exhibition

The creative component is presented in a final exhibition and will include an appropriate installation ceremony. The most suitable situation would be for this to take place in a location appropriate to Christian iconography, for example, a church or monastery. This is preferred even if it is not possible for the icons to remain there permanently. This will require negotiation with appropriate individuals. If this is not possible, and an alternative location is required, additional information material may need to be presented to people who come to view the icons, to provide some additional context and explanation. As the time for a final exhibition approaches, possible forms of examination will need to be considered. While the exegesis can be delivered to the examiners by post or electronically by email, it would be ideal if the examiners could attend the exhibition personally. However, as a part of the documentation process, the exhibition will need to be documented. This may occur through videos, photos, or any other means as appropriate.

Exegesis

The exegesis for this project will perform a number of functions. Firstly, its role will be to investigate discussions of the language used to describe the Trinity and what might be some of the theological implications. The aim here will be to tease out some of the core ideas and symbols within descriptions of the Trinity in order to begin the second task: how the descriptions might be translated into visual language. This material will form a basis for the creation of the icons and will include an investigation of the traditional symbolism used in icons and its translation into the contemporary context. The exegesis will investigate the theology of icons, making, purpose and use, but with a specific focus on Trinitarian icons and, where appropriate, icons of the individual members of the Trinity. The exegesis will also investigate contemporary movements in iconography, the theory and motivations behind them, and how these ideas may impact on the current project. The exegesis will also provide some additional discussions on the creative component and the methods and processes that are involved.

Timeline

Year One:

Semester One: Prepare and submit proposal, complete ethics approval.

Semester Two: Document research. Conduct, transcribe, and analyze interviews with iconographers

Year Two:

Semester One: Commence studio work.

Semester Two: Continue studio work, closed exhibition of work completed to this time. Commence writing of exegesis.

Year Three:

Semester One: Continue studio work and writing.

Semester Two: Writing, review and submission. Preparation for final exhibition.

Ethical Considerations

The early stages of research may benefit from interviews with contemporary iconographers—there are only a small number operating in Australia—to discuss their methods of creation and theological contexts. Benefits to this project will also come from the spiritual exercises they engage in as a part of their icon writing process. Ethical approval will be sought prior to these interviews taking place. No live models will be used for the creation of the icons, so no ethical issues present themselves in this regard. Ethical clearance may be needed to approach churches and/or monasteries for display of the icons and to conduct the installation ceremony.

Ethical approval will be needed in order to seek feedback from individuals attending the final exhibition and will be sought for the proposed workshop. The material from exhibition attendees will be of

Application: A Project Proposal

a general nature and easily de-identified. More detailed engagement is entailed in the workshop and the appropriate procedures will be put in place as requested by the ethics committee.

Budget

Peter Pearson has variously described a debate amongst iconographers as the "Egg Wars"[66] or "the egg thing."[67] It relates to the question of whether icons must use egg tempera as the medium. His view, and the project's view, is that this is not a requirement, and acrylics are perfectly acceptable. He points out that the oldest icons were not egg tempera but used the encaustic method of melted coloured wax on a wooden panel.[68] As a result of this decision, paints need only be obtained in the right colour. Pearson uses *Jo Sonja* colours, such as Turner's Yellow.[69] It is not possible at this stage to determine the breadth of the colour palette that will be needed. This will be determined as the research progresses and decisions are made on the representation of the various figures. A number of options are used for the panels and, where possible, Australian wood will be used.

The only other significant expense is the gold leaf used in the process. This expense is not high, or avoidable, but manageable. It is not anticipated that the series of icons produced will be large, and the size of the icons will fall in the range of about 30 cm x 40 cm (3:4 ratio). At this size, between 9–11 standard 80 mm x 80 mm leaves would be needed per board (since the leaf does not fully cover the board). Therefore, one standard 25 leaf booklet would cover two icons, with some leftover for the next. At 2013 prices, about 4 booklets may be required at about $55 each.[70]

There may be costs involved in the final exhibition. These will depend on the final location negotiated and what facilities the site has as

---

66. Pearson, *Brush with God*, 63.
67. Pearson, *Another Brush with God*, 80.
68. Pearson, *Brush with God*, 63.
69. Pearson, *Another Brush with God*, 52.

70. All these figures are estimates. Some information obtained from the website of an Australian manufacturer/distributor based in Victoria, *The Golf leaf Factory International* (http://www.goldleaf.com.au).

well as any associated hiring fees. The icons can be hung or displayed on easels (available in-house and transportable to the location). No additional costs are anticipated for the workshop. An on-campus studio is highly suitable and only an appropriate booking would need to be made in advance. No materials are required other than those that would normally be available in the studio.

Chapter 9

Conclusions

INTRODUCTION

THIS PROJECT SET OUT to examine how a methodology developed in the creative arts—practice-led research—could be applied in a new context, that of theological and faith-based research. It is now possible to draw all the conclusions together. The chapter is divided into two parts. The first part highlights key linkages between chapters of the tbook. This process will also address challenges, important limitations and possible weaknesses raised by some of the arguments and conclusions of the research. This part also incorporates areas of further research. The ideas suggested spring either directly from issues not covered in the book or arise as a result of the implications of the ideas developed in the various chapters. The second stage is to consider the key research outcomes of the book as a whole, bringing out their importance and implications for the wider debate on the methodology as well as its application generally but also specifically in theology. This section will also directly address the research questions presented in chapter 1.

PART ONE: LINKAGES, CHALLENGES, AND FUTURE RESEARCH

This section presents each chapter in order of appearance to demonstrate the purpose of the chapter and its broader role in the argument of the project. Chapter 1 presented a dichotomy in approaches to understanding the world. These are what might be called two naiveties: on one hand, a one-dimensional rationalism, and on the other, a simplistic experientialism. Although existing at the same time in various forms, it can also be seen as a swinging pendulum; a changing emphasis over time. The chapter aimed to show the presence of these two, sometimes opposing, approaches in academic research, general scholarly thinking and in theology and the church.

Chapter 1 provides the interconnecting framework for all consequent chapters. It outlines the primary objective as well as presenting the research questions, preliminary limitations and indicators of significance. That main objective is to present a relatively new research methodology—practice-led research—as a means of possibly achieving this goal.

The introductory chapter included a short section containing three possible limitations seen at the outset of the project. The first was that practice-led research would be framed for an academic research context only, that is, for use in universities and colleges. The second possible limitation suggested was the Christian context in and for which the methodology is being developed. Thirdly, a possible limitation seen at the outset was that as a researcher, I am essentially working from the outside of practice-led research.

Practice-led research was seen to have originally developed within academic environments as a response to the need to contribute to the research output of universities and this project has attempted to strengthen the methodology for this environment. Further, in the same way that it was seen as an opportunity for artist/practitioners to contribute scholarly work, it is also an opportunity of faith practitioners to contribute scholarly work to disciplines. The narrow framing of practice-led research in this project to a university context is only a restriction if it is thought that the methodology has no application outside of this, its original home. However, there is nothing inherent in practice-led research as a model restricting it to a university environment. Wider applications of the methodology would only need to adapt the model and definition presented to suit that context.

Conclusions

Another possible limitation offered is that the arguments and conclusions presented in this project may be dismissed (by critics) since I am not a practice-led researcher. However, this argument confuses the outcomes with the origins of those outcomes. As such, it is a version of a combined genetic fallacy and an *argumentum ad hominem,* or *against the person.* The genetic fallacy is the error of drawing a good or bad conclusion about a certain argument based on whether the origin of that argument is good or bad.[1] This is often seen in combination with the *ad hominem* fallacy which "condemns a prior argument by condemning its source or proponent."[2] The point to be noted here is that it is not possible to dismiss the arguments presented in this project based on the researcher's circumstances as such; criticisms must address the arguments and proposals directly. Additionally, an outside perspective may be a unique one unclouded by disciplinary blind spots. It is worth noting that apart from the wide range of literature consulted, I have had significant input from practice-led researchers, in formal interviews, workshops and discussion groups.

Yet this dilemma of theoretically and practically developing practice-led research while remaining not a practice-led research project itself presents an area of further research. A significant area of future investigation will be assessing how the definition and model function when implemented by practice-led researchers generally and faith-based researchers particularly. What are the weaknesses of the model and definition? What are its strengths? What components are still unclear and what needs clarification? Are there areas in the theoretical underpinnings that fail to support it and what might need reinforcing?

In chapter 2, the theoretical perspectives and methodologies for bringing about the objectives outlined in the first chapter are detailed. The chapter lays out the basic assumptions and frameworks upon which the main arguments of the thesis are built: a Christian worldview, the theoretical perspective of critical realism and the nature of the project as *public* and *private*.

It is clear that the Christian worldview presented here pervades the project and drives its main aims, that is, to apply practice-led

---

1. Walton, "Informal Fallacy," 431.
2. Walton, "Informal Fallacy," 431.

research in a theological context. This may be raised as a criticism that it restricts the applicability of the definition and model proposed in this book. A similar reply can be offered for the Christian context within which the methodology is developed as was given for the restricted environment the model is developed for. There is nothing inherent in the model of practice-led research developed by this project that restricts its use to a Christian faith context; it could be readily applied in the other faiths or for practitioners of no faith (in the religious sense). More broadly, it could be applied in any area where practice is important. This limitation is addressed in part by framing the definition in a way that somewhat detaches it from its original setting and reframing it in a way less dependent on its origins.

However, a clear outlining of the Christian perspective of the project is present for reasons that go beyond the context of framing practice-led research. It is argued at various points in the book but especially in chapter 2, that no matter an individual's worldview, be it a religious one, a non-religious or some socio-economic position, it will have an impact on the decisions and the direction a project takes. Therefore, in order to assess a project's conclusions and determine whether to accept or reject them, or even to follow the logic, these should be known.

Despite these possible criticisms, it opens an area of investigation. Further research will relate to how well it has been possible to use it in other faith areas. Has the definition and model been *translatable* by other belief systems and secular contexts? If so, how much adjustment was needed? This is a question of interest especially in terms of how robust the original model and definition are.

Chapter 3 is placed at an important point in the logic of the project and performs a number of functions. The chapter provides parallel arguments to those in chapter 1 and in chapter 2 by following the theme of the relationship between the *two knowledges*. However, it broadens the principles to the relationship of theory with practice through time primarily through the eyes of the creative disciplines and the academic or theoretical disciplines.

It lays additional groundwork in demonstrating that there has always been a close relationship between theology and the church with the creative disciplines and, by extension, practice-based disciplines.

Conclusions

This relationship has not always been amicable. These disciplines are neither independent of each other or of the community of which they are a part. It serves here also to head off a possible criticism that creativity and practice have little to do with theology proper. Further, given the absence of a specific literature review chapter, these discussions provide explanatory support on some of the views scholars have on the nature of practice-led research.

Chapters 4–7 are closely linked together. They each work as a part of the broader plan of developing a comprehensive foundation for practice-led research projects. Chapters 4–5 work on the task of what practice-led research is and how it might be understood. Chapter 6 develops a model for the operation and application of the methodology while chapter 7 outlines a plan for the completion of a practice-led project discussing examination, presentation and dissemination of research results.

These chapters systematically analyze three key concepts that make up what practice-led research is and attempts to do. Those concepts—*knowledge*, *practice*, and *research*—are then expanded and developed, culminating in a broad and robust definitional framework. Based on the definition, the project adopts and adapts a *research-question model* arguing that a research question provides structure for a project, provides a base for demonstrating a project's contribution to the *stock of knowledge*, and helps to address other issues of rigour and dissemination of research outcomes. The definition and model are key outcomes of the project (discussed later in this concluding chapter).

A number of possible challenges in the development of the definition and model present themselves. Firstly, each of the conclusions on *knowledge*, *practice*, and *research* might be disputed. Secondly, the research-question model was not the most common choice among those that currently use the methodology and may be seen as imposing restrictions on a researcher's creativity. The research-question model was presented as a means for increasing the quality of research produced by the methodology and any case that this impedes creativity will need to be argued for rather than asserted. These are wide ranging philosophical questions of epistemology and ontology and considerable time was dedicated to formulating them in a robust way for its successful use by practice-led researchers.

There are two specific areas of criticism the definition and model may receive. These relate to the underlying requirement for *accountability* in research and the use of *spiritual intelligence*.

There is a stream in the literature which contends that any requirement by creative practitioners to be accountable for and to justify what they do as research should be resisted. The model and definition presented in this book can be viewed as imposing this need for justification on creative disciplines where it is not needed and certainly not wanted. It might therefore be rejected out of hand. These concerns are addressed in two ways.

Firstly, the arguments of chapter 3 partly address this issue by noting that artists (particularly) and practice-based activities have always been accountable in some way to the society that supports them. The justification expected of those creative practitioners located in an academic environment is a matter of type and degree rather than something additionally imposed upon them.

Secondly, there is the view that justification and accountability include the contention that attempts to define practice-led research or to suggest a model and strategies will somehow restrict creativity and practice. This argument conflates practice in a general sense with practice in a research context which might further be seen as a subcategory of practice in the general sense. The concern has been addressed by the discussion at the end of chapter 5 on what practice-led research is not. That discussion makes the distinction between *practice with research* and *practice alone*. None of the arguments presented in this book proscribe that practice *must be* a particular set of skills nor do they argue that creativity is only one particular thing. It only presents a theoretical framework of how the concept should be understood in this context. Further, there is no argument on what the outcomes of research are to be, only that there should be some.

The criticism represents a deeper concern this project has tried to address: a lack of any clear understanding of what practice-led research is and does and that the often poorly articulated research outcomes will, in the long term, undermine the methodology as a legitimate academic tool.

This fear stems partly from the conclusions of chapter 3: in an economic environment that is placing pressure on higher education institutions, the demand to clearly justify *research* appears likely to only increase. This fear also grew partly as the research developed and it became clear that the fragmentary definitions and what was acceptable as "practice-led research" was so diverse, the methodology was being undermined from within. The methodology is in danger of only resting on the practice of an individual researcher and so become little more than an inward-looking project recounting a personal journey of experiences and makes little, if any, contribution to the discipline. The aim of clearly developing a definition and model is to help prevent this from occurring and fundamentally supports and affirms the validity of practice-led research.

Another area of possible challenge is the use of *spiritual intelligence* in chapter 5. The question might be asked: Doesn't that argument restrict your model to only researches operating within a faith context? This question can be answered with both a "yes" and "no."

It is correct to answer "yes" in that the use of spiritual intelligence does restrict the use of the definition in the applied form in which it is presented. However, it does include virtually any researcher that is operating out of a faith context and it is important to note again that although this project is framed in a Christian worldview, it is not intended nor is it necessarily restricted to that context. It is important not to read spiritual intelligence as "Christian intelligence."

More broadly, it is also correct to answer this question with "no" since the use of spiritual intelligence is complemented by an argument based on embodied/tacit knowledge and this is not exclusively connected to faith. Additional arguments can also be developed in support of the argument that there are fuller understandings of knowledge.

Another criticism relates to the comparisons with other approaches that bear some resemblance to practice-led research or that seem to share common features at the end of chapter 5. There are two points to be made here. Firstly, what is most important about that discussion as it stands is its purpose. It is intended to bring into relief the *distinctives of the methodology* rather than suggest it is better overall than those it is compared to. Practice-led research is presented as an additional tool in the kit of the theological researcher, one that has advantages over others for certain researchers and in particular situations. From a theological context, there was no attempt to compare practice-led research more broadly with other methodologies or theories in use in the discipline, particularly those that have approaches and assumptions that are significantly different. While this may be considered a challenge to the book—a failure of analysis—it may more productively be seen as an area of further research. Questions such as how might comparisons with other different approaches improve or challenge the definition? In what ways might practice-led research complement or support other approaches to important questions in theology, or for that matter, other disciplines? How might practice-led research facilitate the collaboration between researchers?

PART TWO: KEY RESEARCH OUTCOMES AND SIGNIFICANCE

One of the key themes of the book is well summed up in the phrase "head knowledge versus heart knowledge." This theme led to the key motivation of finding a way to bring the two perspectives into discussion and cooperation, to find a way that will "honor the conclusions of rational theological analysis as well as those of the lived faith experience." Grounded in this motivation, the primary objective of this project was to introduce into theology a methodology developed in a different sphere (the creative disciplines) that addressed this bifurcation. The model needed to be explained, defined, and practically developed as well as illustrated in operation. To this end, a number of research questions were developed:

1. Does practice-led research provide an additional methodology for theology?
2. Can a robust definition and model of practice-led research be developed while maintaining its flexibility as a methodology?

Conclusions

3. How might key concepts such as *research*, *knowledge* and *practice* be defined and expanded to support the process of developing a robust definition?

4. Can practice-led research be theoretically demonstrated as a viable methodology in a theological context?

This section will present the key outcomes of the study.

A Broad-based Definition

Early on in the research process for this project, it was discovered that there was no broadly coherent definition of practice-led research. Two possible reasons were identified for this absence. Firstly, there is a significant amount of assumed understanding in the debate—for example, that everyone knows what *practice* is or what it means to say *research* is being done. Different authors have attempted to clarify various elements of the methodology, but these attempts are distributed across numerous journals and across time. The second possible reason identified was that a lack of a clear definition would mean that it was enough to say "it is a practice-led research project" with no further justification or clarification necessary. The consequent access to funding would follow and a creative practitioner would therefore have little requirement to account for themselves and what they are engaged in.

What is new and unique about the definition presented in chapter 5 is the comprehensive attempt to delineate the borders of a practice-led research project, to clearly state what the methodology consists of, its goals and modes of understanding while at the same time not restricting its application to any one context or discipline. The definition aims not to be too prescriptive, and so hamper the flexibility and adaptability inherent in the methodology, while seeking to prevent an *anything goes* approach to practice-led research. The key concepts of the methodology—knowledge, practice, and research—are clearly outlined. These ideas are more often assumed to be understood by all but rarely detailed.

Application of Practice-Led Research in Theology

The end of chapter 5 contains a section describing methodologies which might be thought similar to practice-led research. Two of these were practical theology and action research within which there is a theological stream. While these two approaches engage practice at various levels, what is unique about this project is the new application of a methodology into the theological enterprise that makes practice a key tool for research as well as a knowledge carrier of the research. Chapter 8 includes a fully developed proposal of one example of how this might work and there are a number of other speculative suggestions in chapters 4–6.

Comprehensive Model for Use

Growing partly out of this new application into theology is the development of a comprehensive model for the methodology's use. As was the case with a definition, various elements existed in various forms across time and place. Academic institutions had too many of these forms for a practice-led project to be presented (exegesis and creative component); varying expectations on the nature of the exegesis itself (for example, a commentary or context model); and varying guidelines on the nature and actions for examination of a completed project. The literature often contained only fragmentary suggestions for a potential practice-led researcher as to how to go about such a project in its fundamental form.

What is unique about this project, then, is the presentation of a *complete model for the use, examination, documentation and dissemination of a practice-led project*, and specifically, one in theology. The project provides the theoretical and practical support for the use and justification of the methodology within the academic research environment and does so by not only offering a string of examples but by distilling it down to the essentials so that the methodology may be broadly applied in a variety of contexts.

Conclusions

Historical Context of Practice-Led Research

A common scenario given for the original development of practice-led research is one of external economic political pressures applied to the higher education sector that necessitated the creative disciplines to give an account for themselves and justify what they were doing. This need for accountability and justification is often seen as unreasonable. This approach is, at best, incomplete, and at worst, an overly energetic polemic.

One of the goals of chapter 3 was to establish important foundations for the rest of the thesis, such as demonstrating the close, though not always amicable, relationship between the creative/practice-based disciplines and what might be called the *propositional* disciplines, as represented by theology. However, what is unique about the work done in chapter 3 is the development of a richer understanding of the origins and drivers of practice-led research. The argument is essentially that the events often cited as the beginnings of the methodology are part of a much broader debate on the nature, role and support of the creative disciplines (and of theology) in the public arena.

The arguments especially in chapter 3 are unique in two ways. Firstly, by following the social, political and economic status and role of the artist, the discussion demonstrates that there has *always* been a close link between the artist/practitioner and the means of support of the artist/practitioner. Arguments that contend that this obsession with accountability is new are historically near-sighted.

The second unique feature of the discussions in chapter 3 is the perspective it takes as a result of the conclusions of the first point. Rather than seeing the situation as a burden of increased accountability, it can be seen as an opportunity for disciplines to participate in scholarly debates that they have been largely excluded from throughout history. Although there are streams in the literature that are more positive, the approach taken here is different and presents a more detailed and nuanced understanding of the origins of practice-led research, the comprehensive nature of which is not present in the literature of the methodology.

CONCLUSION: FINAL REMARKS

It has been argued throughout this book that the life of faith is both an intellectual activity and a lived experience and that it is not possible to truly separate these two elements. Practice-led research has been developed as a means to pursue rigorous academic research in and through the active practice of a researcher with the outcomes of research presented in multiple forms and "languages."

The project has come full circle. It began with a statement from the Dutch theologian Herman Bavinck suggesting that "religion is not limited to one single human faculty but embraces the human being as a whole."[3] It is the contention of this project that practice-led research embraces the multiple intellectual and practical faculties of the human.

---

3. Bavinck, *Prolegomena*, 268.

Appendix 1

Interview Guide Questions

THE FOLLOWING TWO INTERVIEW guides were developed to direct the interview process. Only two of the guides used are reproduced here, the first and the last used. Each guide had the set of questions on one side and a selection of quotes to aid discussion if needed on the other side. For further information see the discussion on the interviews in chapter 2.

INTERVIEW GUIDE 1

| Date: |
| Time: |
| Interviewee: |

Introductions

Consent

Purpose of study (Plain language statement)

1. Would you describe for me the topic you chose for your PhD? How did you come to choose this area?

2. Tell me about your methodology?

3. Why did you choose a PLR? What did you see as the advantages? Did there seem to be any disadvantages?

4. Describe for me the processes or strategies you employed to make PLR work for you. Were there tools and methods you had as an artist that were *repurposed* for you research?

5. Was there a written component needed for your degree? What percentage weight was given to it and/or how many words did you need to complete?

6. How would you describe your contribution to knowledge? What did "knowledge" mean for your research?

Conclusion and summary

Follow-up and transcript

Caroel Gray (1996)

By "practice-led" I mean, firstly, research which is initiated in practice, where questions, problems, challenges are identified and formed by the needs of practice and practitioners; and secondly, that the research strategy is carried out through practice, using predominantly methodologies and specific methods familiar to us as practitioners in the visual arts.

Brad Haseman (2006)

However, many practice-led researchers do not commence a research project with a sense of *a problem*. Indeed, they may be led by what is best described as "an enthusiasm of practice."

Henk Borgdorff (2007)

More particularly, the issue is whether this type of research distinguishes itself from other research in terms of the nature of its research object (an ontological question), in terms of the knowledge it holds (an epistemological question) and in terms of the working methods that are appropriate to it (a methodological question).

Brad Haseman (2009)

Practice-led research, particularly for the creative practice-led researcher, is unruly, ambiguous and marked by extremes of interpretive anxiety for the reflexive researcher. It is this way *because* it is deeply emergent in nature and the need to tolerate the ambiguity and make it sensible through heightened reflexivity is a part of what it is to be a successful practice-led research in the creative arts.

INTERVIEW GUIDE 2

Date:
Time:
Interviewee:

Introductions

Consent

Purpose of study (Plain language statement)

1. Definition of PLR
2. Why students would choose the method? What discipline areas?
3. How would a student *set up* a PLR project?
4. What texts or articles do you refer students to?
5. What sort of problems do students encounter?
6. What benefits and disadvantages to students see at the start? How do these change as the project progresses?
7. What benefits and weaknesses do you see with the methodology?

Conclusion and summary

Follow-up and transcript

Appendix 2

Plain Language Statement

THE PLAIN LANGUAGE STATEMENT was produced as a part of the ethics approval process and provided to all interviewees. It was printed on an approved University of Notre Dame, Australia letterhead. This document is discussed in relation to the interviews in chapter 2

PLAIN LANGUAGE STATEMENT

Please be advised that your participation in this study is completely voluntary. Should you wish to withdraw at any stage, or to withdraw any unprocessed data you have supplied, you are free to do so without prejudice. The researchers are not involved in the ethics application process. Your decision to participate or not, or to withdraw, will be completely independent of your dealings with the ethics committee, and we would like to assure you that it will have no effect on any applications for approval that you may submit.

Should you require any further information, or have any concerns, please do not hesitate to contact Neil Ferguson on (08) 6262-9255 or 0410 487074 or by email on nkferguson@gmail.com.

Should you have any concerns about the conduct of the project, you are welcome to contact the Executive Officer, Human Research Ethics Committee, The University of Notre Dame Australia, ph: (08) 9433 0941; fax (08) 9433 0519. Ethics approval ID: #011050F.

Appendix 3

Consent Form

THE CONSENT FORM WAS produced as a part of the ethics approval process and provided to all interviewees. It was printed on an approved University of Notre Dame, Australia letterhead. This document is discussed in relation to the interviews in chapter 2.

INFORMED CONSENT FORM

I, (*participant's name*) _____ hereby agree to being a participant in the above research project.

- I have read and understood the Information Sheet about this project and any questions have been answered to my satisfaction.
- I understand that I may withdraw from participating in the project at any time without prejudice.
- I understand that all information gathered by the researcher will be treated as strictly confidential.
- I agree that any research data gathered for the study may be published provided my name or other identifying information is not disclosed.

Participant's Signature _____

Date _____

Researcher's Full Name: _____

Appendix 3

Researcher's Signature _____

Date _____

If participants have any complaint regarding the manner in which a research project is conducted, it should be directed to the Executive Officer of the Human Research Ethics Committee, Research Office, The University of Notre Dame Australia, PO Box 1225 Fremantle WA 6959, phone (08) 9433 0943.

Bibliography

Adams, Nicholas. *Habermas and Theology*. Cambridge: Cambridge University Press, 2006.
"Advice for Examiners: Doctoral Higher Degree by Research Students." *Curtin University*. Online: https://research.curtin.edu.au/local/docs/graduate/TE-AdviceExaminers_Doc.pdf.
Allen, Diogenes, and Eric O. Springsted. *Philosophy for Understanding Theology*. 2nd ed. Louisville: Westminster John Knox, 2007.
Alvesson, Mats, and Kaj Sköldberg. *Reflexive Methodology: New Vistas for Qualitative Research*. 2nd ed. London: Sage, 2009.
Anderson, Elizabeth. "Feminist Epistemology and Philosophy of Science." *The Stanford Encyclopedia of Philosophy*, August 9, 2000. Online: https://plato.stanford.edu/archives/fall2012/entries/feminism-epistemology.
Arnold, Josie. "Practice Led Research: Creative Activity, Academic Debate, and Intellectual Rigour." *HES* 2 (2012) 9–24.
Australia Council for the Arts. "Arts Funding Guide 2012." Surrey Hills: Australian Government, 2012.
Australian Government. "Higher Education Research Data Collection: Specifications for the Collection of 2011 Data." Canberra: Australian Government, 2012.
Australian Research Council. "Era 2012 Discipline Matrix." Canberra: Australian Government, 2011.
———. "Era 2012 Submission Guidelines." Canberra: Australian Government, 2011.
———. "Factsheet: Australian Research Council." Canberra: Australian Government, 2011.
———. "Glossary." *Australian Government*. No pages. Online: https://www.arc.gov.au/news/glossary.
Bacon, Hannah. *What's Right with the Trinity? Conversations in Feminist Theology*. ANCTRTBS. Farnham: Ashgate, 2009.

Bibliography

Baker, Gordon P., and Katherine J. Morris. *Descartes' Dualism*. London: Routledge, 1996.

Barasch, Moshe. *Theories of Art*. 3 vols. New York: Routledge, 1985–98.

Barnes, Robert. "Religious Studies and Theology." In *Knowing Ourselves and Others: The Humanities in Australia into the 21st Century*, edited by Australian Research Council, 231–38. Canberra: Australian Research Council, 1998.

Barone, Tom, and Elliot W. Eisner. *Arts Based Research*. London: Sage, 2012.

Barrett, Estelle, and Barbara Bolt. *Practice as Research: Approaches to Creative Arts Enquiry*. London: I. B. Tauris, 2007.

Barsalou, Lawrence W., et al. "Embodiment in Religious Knowledge." *JCC* 5 (2005) 14–57.

Barzun, Jacques. "An Insoluble Problem: The Patronage of Art." *PAPS* 131 (1987) 121–31.

Battaglia, Michael P. "Nonprobability Sampling." In *Encyclopedia of Survey Research Methods*, edited by Paul J. Lavrakas, 524–26. London: Sage, 2008.

Bavinck, Herman. *Prolegomena*, edited by John Bolt. Vol. 1 of *Reformed Dogmatics*. 4 vols. Translated by John Vriend. Grand Rapids: Baker Academic, 2003.

Beckwith, John. *Early Christian and Byzantine Art*, edited by Nicholas Pevsner. PHA 33. Harmondsworth, UK: Penguin, 1970.

Benton, Ted, and Ian Craib. *Philosophy of Social Science: The Philosophical Foundations of Social Thought*. TST. New York: Palgrave, 2001.

Bettenson, Henry, and Chris Maunder. *The Documents of the Christian Church*. 3rd ed. Oxford: Oxford University Press, 1999.

Biggs, Michael, and Daniela Büchler. "Eight Criteria for Practice-Based Research in the Creative and Cultural Industries." *ADCHE* 7 (2008) 5–18.

———. "Rigor and Practice-Based Research." *Design Issues* 23 (2007) 62–69.

Biggs, Michael, and Henrik Karlsson, eds. *The Routledge Companion to Research in the Arts*. New York: Routledge, 2010.

Bloesch, Donald G. *Essentials of Evangelical Theology*. 2 vols. San Francisco: Harper & Row, 1978–79.

Bobonich, Chris. "Aristotle's Ethical Treatises." In *The Blackwell Guide to Aristotle's Nicomachean Ethics*, edited by Richard Kraut, 12–36. BGGW 4. Malden, MA: Blackwell, 2006.

Bolt, Barbara. *Heidegger Reframed: Interpreting Key Thinkers for the Arts*. CTRS. London: I. B. Tauris, 2011.

———. "The Magic Is in the Handling." In *Practice as Research: Approaches to Creative Arts Enquiry*, edited by Estelle Barrett and Barbara Bolt, 27–34. London: I. B. Tauris, 2007.

Bibliography

Booth, Wayne C., et al. *The Craft of Research*. CGWEP. 3rd ed. Chicago: University of Chicago Press, 2008.

Borg, Erik. "Writing in Fine Arts and Design Education in Context." *JWCP* 1 (2008) 85–101.

Borgdorff, Henk. "The Debate on Research in the Arts." *TVM* 12 (2007) 1–18.

Bredin, Hugh. "Medieval Art Theory." In *A Companion to Art Theory*, edited by Paul Smith and Carolyn Wilde, 29–39. BCCS 5. Oxford: Blackwell, 2002.

Brown, C. "Historical Jesus, Quest of." In *Dictionary of Jesus and the Gospels*, edited by Joel B. Green and Scot McKnight, 326–41. IVPBDS 6. Downers Grove, IL: InterVarsity, 1992.

Brown, Lesley. "Plato and Aristotle." In *The Blackwell Companion to Philosophy*, edited by Nicholas Bunnin and E. P. Tsui-James, 601–18. Malden, MA: Blackwell, 2003.

Browning, Don S., et al. "Series Foreword." In *Practical Theology: History, Theory, Action Domains: Manual for Practical Theology*, edited by Gerben Heitink, xv–xvi. SPT. Grand Rapids: Eerdmans, 1999.

Buxton, Graham. *Dancing in the Dark: The Privilege of Participating in the Ministry of Christ*. Cumbria: Paternoster, 2001.

Calvin, John. *Institutes of the Christian Religion*. Translated by Henry Beveridge. Peabody, MA: Hendrickson, 2008.

Candlin, Fiona. "A Dual Inheritance: The Politics of Educational Reform and PhDs in Art and Design." *IJADE* 20 (2001) 302–10.

Candy, Linda. *Practice Based Research: A Guide: CCS Report*. Sydney: University of Technology, 2006.

Candy, Linda, and Ernest Edmonds. "The Role of the Artefact and Frameworks for Practice-Based Research." In *The Routledge Companion to Research in the Arts*, edited by Michael Biggs and Henrik Karlsson, 120–37. New York: Routledge, 2010.

Castiglione, Baldassarre, and George Bull. *The Book of the Courtier*. PC 192. Harmondsworth: Penguin, 1967.

Centre for Research in Entertainment, Arts, Technology, Education and Communications (CREATEC) [n.d.]. https://ro.ecu.edu.au/rcreatec.

Charmois, Martin de. "Petition to the King and to the Lords of His Council." In *Art in Theory 1648–1815: An Anthology of Changing Ideas*, edited by Charles Harrison et al., 81–86. Oxford: Blackwell, 2000.

Clark, Kelly James, and Michael Rea, eds. *Reason, Metaphysics, and Mind: New Essays on the Philosophy of Alvin Plantinga*. New York: Oxford University Press, 2012.

Clough, Peter, and Cathy Nutbrown. *A Student's Guide to Methodology: Justifying Enquiry*. London: Sage, 2002.

Bibliography

Clouse, R. G. "Duns Scotus, John." In *Evangelical Dictionary of Theology*, edited by Walter A. Elwell, 357–58. BRL. 2nd ed. Grand Rapids: Baker Academic, 2001.

"Code of Practice for the Assurance of Academic Quality and Standards in Higher Education: Postgraduate Research Programmes." *Gloucester, Australia: Quality Assurance Agency for Higher Education*, 2004. Online: https://core.ac.uk/download/pdf/4154983.pdf.

Combrink, L., and I. R. Marley. "Practice-Based Research: Tracking Creative Creatures in a Research Context." *Literator* 30 (2009) 177–206.

Crisp, Roger. "Form." In *The Cambridge Dictionary of Philosophy*, edited by Robert Audi, 315. 2nd ed. Cambridge: Cambridge University Press, 1999.

Crotty, Michael. *The Foundations of Social Research: Meaning and Perspective in the Research Process*. St. Leonards, Australia: Allen & Unwin, 1998.

Damasio, Antonio R. *Descartes' Error: Emotion, Reason, and the Human Brain*. New York: G. P. Putnam, 1994.

Davis-Weyer, Caecilia. *Early Medieval Art, 300–1150: Sources and Documents*. SDHAS. Englewood Cliffs, NJ: Prentice-Hall, 1971.

Dempsey, Charles. "Some Observations on the Education of Artists in Florence and Bologna During the Later Sixteenth Century." *AB* 62 (1980) 552–69.

Denzin, Norman K., and Yvonna S. Lincoln. *Collecting and Interpreting Qualitative Materials*. 3rd ed. Thousand Oaks, CA: Sage, 2008.

———. "Introduction: Entering the Field of Qualitative Research." In *Handbook of Qualitative Research*, edited by Norman K. Denzin and Yvonna S. Lincoln, 1–17. Thousand Oaks, CA: Sage, 1994.

———. "Introduction: The Discipline and Practice of Qualitative Research." In *Collecting and Interpreting Qualitative Materials*, edited by Norman K. Denzin and Yvonna S. Lincoln, 1–43. 3rd ed. Thousand Oaks, CA: Sage, 2008.

Dingemans, Gijsbert D. J. "Practical Theology in the Academy: A Contemporary Overview." *JR* 76 (1996) 82–96.

"Doctor of Philosophy Course Regulations." *Queensland University of Technology*. Online: https://qutvirtual4.qut.edu.au/group/research-students/your-research-journey/milestones/phd-milestones.

Edmonds, Ernest, and Linda Candy. "Relating Theory, Practice and Evaluation in Practitioner Research." *Leonardo* 43 (2010) 423, 470–76.

Education and Training Department of Employment. "Higher Education: A Policy Statement." Canberra: Australian Government, 1988.

Ellis, Carolyn, and Laura Ellington. "Qualitative Methods." In *Encyclopedia of Sociology*, edited by Edgar F. Borgatta and Rhonda Montgomery, 4:2287–96. 2nd ed. New York: Macmillan, 2000.

Bibliography

Ellis, Carolyn, and Leigh Berger. "Their Story/My Story/Our Story: Including the Researcher's Experience in Interview Research." In *Postmodern Interviewing*, edited by Jaber F. Gubrium and James A. Holstein, 156–83. Thousand Oaks, CA: Sage, 2003.

Emmons, Robert A. "Is Spirituality an Intelligence? Motivation, Cognition, and the Psychology of Ultimate Concern." *IJPR* 10 (2000) 3–26.

Erickson, Millard J. *Christian Theology*. 2nd ed. Grand Rapids: Baker, 1998.

———. *Evangelical Interpretation: Perspectives on Hermeneutical Issues*. Grand Rapids: Baker, 1993.

Evans, G. R. *Philosophy and Theology in the Middle Ages*. London: Routledge, 1993.

Evans, Stuart, and Malcolm Le Grice. "The State of the Art: Research in the Practical Arts—Doctorates—Autonomous Methodologies." *EJAE* 3 (2001) 105–13.

Fantl, Jeremy. "Knowledge How." *The Stanford Encyclopedia of Philosophy*, April 20, 2021. Online: https://plato.stanford.edu/entries/knowledge-how.

Fee, Gordon D. *New Testament Exegesis: A Handbook for Students and Pastors*. Philadelphia: Westminster, 1983.

Fletcher, Julie, and Alan Mann. "Illuminating the Exegesis, an Introduction." *TEXT* 3 (2004). No pages. Online: http://www.textjournal.com.au.libaccess.lib.mcmaster.ca/speciss/issue3/fletchermann.htm.

Frayling, Christopher. "Research in Art and Design." *RCARP* 1 (1994) 1–5.

Gadamer, Hans-Georg. *Truth and Method*. Translated by Joel Weinsheimer and Donald G. Marshall. Rev. ed. New York: Continuum, 2003.

Gardner, Howard. "A Case against Spiritual Intelligence." *IJPR* 10 (2000) 27–34.

———. *Frames of Mind: The Theory of Multiple Intelligences*. New York: Basic, 1993.

———. *Intelligence Reframed: Multiple Intelligences for the 21st Century*. New York: Basic, 1999.

———. *Multiple Intelligences: The Theory in Practice*. New York: Basic, 1993.

Garwood, Jeanette. "Quantitative Research." In *The Sage Dictionary of Social Research Methods*, edited by Victor Jupp, 250–51. London: Sage, 2006.

Geisler, Norman L. "Thomas Aquinas." In *Evangelical Dictionary of Theology*, edited by Walter A. Elwell, 1197–98. BRL. 2nd ed. Grand Rapids: Baker Academic, 2001.

"General Information: Academic Planning, Western Australian College of Advanced Education." *Edith Cowan University*, 1986. Online: https://ro.ecu.edu.au/cgi/viewcontent.cgi?article=8046&context=ecuworks.

Gill, Robin. "The Practice of Faith." In *The Blackwell Companion to Modern Theology*, edited by Gareth Jones, 3–17. BCR. Malden, MA: Blackwell, 2004.

Gillespie, Thomas W. "Biblical Authority *and* Interpretation: The Current Debate on Hermeneutics." In *A Guide to Contemporary Hermeneutics: Major Trends in Biblical Interpretation*, edited by Donald K. McKim, 192–219. Grand Rapids, Eerdmans, 1986.

Goonan, Michael G., et al. *St Pauls Sunday Missal: Sunday Masses for the Three-Year Cycle*. Strathfield, Australia: St Pauls, 2012.

González, Justo L. *The Story of Christianity*. 2 vols. 2nd ed. San Francisco: HarperCollins, 1984–85.

Gottlieb, Paula. "The Practical Syllogism." In *The Blackwell Guide to Aristotle's Nicomachean Ethics*, edited by Richard Kraut, 218–33. BGGW 4. Malden, MA: Blackwell, 2006.

Graham, Elaine L. *Transforming Practice: Pastoral Theology in an Age of Uncertainty*. Eugene, OR: Wipf & Stock, 2002.

Gray, Carole. "Inquiry through Practice: Developing Appropriate Research Strategies." In *No Guru, No Method? Discussions on Art and Design Research*, edited by Pia Standman, 1–28. TKJ B.55. Helsinki: University of Art and Design, 1998.

Gray, Carole, and Julian Malins. *Visualizing Research: A Guide to the Research Process in Art and Design*. Aldershot: Ashgate, 2004.

Green, Lelia. "Creative Writing as Practice-Led Research." *AJC* 33 (2006) 175–88.

———. " Recognising Practice-Led Research . . . At Last!" Paper presented at the Hatched 07 Arts Research Symposium, Perth, Australia, April 20, 2007.

Greene-McCreight, Kathryn. "Feminist Theology and a Generous Orthodoxy." *SJT* 57 (2004) 95–108.

Grenz, Stanley J. *Theology for the Community of God*. Grand Rapids: Eerdmans, 1994.

Grenz, Stanley J., and Roger E. Olson. *20th-Century Theology: God and the World in a Transitional Age*. Downers Grove, IL: InterVarsity, 1992.

Grix, Jonathan. *The Foundations of Research*. PSG. New York: Palgrave Macmillan, 2004.

Grondin, Jean. *Introduction to Philosophical Hermeneutics*. Translated by Joel Weinsheimer. YSH. New Haven: Yale University Press, 1994.

Grudem, Wayne A. *Systematic Theology: An Introduction to Biblical Doctrine*. Leicester: InterVarsity, 1994.

Gruenler, Royce Gordon. *Meaning and Understanding: The Philosophical Framework for Biblical Interpretation*. FCI 2. Grand Rapids: Zondervan, 1991.

Bibliography

"Guideline: Thesis by Publication," *University of Notre Dame Australia*, Apr 1, 2011. Online: https://www.notredame.edu.au/__data/assets/pdf_file/0011/2009/GUIDELINE-Thesis-by-Publication.pdf.

"Guidelines for Thesis Preparation and Submission." *Curtin University*. Online: https://www.curtin.edu.au/students/wp-content/uploads/2021/11/Guidelines-for-Thesis-Preparation-and-Submission.pdf.

Habermas, Jürgen. *Between Naturalism and Religion: Philosophical Essays*. Translated by Ciaran Cronin. Cambridge: Polity, 2008.

———. "Religion in the Public Sphere." *EJP* 14 (2006) 1–25.

Habermas, Jürgen, et al. "The Public Sphere: An Encyclopedia Article (1964)." *NGC* 3 (1974) 49–55.

Hall, Christopher A. *Learning Theology with the Church Fathers*. Downers Grove, IL: InterVarsity, 2002.

Hamilton, Jillian, and Luke Jaaniste. "A Connective Model for the Practice-Led Research Exegesis: An Analysis of Content and Structure." *JWCP* 3 (2010) 31–44.

Harding, Sandra G. "Introduction: Is There a Feminist Method." In *Feminism and Methodology: Social Science Issues*, edited by Sandra G. Harding, 1–14. Bloomington: Indiana University Press, 1987.

Harper, Graeme. "Creative Writing: Words as Practice-Led Research." *JVAP* 7 (2009) 161–71.

Harrington, Austin. *Art and Social Theory: Sociological Arguments in Aesthetics*. Cambridge: Polity, 2004.

Harrison, Charles, et al., eds. *Art in Theory 1648–1815: An Anthology of Changing Ideas*. Oxford: Blackwell, 2000.

Hart, David Bentley. *Atheist Delusions: The Christian Revolution and Its Fashionable Enemies*. New Haven: Yale University Press, 2009.

———. *The Beauty of the Infinite: The Aesthetics of Christian Truth*. Grand Rapids: Eerdmans, 2003.

Harwood, Nigel. "(In)Appropriate Personal Pronoun Use in Political Science: A Qualitative Study and a Proposed Heuristic for Future Research." *Written Communication* 23 (2006) 424–50.

———. "'We Do Not Seem to Have a Theory . . . the Theory I Present Here Attempts to Fill This Gap': Inclusive and Exclusive Pronouns in Academic Writing." *AL* 26 (2005) 343–75.

Hasan, Ali, and Richard Fumerton. "Knowledge by Acquaintance vs. Description." *The Standford Encyclopedia of Philosophy*, Mar 10, 2014. Online: https://plato.stanford.edu/archives/spr2014/entries/knowledge-acquaindescrip.

Haseman, Brad. "A Manifesto for Performative Research." *MIA* 118 (2006) 98–106.

———. "Rupture and Recognition: Identifying the Performative Research Paradigm." In *Practice as Research: Approaches to Creative Arts Enquiry*, edited by Estelle Barrett and Barbara Bolt, 147–57. London: I. B. Tauris, 2007.

Haseman, Brad, and Daniel Mafe. "Acquiring Know-How: Research Training for Practice-Led Researchers." In *Practice-Led Research, Research-Led Practice in the Creative Arts*, edited by Hazel Smith and Roger T. Dean, 211–28. RMAH. Edinburgh: Edinburgh University Press, 2009.

Haug, Wolfgang Fritz. "From Marx to Gramsci, from Gramsci to Marx: Historical Materialism and the Philosophy of Praxis." *RM* 13 (2001) 69–82.

Haynes, Deborah J. *The Vocation of the Artist*. Cambridge: Cambridge University Press, 1997.

Heinze, Rudolph W. *Reform and Conflict: From the Medieval World to the Wars of Religion*, edited by John D. Woodbridge et al. BHC 4. Grand Rapids: Baker, 2004.

"Higher Degrees by Research: Thesis Submission and Examination Guidelines," *University of Canberra*. Online: https://www.canberra.edu.au/research/graduate-research/current-research-students/forms/documents/HDR-Thesis-Submission-and-Examination-Guidelines-v1.pdf.

Hocken, Peter D. "Charismatic Movement." In *The New International Dictionary of Pentecostal and Charismatic Movements*, edited by S. M. Burgess and E. M. van der Maas, 477–519. Rev. ed. Grand Rapids: Zondervan, 2003.

Holbrook, Allyson, et al. "Examiner Comment on the Literature Review in Ph.D. Theses." *SHE* 32 (2007) 337–56.

Hughes, Anthony. "'An Academy for Doing.' I: The Accademia Del Disegno, the Guilds and the Principate in Sixteenth-Century Florence." *OAJ* 9 (1986) 3–10.

Hughes, Graham. *Worship as Meaning: A Liturgical Theology for Late Modernity*. CSCD 10. Cambridge: Cambridge University Press, 2003.

Hyland, Ken. "Authority and Invisibility: Authorial Identity in Academic Writing." *JP* 34 (2002) 1091–112.

———. "Humble Servants of the Discipline? Self-Mention in Research Articles." *ESP* 20 (2001) 207–26.

———. "Options of Identity in Academic Writing." *ELT Journal* 56 (2002) 351–58.

Junker-Kenny, Maureen. *Habermas and Theology*. ELPT. London: Continuum, 2011.

Bibliography

Kälvermark, Torsten. "University Politics and Practice-Based Research." In *The Routledge Companion to Research in the Arts*, edited by Michael Biggs and Henrik Karlsson, 3–23. New York: Routledge, 2010.

Keener, Craig S. *The IVP Bible Background Commentary: New Testament.* Downers Grove, IL: InterVarsity, 1993.

Kemmis, Stephen. "Action Research as a Practice-Based Practice." *EAR* 17 (2009) 463–74.

Kill, Rebekka. "Coming in from the Cold: Imperialist Legacies and Tactical Criticalities." *IJADE* (2006) 308–17.

Klein, William W., et al. *Introduction to Biblical Interpretation.* Rev. ed. Nashville: Nelson, 1993.

Kraut, Richard. "Introduction." In *The Blackwell Guide to Aristotle's Nicomachean Ethics*, edited by Richard Kraut, 1–11. BGGW 4. Malden, MA: Blackwell, 2006.

Ladd, George Eldon. *A Theology of the New Testament*, edited by Donald A. Hagner. Rev. ed. Grand Rapids: Eerdmans, 1993.

Laming, Madeline M. "Seven Key Turning Points in Australian Higher Education Policy 1943–1999." *PS* 2 (2001) 239–73.

LaSor, William Sanford, et al. *Old Testament Survey: The Message, Form, and Background of the Old Testament.* 2nd ed. Grand Rapids: Eerdmans, 1996.

Lawrence, Gavin. "Human Good and Human Function." In *The Blackwell Guide to Aristotle's Nicomachean Ethics*, edited by Richard Kraut, 37–75. BGGW 4. Malden, MA: Blackwell, 2006.

Lear, Gabriel Richardson. "Happiness and the Structure of Ends." In *A Companion to Aristotle*, edited by Georgios Anagnostopoulos, 387–403. BCP 42. Chicester, UK: Wiley-Blackwell, 2009.

Leff, Gordon. "The Trivium and the Three Philosophies." In *A History of the University in Europe: Universities in the Middle Ages*, edited by Hilde de Ridder-Symoens and Walter Ruegg, 1:307–36. 4 vols. Cambridge: Cambridge University Press, 1992.

Letherby, Gayle. "Standpoint Research." In *The Sage Dictionary of Social Research Methods*, edited by Victor Jupp, 288–90. London: Sage, 2006.

Levine, Michael P. "Mystical Experience and Non-Basically Justified Belief." *RS* 25 (1989) 335–45.

"Liberal Arts." *Encyclopædia Britannica Online*, August 2010. No pages. Online: https://www.britannica.com/topic/liberal-arts.

Mao, Luming R. "I Conclude Not: Toward a Pragmatic Account of Metadiscourse." *RR* 11 (1993) 265–89.

Martin, Dennis D. "Mysticism." In *Evangelical Dictionary of Theology*, edited by Walter A. Elwell, 806–8. BRL. 2nd ed. Grand Rapids: Baker Academic, 2001.

Bibliography

Martindale, Andrew. *The Rise of the Artist: In the Middle Ages and Early Renaissance*. LMC. London: Thames and Hudson, 1972.

McFague, Sallie. *Models of God: Theology for an Ecological, Nuclear Age*. Philadelphia: Fortress, 1987.

———. "The Language of Inner Experience in Christian Mysticism." *SJCS* 1 (2001) 156–71.

McGinn, Bernard. *The Presence of God: A History of Western Christian Mysticism: Volume One. The Foundations of Mysticism*. New York: Crossroad, 1991.

———. "Theologians as Trinitarian Iconographers." In *The Mind's Eye: Art and Theological Argument in the Middle Ages*, edited by Jeffrey Hamburger and Anne-Marie Bouché, 186–207. Princeton: Princeton University Press, 2006.

McGrath, Alister E. *Christian Theology: An Introduction*. 3rd ed. Malden, MA: Blackwell, 2001.

———. *A Scientific Theology: Volume One. Nature*. Grand Rapids: Eerdmans, 2001.

McNamara, Andrew. "Six Rules for Practice-Led Research." *TEXT: Journal of Writing and Writing Courses* 14 (2012) 1–15.

McNiff, Shaun. "Art-Based Research." In *Handbook of the Arts in Qualitative Research: Perspectives, Methodologies, Examples, and Issues*, edited by J. Gary Knowles and Ardra L. Cole, 29–40. Los Angeles: Sage, 2008.

McWilliam, Erica, et al. "Transdisciplinarity for Creative Futures: What Barriers and Opportunities?" *IETI* 45 (2008) 247–53.

Meyendorff, John. "Is 'Hesychasm' the Right Word? Remarks on Religious Ideology in the Fourteenth Century." *HUS* 7 (1983) 447–57.

Migliore, Daniel. *Faith Seeking Understanding*. 2nd ed. Grand Rapids: Eerdmans, 2004.

Milech, Barbara H., and Ann Schilo. "'Exit Jesus': Relating the Exegesis and Creative/Production Components of a Research Thesis." *TEXT* 3 (2004). No pages. Online: http://www.textjournal.com.au.libaccess.lib.mcmaster.ca/speciss/issue3/milechschilo.htm.

Miller, Fred D., Jr. "Aristotle on the Ideal Constitution." In *A Companion to Aristotle*, edited by Georgios Anagnostopoulos, 540–54. BCP 42. Chichester: Wiley-Blackwell, 2009.

Miller-McLemore, Bonnie J., ed. *The Wiley-Blackwell Companion to Practical Theology*. WBCP. Malden, MA: Wiley-Blackwell, 2012.

Moreland, James Porter, and William Lane Craig. *Philosophical Foundations for a Christian Worldview*. Downers Grove, IL: InterVarsity, 2003.

Morris, Michael Rowland. *An Introduction to the Philosophy of Language*. CIP. Cambridge: Cambridge University Press, 2007.

Bibliography

Moser, Paul K. "Epistemology." In *The Cambridge Dictionary of Philosophy*, edited by Robert Audi, 273-78. 2nd ed. Cambridge: Cambridge University Press, 1999.

Mottram, Judith, and Chris Rust. "The Pedestal and the Pendulum: Fine Art Practice, Research and Doctorates." *JVAP* 7 (2008) 133-51.

Mounce, William D. *The Analytical Lexicon to the Greek New Testament*. Grand Rapids: Zondervan, 1993.

Mullins, Gerry, and Margaret Kiley. "'It's a PhD, Not a Nobel Prize': How Experienced Examiners Assess Research Theses." *SHE* 27 (2002) 369-86.

Nes, Solrunn. *The Mystical Language of Icons*. 2nd ed. Grand Rapids: Eerdmans, 2005.

Nichols, Aidan. *Redeeming Beauty Soundings in Sacral Aesthetics*. ASTIA. Aldershot: Ashgate, 2007.

Niedderer, Kristina, and Linden Reilly. "New Knowledge in the Creative Disciplines: Proceedings of the First Experiential Knowledge Conference 2007." *JVAP* 6 (2007) 81-87.

OECD. *Frascati Manual 2002: Proposed Standard Practice for Surveys on Research and Experimental Development*. Paris: OECD, 2002.

———. *Frascati Manual 2012: Proposed Standard Practice for Surveys on Research and Experimental Development*. Paris: OECD, 2012.

———. *Oslo Manual: Guidelines for Collecting and Interpreting Innovation Data*. 3rd ed. Paris: OECD, 2005.

Oliver, Paul. "Purposive Sampling." In *The Sage Dictionary of Social Research Methods*, edited by Victor Jupp, 245. London: Sage, 2006.

Osborne, Grant R. *The Hermeneutical Spiral: A Comprehensive Introduction to Biblical Interpretation*. Rev. ed. Downers Grove, IL: InterVarsity, 2006.

Outhwaite, William. *The Habermas Reader*. Cambridge: Polity, 1996.

Palmer, Richard E. *Hermeneutics: Interpretation Theory in Schleiermacher, Dilthey, Heidegger and Gadamer*. NUSPEP. Evanston, IL: Northwestern University Press, 1969.

Paltridge, Brian. "The Exegesis as a Genre: An Ethnographic Examination." In *Analysing Academic Writing: Contextualized Frameworks*, edited by Louise J. Ravelli and Robert A. Ellis, 84-103. OLS. London: Continuum, 2004.

Panksepp, Jaak. "On the Embodied Neural Nature of Core Emotional Affects." *JCS* 12 (2005) 158-84.

Pearse, Meic. *The Age of Reason: From the Wars of Religion to the French Revolution, 1570-1789*. BHC 5. Grand Rapids: Baker, 2006.

Pearson, Peter. *A Brush with God: An Icon Workbook*. Harrisburg, PA: Morehouse, 2005.

———. *Another Brush with God: Further Conversations about Icons.* Harrisburg, PA: Morehouse, 2009.

Pelikan, Jaroslav. *The Christian Tradition: A History of the Development of Doctrine: Volume 3. The Growth of Medieval Theology (600–1300).* Chicago: University of Chicago Press, 1978.

Penner, Terry. "The Forms in the Republic." In *The Blackwell Guide to Plato's Republic*, edited by Gerasimos Santas, 234–62. BGGW. Malden, MA: Blackwell, 2006.

Pensky, Max. "Society, Morality, and Law: Jürgen Habermas." In *The Blackwell Companion to Political Sociology*, edited by Kate Nash and Alan Scott, 49–59. Malden, MA: Blackwell, 2004.

Peterson, Gregory R. "In Praise of Folly? Theology and the University." *ZJRS* 43 (2008) 563–77.

Phillips, Maggi, et al. *Dancing between Diversity and Consistency: Refining Assessment in Postgraduate Degrees in Dance.* Mt Lawley, Australia: West Australian Academy of Performing Arts at Edith Cowan University, 2009.

Pittenger, W. Norman. "Process Thought as a Conceptuality for Reinterpreting Christian Faith." *Encounter* 44 (1983) 109–17.

Plantinga, Alvin. "Advice to Christian Philosophers." *FP* 1 (1984) 253–71.

———. "Justification and Theism." In *The Analytic Theist: An Alvin Plantinga Reader*, edited by James F. Sennett, 162–86. Grand Rapids: Eerdmans, 1998.

Polanyi, Michael. *The Tacit Dimension.* Chicago: University of Chicago Press, 2009.

Pope Paul VI. "Sacrosanctum Concilium." *La Santa Sede*, Dec 4, 1963. Online: https://www.vatican.va/archive/hist_councils/ii_vatican_council/documents/vat-ii_const_19631204_sacrosanctum-concilium_en.html.

Pratt, John. "Higher Education in England and Wales: Unification, Stratification or Diversification?" *TC* 7 (2001) 19–27.

"Preparing and Presenting a Research Thesis for Examination." *Curtin University.* Online, http://research.curtin.edu.au/local/docs/graduate/TE-ThesisPrepPres.pdf.

Preziosi, Donald. "Introduction." In *The Art of Art History: A Critical Anthology*, edited by Donald Preziosi, 21–30. OHA. Oxford: Oxford University Press, 1998.

Raein, Maziar. "Where Is the 'I'?" *Writing PAD* (2003) 1–4. Online: https://www.academia.edu/27954645/Where_is_the_I_.

Roberts, Jean. "Excellences of the Citizen and of the Individual." In *A Companion to Aristotle*, edited by Georgios Anagnostopoulos, 555–65. Chichester: Wiley-Blackwell, 2009.

Bibliography

Rojek, Pawel. "The Logic of Palamism." *SH* 2 (2013) 3–25.

"Rule No. 10 Made Pursuant to Statute No. 12—Enrolment: Degree of Doctor by Research," *Curtin University*. Online: https://policies.curtin.edu.au/local/docs/statutes-rules/Rule_No_10_to_Statute_12_Enrolment_Degree_of_Doctor_by_Research.pdf.

Rust, Chris, et al. *Practice-Led Research in Art, Design and Architecture*. AHRCRR. Swindon, UK: AHRC, 2007.

Schleiermacher, Friedrich. *The Christian Faith*, edited by H. R. Mackintosh and J. S. Stewart. 2 vols. HTCL. New York: Harper & Row, 1963.

———. *On Religion: Speeches to Its Cultured Despisers*, edited by Rudolf Otto. Translated by John Oman. LRC. New York: Harper & Brothers, 1958.

Schön, Donald A. *The Reflective Practitioner: How Professionals Think in Action*. New York: Basic, 1983.

Schwandt, Thomas A. "On Understanding Understanding." *QI* 5 (1999) 451–64.

Searle, John R. "Contemporary Philosophy in the United States." In *The Blackwell Companion to Philosophy*, edited by Nicholas Bunnin and E. P. Tsui-James, 1–22. BCP. Malden, MA: Blackwell, 2003.

Segal, Robert Alan. "Introduction." In *The Blackwell Companion to the Study of Religion*, edited by Robert Alan Segal, xiii–xix. BCR. Malden, MA: Blackwell, 2006.

Sennett, James F., ed. *The Analytic Theist: An Alvin Plantinga Reader*. Grand Rapids: Eerdmans, 1998.

Silverman, David. *Doing Qualitative Research: A Practical Handbook*. 3rd ed. London: Sage, 2010.

Sire, James W. *The Universe Next Door: A Basic World View Catalog*. 5th ed. Downers Grove, IL: InterVarsity, 2009.

Smith, David. "Economic Support of Art in America Today." In *Art in Theory 1900–1990: An Anthology of Changing Ideas*, edited by Charles Harrison and Paul Wood, 663–65. Oxford: Blackwell, 1992.

Smith, David L. *A Handbook of Contemporary Theology*. BPB. Wheaton, IL: Victor, 1992.

Snodgrass, Klyne. "Exegesis." In *Dictionary for Theological Interpretation of the Bible*, edited by Kevin J. Vanhoozer, 203–6. Grand Rapids: Baker Academic, 2005.

Sörbom, Göran. "The Classical Concept of Mimesis." In *A Companion to Art Theory*, edited by Paul Smith and Carolyn Wilde, 19–28. BCCS 5. Oxford: Blackwell, 2002.

Stark, Rodney. *For the Glory of God: How Monotheism Led to Reformations, Science, Witch-Hunts, and the End of Slavery*. PP. Princeton: Princeton University Press, 2003.

Stember, Marilyn. "Advancing the Social Sciences through the Interdisciplinary Enterprise." *SSJ* 28 (1991) 1–14.

Stephens, Chris. "Sir William Coldstream 1908–1987." *Tate*, August 1998. No pages. Online: https://www.tate.org.uk/art/artists/sir-william-coldstream-927.

Stewart, Robyn Anne. "Practice vs Praxis: Constructing Models for Practitioner-Based Research." *TEXT: Journal of Writing and Writing Courses* 5 (2001). No pages. Online: https://eprints.usq.edu.au/2498/1/Stewart_R.A._Practice_Vs_Praxis_Text_publication.htm.

Stock, Cheryl. "Approaches to Acquiring 'Doctorateness' in the Creative Industries: An Australian Perspective." In *Doctoral Education in Design Conference 2011*, edited by L. Justice and K. Friedman, 1–11. Hong Kong: Hong Kong Polytechnic University, 2011.

Strand, Dennis. *Research in the Creative Arts*. EIPR 98.6. Canberra: Department of Employment, Education, Training and Youth Affairs, 1998.

Sullivan, Graeme. *Art Practice as Research: Inquiry in Visual Arts*. 2nd ed. Thousand Oaks, CA: Sage, 2010.

Sumner, Maggie. "Qualitative Research." In *The Sage Dictionary of Social Research Methods*, edited by Victor Jupp, 248–49. London: Sage, 2006.

Swinton, John, and Harriet Mowat. *Practical Theology and Qualitative Research*. London: SCM, 2006.

Taliaferro, Charles, and Elsa J. Marty. "The Coherence of Theism." In *Contending with Christianity's Critics: Answering New Atheists & Other Objectors*, edited by Paul Copan and William Lane Craig, 184–204. Nashville: B&H Academic, 2009.

"The Tertiary Education Strategy," *Tertiary Education Commission*, November 13, 2020. No pages. Online: https://www.tec.govt.nz/focus/our-focus/tes.

Tertiary Education Commission. "Performance-Based Research Fund: Creative and Performing Arts Panel-specific Guidelines 2012 Quality Evaluation." Wellington, Australia: Tertiary Education Commission, 2012.

———. "Performance-Based Research Fund: Humanities and Law Panel-Specific Guidelines 2012 Quality Evaluation." Wellington, Australia: Tertiary Education Commission, 2012.

———. "Performance-Based Research Fund: Quality Evaluation Guidelines 2012." Wellington, Australia: Tertiary Education Commission, 2013.

"Thesis by Creative Works Guidelines." *Queensland University of Technology*. Online: https://cms.qut.edu.au/__data/assets/pdf_file/0013/7231/phd-thesis-by-creative-works-guidelines.pdf.

Bibliography

Thiselton, Anthony C. *The Two Horizons: New Testament Hermeneutics and Philosophical Description with Special Reference to Heidegger, Bultmann, Gadamer, and Wittgenstein.* Grand Rapids: Eerdmans, 1980.

Thomas, R. Murray. *Blending Qualitative and Quantitative Research Methods in Theses and Dissertations.* Thousand Oaks, CA: Corwin, 2003.

Tiberius, Valerie. "Blackburn, Simon." In *The Oxford Dictionary of Philosophy*, edited by Robert Audi, 138. 2nd ed. Cambridge: Cambridge University Press, 1999.

Tsakiridou, Cornelia A. *Icons in Time, Persons in Eternity: Orthodox Theology and the Aesthetics of the Christian Image.* Farnham, VT: Ashgate, 2013.

Veling, Terry A. *Practical Theology: On Earth as It Is in Heaven.* Maryknoll, NY: Orbis, 2005.

Vinci, Leonardo da. *The Notebooks of Leonardo da Vinci*, edited by Irma A. Richter. WC. Oxford: Oxford University Press, 1980.

Walton, Douglas. "Informal Fallacy." In *The Cambridge Dictionary of Philosophy*, edited by Robert Audi, 431–35. 2nd ed. Cambridge: Cambridge University Press, 1999.

Walton, John H., et al. *The IVP Bible Background Commentary: Old Testament.* Downers Grove, IL: InterVarsity, 2000.

Webb, Jen, et al. "Examination of Doctoral Degrees in Creative Arts: Process, Practice and Standards." *University of Canberra*, 2013. Online: https://d3n8a8pro7vhmx.cloudfront.net/theaawp/pages/20/attachments/original/1384907851/PP10-1801_UC.Webb_Final_Report.pdf?1384907851.

———. "Examining Doctorates in the Creative Arts: A Guide." *Australasian Association of Writing Programs.* Online: https://d3n8a8pro7vhmx.cloudfront.net/theaawp/pages/20/attachments/original/1384907948/Examiners_booklet_final_0.pdf?1384907948.

Whitehead, Alfred North. *Process and Reality: An Essay in Cosmology.* New York: Humanities, 1929.

Williams, A. N. "Mystical Theology Redux: The Pattern of Aquinas' Summa Theologiae." *MT* 13 (1997) 53–74.

Williams, J. Rodman. *Renewal Theology.* 3 vols. Grand Rapids: Zondervan, 1988–92.

Wilken, Robert Louis. *The Spirit of Early Christian Thought: Seeking the Face of God.* New Haven: Yale University Press, 2003.

Winter, Richard. "Some Principles and Procedures for the Conduct of Action Research." In *New Directions in Action Research*, edited by Ortrun Zuber-Skerritt, 13–27. London: Falmer, 1996.

Wright, Andrew. *Christianity and Critical Realism: Ambiguity, Truth, and Theological Literacy.* NSCRS. London: Routledge, 2013.

Bibliography

Wright, N. T. *The Christian Origins and the Question of God: Volume 1. The New Testament and the People of God*. Minneapolis: Fortress, 1992.

Index of Names

Adams, Nicholas, 24, 28–29
Allen, Diogenes, 51, 70
Alvesson, Mats, 20, 22, 37, 42–43, 122, 240–41
Anderson, Elizabeth, 188
Arnold, Josie, 164, 167–68

Bacon, Hannah, 232–33
Baker, Gordon P., 136
Barasch, Moshe, 50, 52–62, 64–65, 69–71, 76
Barnes, Robert, 88
Barone, Tom, 112
Barrett, Estelle, 99, 177, 180, 213
Barsalou, Lawrence W., 134–35
Barzun, Jacques, 54, 58, 60, 72
Battaglia, Michael P., 38
Bavinck, Herman, 1–2, 18, 258
Beckwith, John, 55
Benton, Ted, 23,
Berger, Leigh, 39–40
Bettenson, Henry, 226
Biggs, Michael, 155–56, 174, 180
Bloesch, Donald G., 18–19, 21, 30
Bobonich, Chris, 55
Bolt, Barbara, 99, 142–43, 177, 180, 213, 239
Borg, Erik, 57–58, 62, 67, 71–72, 74–76
Borgdorff, Henk, 84, 98, 260
Bredin, Hugh, 55–56
Brown, C., 20
Brown, Lesley, 51
Browning, Don S., 148
Büchler, Daniela, 155–56, 174

Buxton, Graham, 233

Calvin, John, 68, 186
Candlin, Fiona, 48, 73, 75, 77–79, 82–83
Candy, Linda, 85, 140, 168
Castiglione, Baldassarre, 63
Charmois, Martin de, 66
Clark, Kelly James, 25
Clough, Peter, 100, 190
Clouse, R. G., 60
Combrink, L., 85
Craib, Ian, 23
Craig, William Lane, 21–22, 27, 33–34, 116, 186
Crisp, Roger, 50–51
Crotty, Michael, 19–20, 205

Damasio, Antonio R., 134, 136
Davis-Weyer, Caecilia, 56, 58
Dempsey, Charles, 65,
Denzin, Norman K., 19, 29, 111, 124
Dingemans, Gijsbert D., 147–48

Edmonds, Ernest, 140, 168
Eisner, Elliot W., 112
Ellington, Laura, 19
Ellis, Carolyn, 19, 39–40
Emmons, Robert A., 129–31, 238–39
Erickson, Millard J., 18, 20–21, 171
Evans, G. R., 70
Evans, Stuart, 76–77, 85, 175

Fantl, Jeremy, 198
Fee, Gordon D., 171–72

Index of Names

Fletcher, Julie, 164
Frayling, Christopher, 146–48, 152–53
Fumerton, Richard, 198

Gadamer, Hans-Georg, 5
Gardner, Howard, 125–32, 136, 141, 238
Garwood, Jeanette, 191
Geisler, Norman L., 60
Gill, Robin, 147–48
Gillespie, Thomas W., 5
González, Justo L., 2–3, 69, 187
Gottlieb, Paula, 53
Graham, Elaine L., 150
Gray, Carole, 85, 97–98, 139–40, 175, 260
Green, Lelia, 6, 153–54, 173–74
Greene-McCreight, Kathryn, 233
Grenz, Stanley J., 1, 3, 25, 64, 183, 229–32
Grix, Jonathan, 205
Grondin, Jean, 170
Grudem, Wayne A., 181, 231–32
Gruenler, Royce Gordon, 6

Habermas, Jürgen, 24–25, 27–34, 45, 89–90, 209
Hall, Christopher A., 2
Hamilton, Jillian, 96, 163, 165–67, 169
Harding, Sandra G., 187
Harper, Graeme, 85, 96
Harrington, Austin, 53, 59–60, 62, 67, 71–72, 81
Hart, Chris, 10
Hart, David Bentley, 17, 87
Harwood, Nigel, 206–8
Hasan, Ali, 198
Haseman, Brad, 96–97, 112, 154–56, 173, 175, 213, 216, 260
Haug, Wolfgang Fritz, 117
Haynes, Deborah J., 70–72
Heinze, Rudolph W., 68
Hocken, Peter D., 4
Hughes, Anthony, 65–66
Hughes, Graham, 183
Hyland, Ken, 206–9

Jaaniste, Luke, 96, 163, 165–67, 169
Junker-Kenny, Maureen, 31, 33

Kälvermark, Torsten, 84, 89
Karlsson, Henrik, 180
Keener, Craig S., 19, 144
Kemmis, Stephen, 152
Kiley, Margaret, 221
Kill, Rebekka, 48, 74–75, 138, 178–79
Kraut, Richard, 53, 55

Ladd, George Eldon, 20, 144
Laming, Madeline M., 79–80
Lawrence, Gavin, 141
Lear, Gabriel Richardson, 141
Leff, Gordon, 62
Le Grice, Malcolm, 76–77, 85, 175
Letherby, Gayle, 187
Levine, Michael P., 186
Lincoln, Yvonna S., 19, 29, 111, 124

Mafe, Daniel, 96, 175
Malins, Julian, 139–40
Mann, Alan, 164
Mao, Luming R., 208
Marley, I. R., 85
Martin, Dennis D., 185
Martin, Leslie, 79
Martindale, Andrew, 61, 65
Maunder, Chris, 226
McFague, Sallie, 233
McGinn, Bernard, 185–86, 227, 234
McGrath, Alister E., 16–18, 55, 60, 117, 230
McNamara, Andrew, 123, 169, 196, 210–11, 214
McNiff, Shaun, 115
Marty, Elsa J., 231
Meyendorff, John, 237
Migliore, Daniel, 2, 87–88, 181, 230–31
Milech, Barbara H., 163–65, 167, 169, 174–75, 178, 201, 212, 219
Miller, Fred D., Jr., 54
Miller-McLemore, Bonnie J., 150
Moreland, James Porter, 21–22, 27, 33–34, 116, 186
Morris, Katherine J., 136

Index of Names

Morris, Michael Rowland, 127, 182
Moser, Paul K., 198
Mottram, Judith, 94, 174
Mounce, William D., 187
Mowat, Harriet, 148–50
Mullins, Gerry, 221

Nes, Solrunn, 64, 238
Niedderer, Kristina, 121
Nutbrown, Cathy, 100, 190

Oliver, Paul, 38
Olson, Roger E., 3, 230–32
Osborne, Grant R., 171
Outhwaite, William, 27–29

Palmer, Richard E., 5, 35
Paltridge, Brian, 164
Panksepp, Jaak, 199
Pearse, Meic, 69, 86–87
Pearson, Peter, 237–38, 245
Pelikan, Jaroslav, 63
Penner, Terry, 51, 52
Pensky, Max, 27
Peterson, Gregory R., 63–64, 86
Pittenger, W. Norman, 231
Plantinga, Alvin, 21, 24–27, 34, 45, 89, 186, 209
Polanyi, Michael, 132–34, 143
Pope Paul, VI, 183
Pratt, John, 79–80, 83
Preziosi, Donald, 65

Raein, Maziar, 115, 179
Reilly, Linden, 121
Roberts, Jean, 54
Rojek, Pawel, 236–37
Rust, Chris, 84, 94, 174

Schleiermacher, Friedrich, 87, 147, 230
Schilo, Ann, 163–65, 167, 169, 174–75, 178, 201, 212, 219
Schön, Donald A., 78, 116–17, 122
Schwandt, Thomas A., 124

Searle, John R., 127
Segal, Robert Alan., 88
Sennett, James F., 24
Silverman, David, 10, 176–78, 212–14, 221–22
Sire, James W., 35–36
Sköldberg, Kaj, 20, 22, 37, 42–43, 122, 240–41
Smith, David, 74
Smith, David L., 232
Snodgrass, Klyne, 172
Sörbom, Göran, 52
Springsted, Eric O., 51, 70
Stark, Rodney, 87
Stember, Marilyn, 9
Stephens, Chris, 74
Stewart, Robyn Anne, 122–23, 168
Stock, Cheryl, 113
Strand, Dennis, 80, 83, 86, 93
Sullivan, Graeme, 20, 73, 82, 84–85, 121–22, 173
Sumner, Maggie, 192
Swinton, John, 148–50

Taliaferro, Charles, 231
Thiselton, Anthony C., 36
Thomas, R. Murray, 111–12, 120
Tiberius, Valerie, 51
Tsakiridou, Cornelia A., 56–57, 59, 226

Veling, Terry A., 150–51

Walton, Douglas, 249
Walton, John H., 182
Whitehead, Alfred North, 49–50, 231–32
Williams, A. N., 184
Williams, J. Rodman, 18, 70, 183–84, 186, 229
Wilken, Robert Louis, 1
Winter, Richard, 151–52
Wright, Andrew, 22, 192–94, 228–29
Wright, N. T., 15, 36–37, 45, 194–95, 197, 201

www.ingramcontent.com/pod-product-compliance
Lightning Source LLC
Chambersburg PA
CBHW071239230426
43668CB00011B/1507